WALKING TALL

PETER CROUCH

WALKING TALL MY STORY

with Sam Wallace

HODDER &
STOUGHTON

Copyright © 2007 by Peter Crouch

First published in Great Britain in 2007 by Hodder & Stoughton
A division of Hodder Headline

The right of Peter Crouch to be identified as
the Author of the Work has been asserted by him in accordance
with the Copyright, Designs and Patents Act 1988.

A Hodder & Stoughton Book

I

A CIP catalogue record for this title is available from the British Library

Trade paperback ISBN 978 0 340 96083 7
Hardback ISBN 978 0 340 93712 9

Typeset in Scala by Hewer Text UK Ltd, Edinburgh
Printed and bound by Clays Ltd, St Ives plc

Hodder Headline's policy is to use papers that are natural, renewable
and recyclable products and made from wood grown in sustainable
forests. The logging and manufacturing processes are expected to
conform to the environmental regulations of the country of origin.

Hodder & Stoughton Ltd
A division of Hodder Headline
338 Euston Road
London NW1 3BH

To my family, friends and all the managers, coaches, players, journalists and fans who have unfashionably believed in me

CONTENTS

ACKNOWLEDGEMENTS

I must thank Sam Wallace, a new breed of young sports journalist who players actually like talking to rather than trying to avoid. His commitment, dedication and perfectionism were inspiring. Now if I can just persuade him to stop having breakfast with Jimmy Hill and his mate . . .

Thanks to Dad for providing the memories, dabbling in the photography, design, marketing and everything else! You've got a mate for life there Sam!

Thanks also to Roddy Bloomfield, a veritable giant in sports book publishing, for supporting the project at Hodder and Stoughton. Hannah Knowles was vital in keeping the whole thing on track.

I would like to thank those people who helped me fill in the gaps in the process of writing this book. First of all, Andy Campbell, my first-ever manager at West Middlesex Colts. Thanks to Tottenham Hotspur's club historian Andy Porter for tracking down my youth team records. I'm grateful to Martin Eede and John Lawrence at Dulwich Hamlet – as well as former captain Les Cleevely – for recalling my time in non-league. At Hässleholm, my former manager Cony Olsen explained the origin of snus.

Thanks also to Des Bulpin, the man who believed in me from day one, and Gerry Francis for their memories of my time at Queens Park Rangers. Graham Taylor also put his memory to good use recalling the ups and downs of my time at Aston Villa.

The design team at Unreal under Tim and Brian have done a great job of the cover. Thanks to photographer Hamish Brown. I'm also grateful to John Ley for compiling the statistics on my career.

To David O'Leary for being wrong.

Mum, Zar and Bet – you know what I think of you. xxx

Photographic Acknowledgements

The author and publisher would like to thank the following for permission to reproduce photographs:

Action Images Digital, Marc Aspland/*The Times*, Paul Barker/AFP/Getty Images, Bildbyran/Offside, Shaun Botterill/Getty Images, Clive Brunskill/Getty Images, Andrew Budd/Action Images, Phil Cole/Getty Images, Colorsport, Andrew Couldridge/Action Images, Andrew Cowie/Colorsport, Michael Craig/Action Images, Adrian Dennis/AFP/Getty Images, Paul Ellis/AP/PA Photos, Mike Finn-Kelcey/Reuters, Nicky Hayes/the *Sun*, Mike Hewitt/Getty Images, Owen Humphreys/PA Photos, ITV Plc, Alex Livesey/Getty Images, John Marsh/Action Images, John Marsh/Empics/PA Photos, Tony Marshall/PA Photos, Jamie McDonald/Getty Images, Simon Mooney/Getty Images, the *News*/Portsmouth, Norwich City Football Club, Ben Radford/Getty Images, David Rawcliffe/Propaganda, Michael Regan/Action Images, Michael Regan/Rex Features, Martin Rickett/PA Photos, Matt Roberts/Offside, Andrew Yates/AFP/Getty Images, Richard Young/Rex Features.

The painting on page 4, plate section two, is by Brian West.

All Other Photographs are from private collections.

1

NO STOPPING ME

It's less than a week before the Champions League final in May 2007 and I'm in a go-kart on a track in La Manga. I hit top speed as I swerve into the pit lane. Ahead of me, my Liverpool team-mates are climbing out of their karts and walking across the track. They're all famous footballers, excited about the biggest game of their careers just a few days away. As for me, I'm terrified. But that's got nothing to do with the match. It's because I'm heading straight for them and my brakes have gone.

It's not easy to describe that feeling of horror as I hurtled towards the lads at 30mph. We were in Spain for a training camp before the final in Athens and this incident is the one everyone remembers. We all laugh about it now but there is still something about the memory of it that makes my blood run cold. The awful realisation, as I turned into the pits, that my brakes had completely gone. The way I pumped the pedal to no avail. How ridiculous can you get? The Champions League final next week and here I was in a go-kart, my knees up by my chin, heading straight for my Liverpool team-mates.

In the pits, the go-karts were parked on the right and there was a low wall to the left. In between was a lane just narrow enough to drive through but the boys were stepping into it as they got out of their karts. I managed to swerve past a couple of lads and then I very clearly remember seeing Dirk Kuyt getting out of his kart right in front of me. There was no way past him. I don't like to think what would have happened if, in that split second, Dirk had not turned to see me flying towards him. Just in time he jumped up in the air, my helmet smashed his knee, he spun over and came down on the tarmac with a crack. I thought I had killed him.

All sorts of things rushed through my head. *People might think I've done this on purpose so that I can play in the final.* It was obvious that Dirk and I were competing for the same place in the side and, more often than not, he had played that season. There might be a rivalry between us but I really like Dirk. But even if I didn't, I certainly wouldn't resort to running him over with a go-kart. I thought about what the manager would think – 'There goes Crouchy, messing around a few days before the biggest game of the season.' But there was nothing I could do. The brakes had gone.

I just avoided the pit-lane wall and shot out the other end of the pits, the go-kart showing no sign of slowing. By then I was panicking. The smart thing would have been to wait until the kart slowed down of its own accord but I wanted to bail out immediately. I steered near to a patch of grass and managed to get up on to my feet in a crouching position. When I was near enough I threw myself off and just hoped for a soft landing. It must have looked ridiculous, like something out of a James Bond film. Some of the boys were watching from up in a gallery overlooking the track and they were all in stitches. They hadn't seen what had happened in the pit lane and thought I was messing about. The go-kart shot off, hit a wall and, just to add to the drama, its petrol tank caught fire.

I lay on the grass by the track. My leg was bleeding and I was praying that Dirk was OK. Our doctor, Mark Waller, came running over to see me. There was a lot of blood and he had to clean up my leg – I've still got the scars on my knee and thigh from where I hit the deck. Dirk was shaken up but, thank God, not badly hurt. 'The brakes have gone,' I told everyone but I was worried that I had got it wrong and it would turn out to be me who had messed up. I was so relieved when the bloke from the go-kart track actually admitted – amid great apologies – that, having examined my now smouldering go-kart, the brakes had indeed gone.

Our manager Rafa Benitez told us that we should slow down and, to make his point, did a lap himself. In fact, he was so slow I reckon the bloke in 'Driving Miss Daisy' would have beaten him. All the boys watching from the gallery were still in fits of laughter but I couldn't stop thinking about the horrible prospect of Dirk and me missing the Champions League final because of go-karting injuries.

Almost mowing down my team-mates in an out-of-control go-kart was a first for me but I think it's fair to say that my football career hasn't always been plain sailing. My proudest day was when I joined Liverpool in July 2005, aged 24, but it had already been quite a journey through the ranks of professional football to get there, from trainee days at Tottenham to Queens Park Rangers, Portsmouth, Aston Villa, Norwich City and Southampton.

My career has been different from the careers of many of the lads I now play alongside for England. They have been stars in the making since they were kids. Steven Gerrard, Wayne Rooney and Michael Owen have been in the Premiership since they were teenagers. They were always absolute certainties to make the grade, to do great things, to play for famous football clubs. The ride has been a bit bumpier for me. I've had to prove myself over and over again. I still have to.

My football story is different. It doesn't make me a better or a worse person than any of my team-mates; it just makes me different. As a kid I had the big-club treatment at Tottenham, where I was a trainee for five years, but I never made it as far as the first team and sometimes it feels like I've been climbing back up ever since I left there.

Six years before I played for England in the World Cup finals in 2006, I turned out in front of 182 people for Dulwich Hamlet at Harrow Borough in the Ryman Premier League – and we lost. I've been bought, sold and loaned. I've even been on loan in the third division in Sweden. I've been bombed out by a few managers, some of whom have liked me, some of whom haven't, and I've known a few. In eight seasons I've played for ten different managers, and for one of them, Harry Redknapp, at two different clubs, those bitter old rivals on the south coast, Portsmouth and Southampton.

I've had good and bad from fans. I've had good and bad from my own teams' fans. I haven't always played in the Premiership or been an England international. I've played in the Championship and non-league as well, and played in struggling teams in front of angry fans. I've played alongside part-timers in Sweden where the club confiscated my passport to stop me going home, I've been relegated with QPR, I've been accosted by a pissed-up Portsmouth fan whom my dad wrestled over a garden hedge.

I'm 6ft 7in. tall but that doesn't make me any different from any other professional footballer who wants success in the game. As a kid dreaming of being a footballer, I idolised the same players as my mates, players with skill and those who scored goals – Diego Maradona, Paul Gascoigne, Gianluca Vialli. I do sometimes wonder whether people would treat me differently if I was just 6ft tall. But it doesn't matter. I'm happy with who I am and the way I look. And I'm doing the one thing I love the most.

Some people think life begins and ends with the Premiership but it hasn't for me. My football career started long before I performed the robot dance for Prince William. Or accidentally almost ran Dirk over in a go-kart. I try not to take myself too seriously, but when it comes to the business of football, scoring goals and winning matches, there's nothing more important.

These days, footballers are in the public eye more than ever before and I accept that – up to a point. But, first and foremost, my story – my life – is not about fame or about money. It's about football.

2

SINGAPORE AND BACK

My story begins in earnest a long way from Liverpool, or Maccles-field, where I was born on 30 January 1981, or Ealing, in west London, where I grew up and first felt a ball at my toes. As a baby, I took my first steps around a courtyard in Singapore – and if my mum and dad had decided to take one of the options offered to them when they lived in the Far East all those years ago, I wouldn't have been playing for England at the last World Cup finals. I'd have been Australian. We lived in Singapore for three years and we nearly didn't come back. Dad had done well in his job there and had been offered another job in Australia. But he was a London boy, from Fulham in south-west London originally, and he wanted the same for his son. Even so, I certainly didn't have the average English kid's start to life.

I don't remember much about Singapore – even from the photo-graphs we still have at home – but Mum and Dad say it was a great time, and the stories about it that have been told over the years are a big part of Crouch family history. Apparently, the first words I spoke were not in English – they were in Japanese. No joke. Not for me anything as simple as 'Mummy' or 'Daddy'. I picked it up at play-school when I was about eighteen months old. I'd be brought home babbling away. Mum and Dad say they didn't pay much attention until it became obvious that the little Japanese kid from next door, Tohru, was answering me back. We were having a conversation. The trouble is, no one in the family can say with any certainty what my first words were – just that they weren't in English. I also picked up a bit of Mandarin from watching the telly. I can't remember a word of it now.

Maybe it's a result of those early days spent abroad but I have always wanted to see the world. I love travelling and in the summers I head off to America with my old gang of mates from Ealing and get off the tourist trail. Even when you're a 6ft 7in. England international, most Americans couldn't care less who you are. As a footballer you do travel quite a bit, but you don't see a lot of the countries you visit. Take the average Champions League away trip – airport, hotel, stadium, hotel, stadium, airport, home. I've been to a lot of interesting places with Liverpool and England, but I can't say I've actually seen much of them.

My father Bruce and my mother Jayne always wanted to travel, too, so when Dad was offered a job at a Singapore advertising agency in 1982, they decided that having a one-year-old kid shouldn't stop them going to the Far East. By today's standards, they were both young when I was born, 21, but they were still determined to see the world. I was simply taken along for the ride.

Dad moved around a lot when he was a kid – his dad was a salesman for Rowntree's. He met my mum in Cheshire when he was in his first job – copywriter at an advertising agency, writing commercials. He has worked in the same business ever since, moving up the career ladder. Somehow, along the way, he has been to just about every single football match I have ever played in, and I don't just mean at Anfield or with England. He helped to run my first serious boys' team, West Middlesex Colts. He's been there with Queens Park Rangers on the away trips to Grimsby and Crewe. He's been there on the worst times of all, the crap Tuesday evenings playing for Southampton reserves when Steve Wigley had struck me out of the first-team reckoning.

The same goes for my mum. She has sat on the sidelines in gyms and parks where I played as a kid. She has ferried me around after school, taking me to games or training. She has sat in the car with the heater on, waiting for me to finish playing on cold winter nights. When I moved clubs – and I've done that a few times – she helped me pack up my stuff in one city and unload it in another. My sister Sarah has always been a real support, too. Sarah has had to put up with a lot, including people wanting to know her because her brother is a professional footballer. It sounds crazy but it does happen, and Sarah has learned how to spot a fake. She has her own career and we are very close. I confide in her a lot.

When I think of Mum, Dad and Sarah parking the car outside Anfield and making their way through the crowds, it makes me feel good to know that my success is theirs too. To the other supporters going to Liverpool or England games, they must look like any other normal family going to the match, but the three of them know what a long journey it has been for me to get there.

Before my parents moved to Singapore they were, my dad says, pretty skint. They lived at my mum's parents' place in Stockport and, when they arrived in Singapore, they didn't have enough money to live in the plush area of the city where the expat businessmen lived – not for my mum and dad the swimming pools and servants of the Brits abroad. The Crouchs had to live on Dad's wages, and that meant living among the ordinary local people in a 'walk-up' apartment.

They say that, as far as I was concerned, there was always a willing babysitter, or 'amah' as they call the local girls who do the child-minding in Singapore. I wasn't a particularly big baby – I weighed 7½ pounds when I was born. What made me unusual in Singapore was my blond hair. I'm told that I was quite a novelty in our little apartment community, and that led to a big panic one day when Mum came home to discover me and the amah gone and our flat empty. There was no note, no explanation. Mum was beside herself. Dad got a search party organised but he admits now that he thought they'd lost me for good.

The whole neighbourhood was on the look-out for a small blond English boy by the name of Peter who had a very basic understanding of Japanese and Mandarin. Dad says they finally found me in a local market where I was causing a great deal of interest. My amah that day had been so overcome with the pride of being asked to look after this strange blond kid that she had taken me on a publicity tour around the neighbourhood.

Mum and Dad threw themselves into the lifestyle of the area where we lived. They bought our food from stalls on the street, like proper locals, and when Dad got time off from work, they took me with them on their travels. 'Great experience,' Dad always says of those years in the Far East, 'although we nearly lost Pete a couple of times.'

The one trip that goes down as a Crouch family legend was when Dad decided we should take the causeway to Malaysia and drive north to the border with Thailand. The only motor he could get his hands on was a Datsun 120, which, even in the 1980s, was already well out of date. That was the least of his worries, though. If only someone had told him about the problems in the countryside around the Thai border, he would have been spared one of the biggest shocks of his life. He pulled the car over to read the map in a quiet village close to the border, and found himself staring down the barrel of an AK47 rifle.

Armed men were everywhere, coming out of the bushes and trees on the side of the road. Dad says it was like a Vietnam war film. He got out of the car with his arms raised above his head and tried to talk to them. Unfortunately, there was only one person in the car who could speak any Mandarin – and at three years old I wasn't going to be much cop as a negotiator. We had just met the armed wing of the Communist Party of Malaysia.

Dad later did a bit of research and found out that these soldiers had been ducking and diving around that part of the world since they fought against the Japanese during the Second World War. In fact, they didn't come in from the cold until the late 1980s, and fought with government forces on both sides of the border. We didn't know what they wanted. Kidnap? Robbery? The Datsun 120's spare wheel?

By pointing to Mum and me, Dad managed to convince the men with guns that we were just an English family travelling around Malaysia rather than secret agents. Fortunately, they let us go. When we got to the next village and saw the police checkpoint, Mum and Dad were more than a little relieved.

The terms of Mum's visa meant that she couldn't do paid work, so instead she joined a voluntary organisation that helped the Vietnamese boat people who were turning up as refugees in Singapore at that time. Both Mum and Dad say that because they were away from family and friends they really had to rely on each other. That's probably one of the reasons why, as a family, we are still so close.

After three years, Dad got a job offer from a company in Australia but part of the deal in getting work permits and visas meant that I would have had to become an Australian citizen. That was the breaking point for my football-crazy father. No chance, he said. He was hoping that one day his baby son would play football for England. Anyway, after three years they both fancied a change and that meant coming back to England. So Dad chucked in his job and we came home.

When we arrived back in England, my parents were skint again, and we had nowhere to live. If Dad was going to keep working in advertising, we had to stay in London, and that was the hardest time of all for Mum and Dad. With nowhere to go and no money, we had to live in the only place we could afford. So we ended up spending six months at the YMCA on Tottenham Court Road.

When I listen to the stories of that time now, it sounds pretty desperate. Mum and Dad refer to it as 'hell'. Back in 1984 it must have seemed pretty grim to my parents, just back from the Far East and worried about their future. All sorts of people drifted through that place. My parents knew that, but they had nowhere else to go.

I was too young to know that we weren't exactly staying in the Ritz Hotel. Our room was barely big enough to hold their bed and mine, and Dad can remember climbing over the bed to lift me out of the cot. During the day the place was really bleak, with all sorts of characters hanging about. So Mum would put me in my pushchair and take me to Hyde Park – anything to get out of the YMCA.

Dad jokes that not many young wives would have put up with living in a refuge for six months while their husband looked for a job, but Mum has always made sacrifices like that for Sarah and me. She just got on with it and tried to make life as normal as possible while they figured out a way of getting out of there. Life wasn't easy for Dad, either. He would spend his days visiting advertising agencies in town, hoping that someone would give him a job.

I have read in some newspapers that my family are middle-class, which people say is rare in a game where most players come from working-class backgrounds. I suppose we are middle-class now but we never used to be, and that's not the background that either of my parents came from. Now, twenty years on, they are comfortable because they've worked hard, which is no different from any other normal family.

Eventually, Dad got a job based in Baker Street, so he decided to take the Metropolitan Line out of London to find us somewhere to live, and settled on Harrow-on-the-Hill. We stayed in a bed-and-breakfast while Mum and Dad saved up the £4,000 deposit to put down on a £40,000 house in Nelson Road. It backed on to the famous Harrow School and, most importantly, there was plenty of room to play football in a nearby park.

I have so many happy memories of Nelson Road. Mum and Dad brought my baby sister Sarah back there when she was born in 1986, and I have my first hazy memories of playing football with my dad on the cricket field behind the house after we bunked in through a hole in the fence. I went to my first school from there, Roxeth Primary. I was a child of the London suburbs and I soon made friends with some of the kids on my streets.

When I look back on my childhood, I can see that I was lucky to have so many opportunities to play sport, and that so many inspirational coaches and parents gave up their time to allow me to play football. I have played ever since I can remember – in gyms, leisure centres, soccer schools, playgrounds, parks, the training pitches at Hanwell Town. If there's a set of goalposts in Ealing, you can bet I've kicked a ball around in the goalmouth.

My first team was Northolt Hotspurs, where I played at the age of five. We played in the gymnasium at Northolt School, and in the summer we played in the park. My love for competitive football grew from there. I was always looking for a chance to have a kickabout. I loved playing football and already, even at that young age, people were noticing that I could play. By then, I was taller than the other kids, but that wasn't what was getting me noticed. I had skills. I could beat players with a trick. I was always dragging my dad out to the local park to pass the ball about and I was always on the look-out for a game. I'd find out where my mates at school were playing and try to persuade Mum and Dad that I should be there too.

Next up was Brentford Football Club's centre of excellence. I was young when I convinced Mum to ferry me across to Bromyard Leisure Centre, where I had discovered another outlet for my passion. A scout from Brentford had spotted me playing for Northolt and invited me to join in, even though technically I wasn't old enough to be playing at that level. They had a simple rule.

'Peter,' the coach told me, 'if the man from the Football Association turns up to check the boys' ages, you have to leg it.'

He pointed to a hole in the fence in the corner of the field. Since I was taller than the rest of the lads, I don't know why they were worried about me being spotted as an under-age player, but Brentford were taking no chances. One minute I'd be in the thick of a game and then the coach would suddenly stop the match, point at me, and then at the corner of the field. The hole in the fence was big enough for me to get through. I didn't mind. I'd do anything for a game. Later at Brentford I also met Barry Quinn, a brilliant coach who was a big influence on my early career and encouraged me to play in the right way.

My mum was the one who took care of all the lifts when Dad was at work. She never let me down when I had a new place to play football. One of my earliest memories is of my cousin Sam Dicken, son of my mum's brother Mike, coming down from Cheshire one summer to join me for a stay at Martin Allen's soccer school in Uxbridge. Martin was still a young player and a bit of a star at Queens Park Rangers. Sam and I were just excited about having our own room and the chance to play football every day.

When you're that age, football is all you think about and the chance to play it all day was all I wanted. Martin roped in a few of his QPR team-mates to come along to coach us. I still have a photograph of me with Justin Channing, the QPR midfielder. OK, so he might not have been the most famous player in the country, but for a boy who would go on to live in Ealing, the heart of QPR territory, this felt like being at the centre of the world. When they gave me the player of the week award, they might as well have been handing me the FA Cup.

I'd made a bit of a name for myself among the Under-7s football fraternity in London W3, and for the first time I found myself in demand. When Mum came to pick me up from Martin Allen's soccer school, a few of the parents who had watched the games came over to ask whether I wanted to join their Sunday football team. At seven years old I would have signed up there and then but my parents were keen for me to join a team where I would be looked after and allowed to enjoy football. Some of the parents, Mum had noticed, watched the game with cans of lager in their hands, shouting and swearing at the kids. She wasn't having that, she told my dad. They both wanted me to play somewhere I could enjoy football, free from pressure to win. We took a long time deciding where I was going to play. Since then, I've had to make up my mind over transfers to different clubs quite a few times. You could say that joining the West Middlesex Colts was as important as any of them.

3

THE FOOTBALL ACADEMY
BY THE A4

The West Middlesex Colts Football Club achieved what all boys' teams dream of – they won trophies and they produced professional footballers. And we did it without our parents screaming and ranting and raving on the touchline. There was no pressure on us. We were encouraged to try our skills and tricks, and that approach paid dividends.

For five years we were the team to beat in the area and from the ranks of 'West Mid' came another three professional football careers. Michael Dobson rose to captain Brentford and is now at Walsall. Left-back Anthony Charles was a trainee at Chelsea and is now at Barnet, and goalkeeper Gavin Kelly played alongside me in Tottenham's youth team.

It was an incredible achievement for an ordinary boys' club in Osterley, west London, based at the White Lodge Club, just off the A4 on the opposite side to the Sky television studios. When I went there to appear on Sky's 'Soccer AM' programme in the 2006–07 season, I went past the place where I played my first proper football. West Mid's success was a testament to our manager, Andy Campbell, as dedicated a football man as you are likely to find in kids' football. Andy is a printer by trade. His son Ian played in the team, and Andy spent all his spare time improving our training sessions and making sure we developed as good footballers.

Andy had approached my parents after my stay at the Martin Allen soccer school and asked if I was interested in playing for a new Under-8s team he was setting up at the West Middlesex Colts club. Mum and Dad were impressed with the way he put the emphasis on skill and technique rather than physical strength. Andy is the sort of bloke whose contribution goes unnoticed in modern English football. We boys could not have hoped for such a good start to our careers.

The philosophy at West Mid was different from most of the boys' teams I played against during my five years there. For a start, we passed the ball. We always trained outside, even in the winter, so that we were never shocked by the cold when it came to matches. But when it got really cold, Andy would let us wear our tracksuit tops under our shirts if that made us more comfortable.

Andy believed in sticking with the squad he recruited as eight-year-olds and he wanted every boy to get a game. He didn't have to, because there were better players queuing up to join West Mid, but Andy thought it was important we played together over the years, so we grew up as a team. He did take a bit of stick from my dad on that one. Dad wanted us to win and that meant he wanted Andy to pick the very best XI every time.

'Why are you playing him?' Dad would quietly ask Andy. But we never had much problem in winning matches. We won a coveted County Cup and reached two further County Cup finals in a row, and twice we won the fiercely competitive Hayes and District League. Pulling on West Mid's green and black striped shirt – complete with our 'corporate' sponsor 'Steve's Removals' – was a huge thrill for me. We quickly gained a reputation as a cultured football team and soon scouts from Chelsea, Queens Park Rangers and Brentford were coming to our games.

Playing for West Mid gave me another taste of life as a footballer.

For the first time I realised what it was to look different from other footballers, and be treated differently. It was not just because I was very tall, but also because I was skinny and skilful.

It was horrible for my dad at times, keeping cool when he was standing on the same touchline as parents catcalling stuff at me. He has had to put up with it all through my career but there is something just as unpleasant about listening to that nonsense when you are on a windswept park in Osterley as when you are sitting in Old Trafford with 70,000 England fans.

Playing for West Mid, I got the shit kicked out of me by opposing Sunday teams, and as I got older and played district and county football, I got the shit kicked out of me there, too. Dad always stopped himself giving it back to the parents on the other side, or nearly always – apart from one game. That was an Under-12s match against a team from Surrey that included Peter Nicholas's son. Nicholas was a Welsh international midfielder who had played for, among others, Crystal Palace, Arsenal and Chelsea, and had a reputation for being a 'hardman'. A few in his son's team were no different. They dished it out and they had me in their sights.

The centre-half was a thug, even at that tender age. He had a ponytail and a bad attitude, and he set about my ankles from the kick-off. It was brutal. He smashed me every time I got the ball. I took a beating out there, and it was being encouraged by a few of the watching parents. Dad swears that he heard one of them shout from the touchline, 'Kick the shit out of him.' Dad had kept a lid on it so far but there is a limit to how much you can take. I was 12 years old and being kicked relentlessly on the orders of another adult. At 6ft 5in., and quite capable of looking after himself, my dad has never been one to dodge a confrontation. He marched down the touchline and confronted the fella, telling him he was 'a fucking disgrace'. The bloke just grinned back at him, and shrugged. Even he didn't seem to fancy calling it on with my old man when he was in a mood like that. Funnily enough, years later, as manager of Barry Town, Peter Nicholas, who was also watching that game, would try to sign me from Tottenham. When it had all settled down, we went on to win the game and I did well. I'd had the shit kicked out of me – no change there – but I had taken it and come out on top. As we walked off, Andy told Dad that I had turned a corner. Andy had always believed in me, always thought I had real talent.

'Look at Pete, he's been kicked black and blue and he's hardly flinched,' he said. 'He's shown what he's made of. I think he's got a real chance of making it in this game.'

Being kicked all over the place is just something you have to overcome, even at that age. Good players will always be kicked and provoked. The opposition wouldn't bother if you weren't any good. It's a way of unsettling you and, sadly, on some talented players, the tactic works. It didn't work on me and, in the main, that has been the case throughout my career.

The West Mid club was a day out for all the families concerned, and visits there became an important part of my own family's week. We all have happy memories from that time. We used to go there on Friday nights. I would train with the other boys and we would all stay on afterwards to play football on our own while our parents were having a drink in the bar of the White Lodge Club. There was a real bond between the boys in the team.

We were obsessed with 'Gazzetta Football Italia' on Channel Four, which started in 1992 – in the days when Paul Gascoigne was in Italy playing for Lazio. On one of his lunch hours, Dad nipped down to Carnaby Street, just off Oxford Circus, to get me a Sampdoria shirt from Soccer Scene. I loved the famous blue shirt, with the red, white and black band. In that shirt I dreamed I was Vialli, then a young Italian striker with a deadly touch in front of goal. Those Asics boots he wore in the late 1980s? I had them too. Italian football caught our imagination – great players, cool kit designs, amazing skills. Those days seemed like a golden age for *Serie A*.

After training at West Mid, the players we emulated in our kickabouts were Marco van Basten, Roberto Mancini, Vialli and Gazza. We took turns to throw ourselves around in the muddy goalmouth trying to connect with overhead kicks and scissor-kicks. It was there that I first got to grips with that skill. Launch yourself into the air, non-striking foot first, then smack it with your other foot. When I scored with scissor-kicks against Galatasaray and Bolton Wanderers, it was no accident. I think I owe those goals to Marco van Basten and Italian football on Channel Four, although on the pitch I would always try to imitate Diego Maradona. Just because I was tall didn't mean I was a fan of tall players. With all respect to Niall Quinn – and I appreciate now what a good player he was – I didn't want to be like him. He wasn't the kind of player I aspired to be. At that age, any kid wants to be the dribbler, the flair player, and that is how I played when I was younger – up front, averaging 60-odd goals a season in a really good West Mid side. It was only when I got older that I played to other strengths as well, and learned the responsibilities of my position.

Andy and Dad were always interested in ways of improving us as footballers. They were, and still are, real believers in the Coerver Coaching method, devised by the old Dutch coach Wiel Coerver. The skills and techniques are named after famous former players, so you have the Cruyff move, the Littbarski and the Rivelino. Andy paid out of his own pocket for a proper Coerver-approved coach to do a session with us and we loved it. He would shout out 'Cruyff' and all of us, with a ball at our feet, would do the Cruyff turn. I still use those core skills. The third goal of my hat-trick against Arsenal in March 2007 was a classic Coerver-style Cruyff turn that took me away from Kolo Toure.

The philosophy was that you could always improve your skills, no matter how good you were, and the more you practised, the better you became. We enjoyed it so much that at the age of 11, a few of us went on a residential Coerver Coaching course at Uppingham in Rutland and spent a week honing our skills. Did it make me a better player? All I can say is that the ability I have on the ball now is not all down to luck.

At West Mid, we were never shouted at when we lost the ball trying a piece of skill, and Andy never discouraged us from trying a trick. It was an environment in which we were told to play without fear. I didn't start training more than once a week at my first club – Queens Park Rangers – until I was 14. Only then did I stop playing for West Mid and concentrate on the club, which, by normal standards, was very old. The general rule was that if you weren't at a club by the age of nine, you weren't going to make it. I stayed at West Mid because Mum and Dad wanted me to remain free of pressure, and I loved it there.

It's very different now. Kids as young as six are playing at club academies. If they make the grade, they are kept on for another year, and every season these boys play in fear of being moved out in favour of another hopeful. Where's the enjoyment in that? At West Mid, we played for the love of it. The professional clubs would come later.

That didn't mean that we took our games lightly. I considered every Sunday match with West Mid a massive game, although nothing beat playing in the County Cup finals. Conquering Middlesex and the surrounding area was no easy feat. The competition took in teams from as far east as Tottenham and inner-city sides from

Paddington. These were tough kids, and good footballers, but the rewards, as I saw it, were huge.

The finals were held at proper grounds and, by the age of 12, I had played twice at Fulham's Craven Cottage and once at Brentford's Griffin Park. I will remember forever the day that my West Mid Under-10s team beat Enfield Rangers at Craven Cottage. My mum's family from the north-west came down to watch the game. They were all Manchester City fans, a great bunch of lads, and I wanted to put on a good show for them. I scored one and we won the game 3–2. About ten years later the same group of relatives watched me score the winner for Portsmouth against their beloved Manchester City at Fratton Park. I got some stick for that in the pub after the game.

We reached the County Cup final for the next two years running but lost both times. Although we were a good team, the physical part of junior football was starting to catch up with us. I still have the programmes from those games. 'Forward Peter is once again the team's top scorer with over 50 goals,' it says in my player profile. 'Combines great skill both on the ground and in the air with a punishing workrate.' Couldn't have put it better myself.

My height had one big drawback in Sunday football. I would always face the accusation from parents of kids on opposing teams that I was too old to play in that age group. I had no facial hair, as kids who hit puberty early do, but I was, of course, taller than the rest. When children are still growing, you determine their age by their height. So that meant parents would take one look at me and complain that I was obviously too old to play in a certain age group. Dad hated it when the other parents came up with that argument. He didn't carry my birth certificate around, but he would get very angry if they started questioning my age. Andy, always the peacemaker, would resolve it by pointing at my dad, 6ft 5in. tall.

'He's Peter's dad and look at the size of him,' he would say to the parents on the other team. 'The boy's tall like his father.'

My height was the first thing people noticed about me, but what became a problem was people's perception of my strength. That has been an issue throughout my career. There were always those who believed that I had the ability to play professional football. What they weren't convinced about was that I would be strong enough. I kept hearing the same criticism as I hit my early teens. 'He's not going to be strong enough, we'll have to build him up.' I still hear it now.

I've never felt that I've been pushed off the ball and I'm tired of hearing people say that I have to put on weight or muscle. Yes, I had to learn to stand up for myself, but I did that and I know that I'm strong enough to hold my own at any level of football. The misconception that I'm not has often held me back and is a snap judgement that has been the bane of my life. Just because I'm not rippling with muscle doesn't mean I'm not strong. Believe me, in the gym at Liverpool's Melwood training ground, I can lift just as much as any of the other lads in the squad.

West Mid filled my weekends but my oldest and best mates are those I met at school. We left our house in Nelson Road when I was aged eight. The area was too expensive for Mum and Dad to buy a place with an extra bedroom for their growing family, so we settled in Ealing. When I go back to Ealing now, I feel most at ease with the people I grew up with. Those friendships hold strong even today, and I met most of them in my first few weeks at North Ealing Primary School.

My parents didn't realise it at the time but our new house in Ealing was within walking distance of QPR's old training ground on Twyford Avenue, near the old Guinness building – convenient when I launched my professional football career there more than ten years later. At eight years old I was more worried about changing schools, leaving Roxeth in Harrow for North Ealing Primary. Walking there on the first day, Mum and I got lost and I was late.

Lucky then that I could play football, and lucky too that I played for West Mid. When you're one of the main men in a good local football team, it makes it a lot easier joining a new school and making friends. I didn't have to look far to find a group of lads who were as obsessed with sport as I was. We went on to the same high school together and we spent our summers together playing football and tennis.

I met my best mate Greg Chapman there. He is now in Dad's line of work. Then there are the twins Rob and Ed Aitken, James Nesbitt, whose nickname is 'Herman' because he's a dead ringer for Herman Munster, Ben Fitzgerald and Greg Jules, who is a fireman. We still go on summer holidays together – depending on what my football commitments will allow – and when I joined Aston Villa I used my Premiership wages to pay for us to go to the west coast of America on holiday.

It was Ben who coined the nickname that has stuck with me through all those years. At Liverpool, and with England, the lads know me as 'Crouchy', but in Ealing the boys have called me 'Tallous' since we were kids. That's obviously the height but as for the weird twist on it, well, don't ask me why. It's just always been Tallous. We have grown up together and the stick that gets dished out among lads definitely helps you develop a thick skin.

I don't know exactly how tall I was when I joined my new school, but I have always been taller than everyone else. The difference is that I just didn't stop growing, although my major growth spurt came at around the age of 14. I think the fact that I have never known any different has probably helped me. I suppose that if I had been the same height as everyone else and then suddenly shot up it would have felt a bit strange, but because I have always been that way it has never fazed me. The teachers were fine with me and, if I'm honest, I didn't get that much stick from older kids, even though my best mate at primary school was Ed Aitken and he was the smallest kid in our class. He's about 6ft 1in. now, but when we were knocking about together we looked ridiculous. I still have a few snaps of him and me, little and large, at school.

One big problem was getting a school uniform that fitted me. For my trousers, Mum had to go to a different shop from the one everyone else used. The other thing that used to kill me was the football kit I had to wear for school or representative teams. When you're a kid, the kits are often too small. On me they looked ridiculous.

The shorts were the worst – so short they would barely cover any of my thighs. They looked like those tiny shorts John Barnes used to squeeze into when he was playing for Liverpool in the 1980s. A couple of times I said to Dad, 'I can't play today because I am not wearing those shorts.' They looked stupid.

The kit never actually stopped me playing, though. Every time I protested, Dad would pull out all the stops and we would manage to find some better kit. Nevertheless, I remember playing in some terrible football strips. I hated not feeling comfortable about how I looked. Even at that age, it seemed so important. If I didn't look right, I couldn't play right and it would put me off my game.

At North Ealing, I got into the habit of arriving early at school, 8 a.m., to play football. It was the same at break and at lunchtime, and after school we would play until it got dark. In the early days at North Ealing, out of all the teachers, I got along best with Phil Wareing, my PE teacher. He's still there and I've sent him a few shirts from my professional career. My memories of North Ealing are about playing football. Mr Wareing was a top man, a great teacher, and he let us boys just enjoy playing our football.

He could have let us play all day. For my mates and me, we just could not get enough football or, when the weather turned nice, tennis. Take a look at Ealing on a map and everywhere you look there are patches of green space – Pitshanger Park, Perivale playing fields, Hanger Hill Park. One of the reasons Dad chose the street we lived in was that there were tennis courts behind it, perfect for his two children, both of whom just loved to play outside.

However, for Greg, the Aitkens, Herms, me and the rest of the lads, a place up by the A40, on the banks of the River Brent, was where we considered our sporting academy to be. The Brentham Club, a sports and social club just by Ealing golf course, is almost ninety years old and it had the lot. There were snooker tables in the clubhouse and, outside, loads of grass and hard tennis courts, football pitches and hockey goals that we would kick around in. It was, and still is, a brilliant club, our unofficial home and the place we would head to every summer day, a football under one arm, a tennis racket under the other.

Nowadays, when I go back to Ealing, I often drop in to watch my mates play football for Brentham's senior men's teams. The pitches are famous in the area for their immaculate condition. Ed and Rob Aitken are on the football committee that organises the club's three teams. People seem to like the fact that, as a group of friends, we virtually grew up at the place. In fact, they have a few pictures of me on the wall in the bar. However, up until now we've kept one small detail secret between the group of us. Through all those happy years spent there as kids, none of us were ever members.

I still have a laugh about it with the lads even now. I don't know how we pulled that one off. I suppose the boys must have finally relented and handed over their subs by now – they've made it on to the committee after all – but for years, when we were skint teenagers, we managed to wing it. We would play football in the hockey goals, play tennis on any surface that was going and try to avoid anyone challenging us to show our membership cards.

If it was quiet, we would always get in and it would be fine. Every now and then an official would come over to us and say, quite rightly, 'You lot aren't members.' I would explain that we'd had trouble getting the right form, or that I was sure my mum had put it in the post. That normally worked. The groundsman was different. He would take more direct measures, driving over in his tractor, and we would have to leg it. Still, I was never one of those kids who got into trouble. I knew where the line was. I just wanted to play football and tennis.

They must have taken pity on us boys, just so desperate to play sport that we would hang about at the Brentham every day. As well as football, I played tennis to a high standard. The technique came very naturally to me. I never had any specialist coaching. I just headed down to the Brentham with my mates and picked it up as I went along.

I play so rarely now, sometimes I can go for a whole year without picking up a racket, but I know if I went down to a court tomorrow it would come back to me. My height does help. I have a reach that makes the court that much smaller when it comes to my opponents trying to pass me, and I can get a fair bit of whip on my serves. The members at the Brentham recognised that I could play and I was invited to sign up for the club's tournaments.

I needed new opposition to be honest, because after a while I grew a bit tired of battering my mates on court. I found a new opponent in Roman Nemeczek, who lived near the Brentham and also played football for West Mid. He was a step up and we had some good battles. I won a few tournaments at the Brentham in my age group and started to get noticed as a player.

In fact, I was invited to train with the Middlesex county squad and my standard steadily improved right up to the point where, as my sporting commitments became even more hectic, I was forced to choose between tennis and football. There was only ever going to be one winner there.

I still love that area of Ealing. I can go to the local pub and not get bothered. I can drop into the local shops and the people there know me well. They've seen me grow up. If you stop at West Kebab, you'll see a picture of me behind the counter. Those guys are all Fenerbahce fans so they loved the scissor-kick goal I scored for Liverpool against Galatasaray in September 2006 as much as anyone. It earned my dad a free kebab.

Drop in for a haircut with Andreas the Greek barber and he'll know me, as will the guys in the Samrat curry house. When they redecorated the place, I bought their famous waterfall picture in the auction. It's a classic bit of curry-house junk and was legendary among my mates. The picture has a twist – you plug it in, turn it on and the waterfall appears to be moving. It brings back memories of some good nights out with the lads.

4

REJECTING CHELSEA

The recent history between Liverpool and Chelsea has made for a rivalry that runs deep. In May 2005, the season before I arrived at the club, Liverpool won that amazing Champions League semi-final second leg at Anfield. Five months later Chelsea stuffed us 4–1 at Anfield. I scored the winner against them in the Community Shield in August 2006 in Cardiff. And then we beat them again in the Champions League semi-final in May 2007. At Liverpool, we love to beat Chelsea, and for me in particular, the fixture has special meaning.

With the wealth of Roman Abramovich, Chelsea have the money to buy some of the most famous footballers in the world, and the team that has been built by Jose Mourinho is very different from the one I watched when I was growing up. Then, the fans didn't expect to win Premiership titles and challenge for the Champions League. The Chelsea I remember were much less successful but the club had a massive impact on my childhood. I was a west London boy, son of a Chelsea fanatic, and Stamford Bridge drew me in from a young age.

How could I have ever escaped? Dad was born a Chelsea fan, even if he follows Liverpool home and away now. The first game he went to was as a seven-year-old in 1967. He was at Wembley to watch Tommy Docherty's Chelsea side lose 2–1 to Tottenham in the FA Cup final. From then on, Dad was hooked.

In fact, the legacy of his loyalty was written on my birth certificate. Why was I called Peter? I was named after the late, great Peter Osgood, the Chelsea legend who my father idolised when he was a kid.

The way my career has developed, and a later bond that grew when I became old enough to go to matches with my mates, means that now I feel closer to another great west London football club. Queens Park Rangers are the other team whose results I look out for. That was where I made my professional debut. It is difficult to remain fond of Chelsea when they are such great rivals of Liverpool, but there is no doubt that I received much of my football education there.

Three generations of the Crouch family once stood together in the Shed End, as it was before the Stamford Bridge ground was rebuilt in the 1990s – my grandfather, Jim, my father and me. I am told that even my great-grandfather, another Jim, was a Chelsea fan. That passion for football runs deep in our family.

My relationship with Chelsea changed through my teens as they became increasingly keen on signing me for their youth teams. Before then I was like any other kid, experiencing the sheer thrill of going to watch Chelsea with my dad. By then he had been watching Chelsea for more than twenty years, a veteran of the 1970s teams with a son of his own to take to matches. When it came to replica kits, I was quite spoilt. Dad would always buy me the latest Chelsea shirt and I would pull one of those jerseys on whenever we went to watch a game.

I liked Andy Townsend and Dennis Wise but my favourite was Kerry Dixon. I was an aspiring young striker and Dixon was the man who scored the goals for Chelsea, 193 in nine years there. In fact, I liked Kerry Dixon so much that at eight years old I bestowed upon him the greatest honour I could give anyone – I named my pet rabbit after him. Unfortunately, Kerry Dixon – the rabbit – turned out to have psychopathic tendencies and would attack without warning. He would go for anyone in his way or, most often, my sister's rabbit Jimbo. In the end, we had to make a choice for our own safety and Kerry Dixon was shown the door. The naming tradition continues, though – Stamford is the Crouch family cat.

Memories of those early days watching Chelsea are vivid. Mum would give Dad and me a lift to Ealing Common tube station and we would take the District Line to Earls Court, where we had to change trains. Up until we reached that station the carriages would be quiet, but once we reached Earls Court the match-day atmosphere would take a grip of my imagination. On the platform we joined hundreds of Chelsea fans, decked out in blue shirts and scarves, waiting for the Wimbledon train to take us to Fulham Broadway. The platform was always packed and the train would be jammed full. I'd be crushed in among the crowd. Although I was tall, I was still a bit smaller than most of the fans who crammed on to those old grey trains.

The crowds pour out of Fulham Broadway station on match-days – up the stairs at the back of the tube station and out the gates that the police open up. Every young kid who loves football loves the experience of going to a football match and I was no different. I loved it all – the crowds, the noise, the conversation, the bad language and the sheer excitement on everyone's face.

In those days at Stamford Bridge we used to sit all over the stadium, depending on where Dad could get tickets. I knew all the songs. I would eat, breathe and sleep Chelsea at that time. We sat in the West Stand for a while and I would always nag at my dad that I wanted to stand in the famous Shed End. That was the heartbeat of the club, where the songs came from. It was where the young lads who were old enough to come on their own would stand, the toughest part of the ground.

For a long time Dad wasn't having it. He said I was too young to go in the Shed. We sat in the East Stand lower for a whole season until finally he relented and we stood in the Shed End, which, in those days, was still the old curving terrace set back from the pitch, not the all-seater stand there now. As we got older, and my passion for standing up at a game diminished, Dad got a season ticket for the upper tier of the Matthew Harding, or North, Stand, at the opposite end of the ground.

I had the same deep-rooted obsession with football that a lot of young kids have. I loved it when new football boots came out. I wanted to know which players had them and what new details the designers had included. When I asked for a player's autograph, I found it just amazing when they even acknowledged me. Now when I'm out and about and I meet kids who support Liverpool, I see how excited they get when I sign an autograph or say hello. I know what they are going through.

As I became absorbed with Chelsea, they began to take an interest in me. Word of the success that Andy Campbell was achieving at West Middlesex Colts had spread around the local area. Osterley, Northolt, Ealing, Perivale, if you are a promising young footballer playing there, you're never too far away from a Chelsea scout. Soon a regular stream of scouts from Chelsea, QPR and Brentford began stopping for a drink in the White Lodge Club and talking to the parents.

The Chelsea scout, Bob Orsborn, constantly asked my dad to bring me to train with them in Battersea, and pulled out all the stops to persuade him to agree. Bob got us tickets for matches. He got me team shirts and arranged for me to meet the players. Best of all, he gave me the chance to be a ball-boy at Stamford Bridge, and Chelsea went the extra mile. Even though they were interested in signing just two of us – my team-mate Michael Dobson and me – they invited most of the West Mid team to be ball-boys, including Andy Campbell's son Ian and his daughter Claire.

Bob was nothing if not persistent. If he found out my dad was in a pub somewhere in Ealing, he would turn up and offer to buy him a drink.

'Bruce, fancy bringing Peter down to Battersea?' he would ask.

'Thanks Bob, but the answer is still no,' Dad would tell him.

Bob had recruited Jody Morris – who was regarded as the best young footballer in the country when he was a teenager – and he was good at his job. He had a few tried and tested ways of impressing his targets and their families with the club's hospitality, in the hope that he could get the parents on side and sign up the kids. In those days, although the Chelsea hospitality was generous, it was more in keeping with the tighter budgets of the pre-Roman Abramovich era. We're not talking yacht trips off the coast of Monte Carlo. When I was 12 years old, Bob treated Dad and me to an evening at Wimbledon greyhound track. Sam Parkin was there, too, with his mother. Sam was another of Bob's discoveries, and Bob's idea was that the two of us would be ideal partners in the Chelsea Under-12s attack. Sam went on to sign for Chelsea but never made it as far as the senior team. He's had a good solid career since then and now plays for Luton Town.

Unfortunately for Bob, a night at the dogs still didn't persuade Dad that Chelsea were the right team for his son. I was keen, though. This was Chelsea, our team. What was the argument? At first, I couldn't believe that the father who had taken me to Stamford Bridge as a little kid didn't want me to play there. But Dad had done his research and found out that Chelsea's hothouse for west London talent based in Battersea was signing up all the good young players in the area, and rejecting plenty of them.

We took everything that was going but we never promised Chelsea that I would sign and I never did. It puzzled and frustrated them, especially once they found out what a passionate Chelsea fan my dad was at the time.

The bottom line was that Dad thought if I went to Chelsea only to be released later, it would break my heart. Worse yet, he felt that if I didn't make it at Chelsea, I might turn my back on football altogether. When I look back now, I don't think anything could have changed my love for football – but who knows? Dad was making a tough decision for the right reasons. I might have come up through the ranks with John Terry, who is just a month older than I am. Then again, I might not have done.

Chelsea really wanted me and it was hard because we were both fans, but Dad wouldn't give in and they never understood it. It drove them mad. Dad still believes that the Chelsea way in those days was the 'sausage factory' approach. Get every good kid in and hope one of them makes it. He reckoned it was a production line for footballers rather than a club that could improve and coach me in the same way as West Mid had done. I took my guidance from my dad when it came to the decision but the clincher for me was that I did not know a lot of lads who were playing at Chelsea. All the best players from the teams that West Mid played against seemed to be training at Chelsea, but not my very best mates. Michael Dobson was staying at Brentford, the team his father George had once played for. When you are a young player, you want to go where you know people. So in the end, when Dad said, 'No,' I wasn't too fussed.

If anything came close to changing my mind about Chelsea it was the best perk of them all – that chance to be a ball-boy at Stamford Bridge. What an experience. You run out with the players, you are in the dressing room and the tunnel, and you have a seat just beyond the advertising boards, yards from the action. It's a strange job because a whole match can pass without you having to do anything. These days, most clubs use the multi-ball system where the ball-boys throw in a spare ball before they retrieve the original. If the home side takes the lead, they might discreetly remove all the spares to waste time.

Sounds simple? Well, maybe, but I sometimes found it difficult, to say the least, to work out exactly what was required of me as a ball-boy at Chelsea. With the atmosphere of the match and the intensity of the crowd swirling around me, I didn't always get my duties right. There was one incident during a game that Chelsea were winning when Dennis Wise kicked the ball into touch. I ran after it, picked it up and was just about to throw it back when Dennis shouted at me, 'Fucking keep hold of it, will you?'

That threw me. I was really worried that I had done something wrong, so I decided to keep hold of it next time. When the ball came in my direction again, I changed my approach. This time I casually walked after the ball and took my time as I rolled it back to the defender Gareth Hall. I was taking ages over it.

'Will you fucking hurry up?' Hall shouted at me.

What a nightmare. I was only young and I was being shouted at by these famous players. It was much more fun during the warm-up when five of us ball-boys would go in goal together and the players would take shots at us.

Offers came in from other clubs, too, most bizarrely Millwall, who were trying to sign up all the good young players in London at the time. You might remember they had a kid called Cherno Samba who was, for a while, the hottest property in schoolboy football. Samba is four years younger than I am and the last I heard, he was playing at Plymouth. Millwall let it be known to my dad, when I was about 12 years old, that they were interested.

This time, however, we weren't talking autographs, free tickets and a chance to be a ball-boy. This time we were talking about a professional contract. The regime in charge of Millwall in those days has long since gone, but back then they told my dad that they could guarantee me a professional deal even before I hit my teenage years. Millwall said they would give me guaranteed associated schoolboy forms at 14 and a Youth Training Scheme place, the equivalent of today's academy scholarships. Not only that, but there would also be a two-year professional contract on top of it.

It was unreal. It was like seeing your future mapped out in front of you right up until the age of 18. When you look at it like that, it is not hard to see why a lot of young English lads were sucked in by the incentives that some clubs offered. Some of my mates came from single parent homes where the security of knowing they had a future would have made a huge difference.

We declined for lots of reasons, but mainly because it just seemed weird. How could they be that sure about me? What pressure would that deal bring? And how the hell was Mum going to get me to training after school when Millwall are miles away in south-east London and we're all the way over the other side of the city in Ealing? Practical considerations are equally important with a young family. We made the decision to refuse Millwall for the right reasons. Dad had worked hard to make life comfortable for us. Nine times out of ten, parents who take the deal on offer find that it all goes wrong because they are not making the decision for football reasons.

When I was old enough to be allowed to go to matches with my mates, Greg Chapman and I would watch QPR if Chelsea were playing away. Their Loftus Road stadium is at White City, just four stops east on the Central Line from Ealing Broadway, and to us going there on our own felt like a proper adventure. It was a fiver to get in to the lower paddock, even when they were in the Premiership, and plenty of kids from my area went to Rangers.

As with Chelsea, I came to have more to do with QPR than watching their first team play. Their west London scout was watching me. The man from Rangers was Pat Nolan, a lovely Irish bloke, who has sadly passed away. He was a scout from the old school, and wore a cloth cap. He knew his stuff.

Pat would watch us play on the pitches at the back of the White Lodge Club no matter how hard the rain fell. He had the kind of insight that comes only with experience, and the parents at West Mid, my dad included, had great respect for him. Dad knew for a while that Pat was interested in me going to QPR. Pat knew that Dad had turned down Chelsea because he was uncertain about how they would handle my future, so Pat never put on any pressure. He just told my dad that he thought I had real promise.

'Any time you want to come down to watch the first team train, you just have to say,' Pat would tell Dad. 'We would love to have Peter at QPR. He's a local boy and it would make it easy for him to get to training. We play the right way at Rangers.'

Pat had another thing in his favour. He had put together one of the best youth teams in QPR's history, including the legendary Kevin Gallen, Nigel Quashie, Danny Dichio, Michael Mahoney-Johnson and Mark Perry, who has since become a friend of mine. When I was deciding on which professional team to join, watching that QPR youth team gave me a very clear idea of just how hard it was going to be, joining an élite side of young players.

Pat had first spotted me at West Mid when he stood behind the goal for a game against a team called Larkspur. I scored one of my best goals that day and I came off the pitch buzzing with excitement. I got in the car and Dad showed me a little card Pat had given him. It had a QPR badge on it and Pat's telephone number. I was chuffed and Dad took me to Twyford Avenue, which was within walking

distance of our house in Ealing, to watch the famous Gallen generation youth team.

Gallen was little more than five years older than I was and had
signed professional forms aged 17. He made his debut for the QPR
senior team against Manchester United aged 18 after smashing all
the club's youth team goalscoring records – an amazing 153 goals in
110 appearances. Injuries may have affected his career later on but, as
a nervous kid, I looked at him in awe during my first visit to QPR.

How quick it all seemed. The crunching tackles that were going in
shocked me – it was just a step above. I wondered how I would ever
get to that level, but as I watched these older players, and saw Gallen
banging in goals, I thought, 'This is where I want to be.' The trouble
was it looked so much more professional than playing for West Mid
on a Sunday. The strength of these boys seemed incredible. I felt a
long way off the mark.

I played at QPR for the first time in a training session. It wasn't
exactly a trial, but even so I was nervous – and I'm not the nervous
type, certainly not now. Just going into the dressing room and
meeting the lads was different. You certainly meet some characters.
Going to a professional club can be a great experience for a young lad.
You do your growing up in the youth team.

I was impressed that we wore the full QPR kit and afterwards I was
given even better news – we were handed vouchers to exchange for a
bag of chips. I thought this was amazing. First you got to play football
in the QPR kit, then you got free chips. It was too good to be true. I
soon settled in when I realised that there were perks to be had in
joining a professional club.

Once I am in with a good set of lads and having a laugh, I can play
at my best. There were some good players at QPR, although at that
age you can never tell. One lad, Eddy Mitchell, was stronger and
quicker than everyone else – he was the man, much better than I was.

I thought he was definitely going to make it, but he didn't develop and he fell by the wayside. Maybe I got stronger as I carried on playing. That's what happens.

The manager of QPR's Under-18s youth team, Des Bulpin, turned out to be a major influence on my career. Des is a straight-talking West Country bloke who has always backed me. He liked me in those early days at QPR, then he took me to Tottenham and then back to Loftus Road when I was 19. Des is not afraid to have an opinion and not frightened to tell people what he thinks. Most recently, he became assistant manager at Plymouth Argyle when Ian Holloway took over.

Like Pat Nolan, Des never put any pressure on Dad. I went to training at QPR once a week and Des would occasionally speak to him. Des would catch up with him at the end of a session and tell him that I had been making good progress. 'We think he'll go a long way' – that sort of thing. There was no pressure to promise to sign the forms when the time came, or to sign them early, but we kept going to watch youth-team games. Kevin Gallen spoke to me and gave me some encouragement and we could see that QPR were producing good young players.

Not until the summer of 1994 did I finally quit West Mid and focus completely on QPR, playing for them on Saturday mornings and training with them more than once during the week. I turned 14 in January 1995, which was when I could sign associated schoolboy forms. That would have kept me at the club until they decided whether I would be worth a YTS trainee contract at the age of 16.

But events at a much higher level than the youth teams at QPR were about to influence my career. In November 1994, Ossie Ardiles was sacked as Tottenham Hotspur manager and, a few months later, QPR's Gerry Francis, who had led the club to a fifth-place finish in 1993, the Premiership's first season, was given the job at White Hart

Lane. It didn't come as a surprise in the Crouch household. We had known that Gerry was likely to get the job ever since Ardiles had been sacked. The word had gone round that Des and Gerry were off to Tottenham and we delayed signing the associated schoolboy forms to see what happened. I was free to move.

That's the way football works sometimes. If QPR had been quicker in providing us with those forms, we would have signed them already and a move would have been out of the question. By the time they finally did offer me the forms, Dad told me not to sign anything. Once Des and Gerry took over at Tottenham, the call came that they wanted us to join them there. A few weeks later, Dad called Chris Gieler, QPR's youth development officer, and told him I was moving to Tottenham.

Dad didn't see eye-to-eye with Gieler and once Des had left we didn't feel much loyalty to QPR. The club bombarded us with offers to try to persuade me to stay, mainly because they didn't want to lose a player to Des and they thought that if I went, even more would leave. But Des had built up our trust and, although training at White Hart Lane would mean a couple of long journeys around the North Circular every week, we thought it was a price worth paying. At the time, Spurs had Teddy Sheringham, Jurgen Klinnsman and Nicky Barmby in their senior team. The club was one of the biggest in the Premiership. It was a step up for me.

Dad and I reckoned that with Des at Tottenham I would stand a chance of getting into the youth team. Despite my increasing height – this was when I began to hit a real growth spurt – Des believed in me. He knew I was good technically and he understood the way my game worked. At QPR I had shown that I could not only hold my own in a professional club's youth team but that I was a sought-after player. The next challenge was at a famous old London club with a serious history.

5

A SCHOOL TOO FAR

What influenced my decisions and filled my dreams when I was 11 years old? Football. The pressing questions of when I would next be playing, and with which team, were the main ones that filled my head when I came to leave North Ealing Primary. I was already nicely established as one of the best players in the area, and I had a close circle of mates. To my mind, the next step in my football development depended on me reaching one educational establishment above all others.

Drayton Manor High School in Hanwell was the place my mates were heading to and I'd set my heart on going there with them. It's a redbrick former grammar school that seems to have gone up in the world since I left. It took its pupils from a wide range of families. The Copley estate and the Drayton Bridge estate are nearby and the students reflected the mix of ethnic minorities and social backgrounds in the area. Like a lot of London comprehensive schools, it had a bit of bad and a lot of good in it, none of which was on my mind. I was more interested in the fact that Drayton Manor had really good football teams.

It all seemed perfect. My mates were going to Drayton Manor, and it had a reputation for football. I was ready to get my name on the list as soon as possible. However, there was a problem on that score – Mum and Dad felt differently.

By then, Dad's career was developing and, having done the sums, he and Mum worked out they could afford to send me to a private school. Lots of parents in London go through the same dilemma – will the local comp be good enough for their kids or should they stretch themselves on school fees? I already knew the answer. I was horrified, distraught at the idea of going anywhere but Drayton Manor. I considered myself a proper Ealing boy. What the hell would going to a posh school do to my street cred?

Mum and Dad had their eye on Latymer Upper School in Hammersmith. Almost 400 years old, it included Hugh Grant and Alan Rickman among its famous old boys. I'm sure that many people have very happy memories of their time at that school, but all I could think about was spending the next five years of my life with lots of little Hooray Henrys while my mates did their growing up at Drayton Manor.

The Latymer question came to dominate the Crouch household for six long months. 'Why would I want to go there?' I pleaded desperately each time the subject was raised. I gathered information on Drayton Manor's many qualities, I gave it the hard sell to Mum and Dad. I listened with desperation to my mates as they looked forward to playing football together in Drayton's Year 7 team. I had to escape the fate of going to Latymer, at all costs.

Things only got worse when we went to the open day at Latymer. 'This is such a nice school,' Mum kept saying approvingly as we were shown round. I wasn't looking at the classrooms. I was obsessed by the terrible haircuts most of the lads at Latymer sported – awful floppy barnets. You could definitely tell that Hugh Grant had been there.

'Look at their haircuts,' I kept whispering to my dad. 'There is NO WAY I can go to this school.' Even though he was sticking to the party line, Dad was honest enough to agree with me on that point.

'You're not wrong there,' he whispered back.

I was still protesting right up until the day arrived to take Latymer's entrance exam. Mum and Dad made me sit it and Dad went along with me to make sure I made it in time. These days he says that he knew I had little chance of passing when we waited in the examination hall. While all the other young hopefuls were swatting up on their revision, I was idly studying the roll of honour of Latymer old boys who had won scholarships or been made school captain. I remember pointing out to Dad that I had found a Hurst, a Charlton and a Peters on one list alone. I think that showed what subject was on my mind at the time, and it certainly wasn't the exam.

My parents may well have worked it out by now but I should get this off my chest once and for all. Hand on heart, I failed that exam on purpose. I was there with another lad from my school, Matt Hobden, and he felt the same as I did. He didn't want to go to Latymer either. I can't remember the questions on the paper but I know I wasn't arsed about getting them right. When I got back home Mum asked me how it had gone.

'Yeah, I think it went all right,' I said, but I knew that I was going to Drayton Manor with my mates. I'd blown the Latymer exam – sorry about that, Mum and Dad.

One more major embarrassment awaited me, though, before the way was clear, and my mates have never let me forget it. When you're 11 years old, there are lots of ways that your mum can embarrass you, but telling the kids at your prospective new school what a brilliant footballer you are is one of the most effective. Good old Mum, she dropped me right in it.

One of the lads who showed Mum and I around on the Drayton Manor open day was Stephen Potter, later to become a friend of mine, and he had a tactic for embarrassing the new kids. It involved asking their parents leading questions to get them talking about their children, along the lines of: 'Is Peter well-behaved?' 'Does he do his homework?' 'Is he any good at football?'

My mum was certainly not one to under-sell her son and she bigged me up in front of these kids like never before. 'Oh yes,' she said, 'Peter's an excellent footballer,' 'He always does his homework,' and so on. The more she praised me, the more the questions came. I knew what they were up to. I just wasn't brave enough to stop it. I could only stand there and listen, my embarrassment rising, as these kids suppressed their giggles at my mum's wholehearted praise for her young son. I was getting the piss taken out of me and I hadn't even started there yet.

Mum may have given my football skills the hard-sell but at least I didn't disappoint on that score. Ted Dale, the PE teacher, made me captain of the Year 7 football team. He even switched me to midfield, which was a bad move for my team-mates. At that age I had a deep aversion to passing the ball. My game was just about pure greed. I wanted to score and I would never pass. Never. I don't think the rest of the lads thought I should have been the captain.

It was a good school but totally different from North Ealing, which had a nice village atmosphere. There were tough kids at Drayton Manor, streetwise and confident, the same as most London comprehensives, I expect, but not what I was used to. At first it was a bit of a shock but I quickly came to enjoy it.

In a rough London school, my defence was that I could always make people laugh. At school, being the joker can go a long way to keeping you safe. My height made me stand out from the crowd, and I had a reputation for being a good footballer, but I never had a fight. As for that other benchmark of status, well, I was crap with girls, at least until quite late on. I had made up my mind that I was not interested because I needed to be focused on playing football all the time. I always felt that football had to come first, and if you wanted to be a success, you just couldn't be involved with a girl. For some reason, I thought that was the way to make it.

Football was my priority but I turned my hand to a few other sports as well. At North Ealing I had come to regard myself as an electric sprinter, capable of winning every race staged on sports day. It was only at secondary school that reality hit and I realised that actually I was not the quickest thing on two legs that Ealing had ever seen. So I switched to the 800m and, inevitably, the high jump.

I was the best at school for the 800m and ran in the Ealing borough championships but, for obvious reasons, I really excelled at the high jump, although it caused the worst injury of my sporting career. In my first year at Drayton I held the Ealing borough record for the high jump and definitely thought that I was the man when it came to that event.

Call it overconfidence, or maybe I was just taking the piss, but I soon came to regret the day I showed off to my mates on the high-jump mats. We were messing about during a lesson and I told the lads to raise the bar higher and higher. Unfortunately, one of my record-breaking attempts finished with me landing, Fosbury flop-style, between the two safety mats instead of on top of them. I hit the floor hard and was in absolute agony.

As I climbed to my feet, the pain almost made me pass out. The problem was that I had a reputation as the joker and, all around me, my mates were still cracking up with laughter at the sight of me disappearing headfirst into the gap between the two mats. Yet again I had amused them and they thought I had meant to do it. I couldn't possibly let them down so I managed to smile through the pain. 'I'm fine,' I said, 'but I think I'm going to take a rest.' Bravely, I waved away the few concerns that were expressed for my well-being but as the last kid left the gym, I burst into tears. I had never known pain like it.

A few mates came back at the end of the PE lesson and were surprised to see a very distressed, and far from happy Peter Crouch being loaded into the back of an ambulance. Worse was yet to come. The hospital bodged the diagnosis and failed to recognise that I had not only broken but dislocated my shoulder. They put me in a sling and sent me home. Thanks a lot for that. By then the pain was severe.

I could barely lie down, let alone sleep that night, so Dad put me in the car again and we decided to give a local private hospital a try. The doctor at the Clementine Churchill Hospital in Harrow said he couldn't believe the first doctor had missed it and they operated immediately. I still have the scars on my arm from where they inserted, and later removed, two pins to support the bone.

The worst thing about it? It was summer, so while all my mates were getting on their bikes to go down to the Brentham Club, I was stuck at home. Not just at home but stuck inside a comedy plaster cast that ran from my shoulder downwards and held my arm rigid out in front of me – for a month I was permanently in the pose of a man raising a glass to his lips. I have been lucky with injuries ever since then, I've never had a really bad one, but my enthusiasm for the high jump was never the same.

6

TOUGHENED UP AT TOTTENHAM

I arrived at Tottenham aged 14 with the skill and technique to make it as a footballer, and it was there that I learned to play the game like a man. Ability will get you so far but in football's harsh world you need the bottle, too. That was a lesson I had to learn the hardest way.

The first day I walked across the training ground at Tottenham I got a few stares and a few double-takes. I was well over 6ft tall and had stepped out of the comfort zone of QPR into a much more competitive world. This was Tottenham, the big time, one of the most famous clubs in the country. Kids from all over Britain were there trying to make it as professionals. I was there on the recommendation of Des Bulpin and, as I would find throughout my career, I would have to do more than anyone else to prove myself.

There was no outcry in the newspapers, no big compensation fees for Tottenham to pay when I left QPR. Des just told Dad to bring me down to White Hart Lane for training one Wednesday night and I signed my associated schoolboy forms not long after that. The first transfer of my career was complete. These days, if one of a club's best young players moves to a big club, it can be back-page news. No one bothered when I moved to Tottenham.

Des had stuck his neck out for me. Like Pat Nolan, he believed that

I had the talent to go a long way in the game. He could see past the fact that I was skinny and tall for my age, and he was prepared to back his judgement against all the Tottenham coaches. I wasn't under any illusions. They didn't all fancy me as a player. I still had a lot of people to win over.

After I had been at Tottenham for a while, Des got me to play and train with the older age groups, the 16- and 17-year-olds. Then when I was 15, I was put in with the Under–18s. It was tough. Teenagers grow quickly and I didn't yet have their strength. I would turn up from a day at school to join these lads who were full-time trainees, a close-knit bunch who spent all their days together.

When the banter was flying among the older boys, I just kept my head down. They were big, strong players while I, on the other hand, was known as 'Sticks'. I was a tall, thin teenage kid trying to hold his own, and I can't say I enjoyed training with them or playing for their teams, but Des pushed me on. He had a reason for wanting me in with the older boys. There was a problem with my game and it took me a while to overcome it.

I wasn't nasty enough, or ruthless enough, and I was up against some really tough kids if I wanted to win a place on the trainee scheme when I turned 16. Ledley King, the boy from Bow, just blew me away when I saw first him play. Ledley became one of my best mates and I have never seen a young footballer who was so obviously destined to make it as a professional.

Ledley had it all from a young age. He was skilful, tough, fast, a natural footballer and a strong athlete. He was always going to make it. He was streets ahead of the rest of us when we were teenagers and, as captain of Tottenham now, and an England international, he hasn't let anyone down. How good was he? So good that when, a few years later, we played an England Under-18 international in Spain, even Real Madrid asked about Ledley's availability.

I lacked that aggression. OK, I wasn't a kid from a tough inner-city estate, but I wanted to be a footballer just as much as the other lads at Tottenham wanted it. Des was ruthless with me on that score. He hated me holding back, or failing to go in to tackles fully committed. He was like a sergeant-major. No sympathy. If I held back, there were punishments, there was more running. 'Crouchy,' he'd shout at me. 'Get stuck in!'

Des wasn't the only one who hated it when I pulled out of a tackle. Dad did, too. He could see how it was going for me. We were being watched all the time at Tottenham, being judged by the youth-team staff. They were sizing up our potential to make it as players. Every time I pulled out of a challenge, that was a black mark against my name. Dad believed I had the ability, so did Des. Neither of them wanted me to squander it just because people thought I wasn't brave enough.

It used to kill me when Dad criticised me. He was so upset sometimes that he couldn't hold back after matches or training sessions. 'You're too nice,' he'd say. 'You're never going to get anywhere in football like that. They'll think you're a pansy.' I was a relaxed, laid-back kid. I probably was too nice, and yes, I did jump out of the odd tackle – there were some big strong kids out there – but I learned to stand my ground at Tottenham and I don't jump out of tackles any more.

Gradually, and with Des's guidance and Dad's encouragement, I drummed it into myself that I wasn't going to be the same kid on the pitch that I was off it. When I played football, I wasn't going to be that easy-going teenager who made everyone laugh at school. It's a harsh lesson to learn when you're young. In the end, it stood me in good stead in my professional career. It changed the way I was as a footballer, but I'll never forget the way I had to learn.

Instead of travelling all the way over to the training ground at Spurs Lodge in Chigwell in Essex, east of London, we would meet to train after school in the gym at White Hart Lane. The issue of me jumping out of tackles had stirred recently between Dad and me and I suppose it had to come to a head some time.

One particular night, I jumped out of a tackle with another Spurs hopeful, Nicky Hunt (not the same player who currently plays for Bolton Wanderers). Nicky was from Wandsworth, a big lad and very strong. He was smashing into everybody that night and then came over for a 50–50 challenge with me. I admit it. I didn't fancy it, but as soon as I pulled out, I regretted it.

The gym had a viewing platform where the players' parents could look down on the action from behind a window. I looked up to spot my dad's face. I could see him but I could not make out his expression. Had he seen it? Had he realised I had pulled out of the tackle? I was in a bit of a panic. My mind was in a spin. *Oh God, what have I done? We've talked about this so much and now I've pulled out of one right in front of his eyes.*

In the past when I had pulled out of tackles, Dad would be quiet when we got into the car after training, but I'd get the vibes that something wasn't right. I would know what was coming and as we drove home he would have his say. The normal stuff would come out that I knew in my heart to be true – 'You're too nice, you've got to be stronger.'

That night, when I came out of the gym at White Hart Lane, Dad wasn't there. I looked around for him but he was nowhere to be seen. All the other lads were meeting parents and making their way out to the car park. The life of a football parent means a tight schedule and rushing home late to reheated dinners. My dad wasn't there. I was 14 and on my own in north London, miles from home. I was panicking. *Oh no. What's happened here?*

Looking back, I should have told someone at the club. I should have explained that I needed a lift home, but I was just so embarrassed. What the hell was I supposed to say? 'I jumped out of a tackle and upset my dad. Now he's not here. Could you take me back to Ealing please?' No chance.

I was desperate and upset. It was dark and these were the days long before mobile phones. I had some money in my tracksuit pocket so I walked out of the ground on to the High Road and looked for a phone box to call home. I trailed through one of the local estates before I found one and called Mum. She was so upset when she picked up the phone. Dad had called her on his way out. She told me, 'You're going to have to get home on your own. He's left you.'

I was in bits but I can still remember the route I took home. First I caught the over-ground train from White Hart Lane to Seven Sisters. From Seven Sisters I got on the Victoria Line to Oxford Street, and from Oxford Street I took the Central Line to Ealing Broadway. I had never made that journey on my own, certainly never at night. I hadn't been much farther than White City to watch QPR without my dad, and I don't mind admitting that there were tears most of the way home.

I was upset because I had upset him, and because this was a very harsh lesson to learn. I loved my dad as much as any 14-year-old kid loves his father, and I hated the feeling that I had let him down. I know he did it in my best interests and it is most definitely a night that I will never forget. I certainly never jumped out of another tackle. In the long run what he did helped me, but I do think he went overboard that night.

Mum was obviously upset when I got in, but relieved I had made it back from my epic adventure across London's rail network. Dad was still angry about the tackle – or the lack of one – and as I lay on my bed he came to speak to me. We made up in the end – we always do.

Dad just wanted me to succeed, and to do all he could to help. For instance, when I look back now, I realise the effect of the extra work I did with him. From the ages of 13 to 14 we got into a routine of getting up before school to practise, just me and him. We would get up really early, 6.30, and get over to the football pitch for seven. We'd have half an hour's practice before we went back to the house and I got ready for school. For a while we would do this about twice a week.

If you want to make it as a player, you have to do extra. There is always a way of improving your touch, improving your shot, working on the little things, but I can't say I would have done it if it had been left to me to decide. I was a teenager and teenagers are not well known for their ability to get out of bed bright and early in the morning. We would drive over to Hanwell Town Football Club's ground, jump over the fence and go around to the back of the first-team pitch to another training pitch. We had a big bag of footballs and I would practise heading, shooting and volleying.

At first I was completely bemused by the whole thing. *What are we doing? None of my mates are doing this.* It wasn't as if I didn't want to play football, because afterwards I would go home, have a shower, get to school at eight and start playing again. It wasn't so much what we were doing, it was the time of the morning we were doing it.

There were times when I would say, 'Dad, I don't want to do this.' He never forced me, never ordered me out of bed, he would just give me a look that said, 'It's up to you.' Once I saw that look I would change my mind. 'I do really, I'm coming,' I would say. We didn't just play football. Sometimes, for a change, we would go swimming.

I really hated getting up early, but once I was there I used to enjoy it. I used to ask myself the question *Why? Why is no one else doing this? Why am I the only one?* I have a good answer to that now. Of all my contemporaries, apart from Ledley King, I am the only one playing in the Premiership and for England. When I think about how I made it as a footballer, I tend to think back to those reluctant early mornings at Hanwell Town FC.

As we got into a routine it wasn't so much the early mornings that bothered me. I was most worried about being seen by someone who knew me. At that age you live in constant fear of being embarrassed in front of your school-mates and this seemed like a prime opportunity for someone at school to find a way to take the piss out of me. The training pitch at Hanwell Town was right by the Perivale exit from the A40, where the cars queue at traffic lights. I could imagine the reaction if someone at school spotted me from the road. 'Isn't that Peter Crouch over there playing football with his dad? What's he doing that for at seven in the morning? What a weirdo!'

Greg Chapman was always sympathetic. His dad had played non-league and was very similar to my dad when it came to pushing Greg as a footballer. When we wanted a moan we would swap gripes about our dads and their expectations of us. 'You know when he has a go at you after you've had a bad game? The silence in the car? Is yours like that too?'

That's how it was. I can't knock it now because I think when people say I have a good touch or quick feet, I honestly believe it was the amount of work I put in when I was younger. It doesn't all come naturally. If you work at it at a young age, you get better and better.

I worked so hard at my football skills on those mornings. I didn't ever tell anyone what I was doing. I just used to get on with it and then go to school. My dad had a simple wish for me. He wanted me to be as good as I could be at the one thing that meant the most to me. He had made the most of his skills in his career and he could see that I obviously had talent. Getting a teenager to respond is not always easy.

He knew I could get somewhere but he also thought that I was too laid-back and didn't have as much drive as I should have. Actually, I did. It just wasn't obvious. I had always wanted to be a footballer and I played every day of my life to get there. Dad has always tried to push me towards that goal but he wasn't doing it for himself. He genuinely had my interests at heart. He would take me all over the place, rearrange his own job commitments, so that I could go to training sessions and play in matches.

Our relationship changed as I grew up. It's brilliant now, although we sometimes disagree. These days I argue more with him. When I was younger I didn't because I worried I was wrong. I think the last time he criticised me for my football was after a West Brom match in August 2000, early in my QPR career, when I crumbled under pressure from the opposition fans.

He has taken a step back the higher I have gone. Now I'm playing for England and Liverpool, I have achieved much of what I set out to do, and what he always hoped I would achieve. He has the utmost respect for it, and is only really complimentary. I don't think I ever had to prove myself to him – he's my dad and he will always support me – but if there were any doubts about my commitment, they have been dispelled a long time ago.

After every game I ring him. As a kid I would get in to the car and, if I had played poorly, he would ask me that loaded question: 'How do you think you played today?' Now if things have gone badly for the team, he's more likely to blame someone else, although what I do get from my dad is honesty. I ask his opinion more than ever now. We have always worked together throughout my career. My achievements have not been mine alone, they have been made possible by his help.

He comes to every game now and I know how proud he is. I realise what a help he has been over the years. We have had our ups and downs but the good far outweighs the bad. And most of all, he is always there for me. If I am worried about something I go to him. A lot of players these days speak to their agents first, but I speak to my dad about everything. I know I can trust him completely and I respect his opinion because he is a clever man as well. And he's been with me every step of the way.

Team Crouch – Dad Bruce, Mum Jayne and sister Sarah.

Left: Dreaming of England, aged six – my first-ever football trophy with Northolt Hotspurs.

Above: In Singapore with my first friend, Tohru, at his birthday party.

Below: Playing football with Dad on the beach in Dubai, a long time before it became the favourite holiday destination for Premiership footballers.

Right: Signed up for my first club, Brentford, aged ten.

Below: QPR superstar Justin Channing. He was a hero to a local lad like me, so that's why I look so nervous receiving my Martin Allen soccer school award.

BRENTFORD
FOOTBALL CLUB

Centre of Excellence Schoolboy 1991/92

Name PETE CROUCH

Signature Pete crouch

My cousin Sam Dicken (*left*) had come to watch Anthony Charles (now at Aldershot) and me play for West Middlesex Colts. We've just won the 1991 County Cup at Griffin Park.

More trophies for Andy Campbell's West Mid team.

Leading out the ballboys for a home game at Stamford Bridge.

Posing with my great mates the Aitken twins, Ed (*left*) and Rob.

Ledley King was always destined for great things. I came through the ranks with him at Spurs.

As an apprentice I cleaned David Ginola's boots – and I learned a thing or two from him about the overhead kick.

Spurs scout John Moncur oversees me signing schoolboy forms. I didn't take life too seriously in those days.

In action for the Spurs youth team in July 1999, aged 18.

Bernard Makufi and I celebrate a goal for Hässleholm against Karlskrona in Sweden in 2000.

Makufi and I worked well together and, in the end, Hässleholm didn't want me to leave.

Relaxing with Alton Thelwell in Hässleholm – even most Swedes haven't heard of the place.

7

SPURS TRAINEE – AND THE LEGEND OF EGGYBOFF

At a professional club, the hierarchy of first team, reserves, pros and YTS apprentices is like a feudal society. Those at the top can do whatever they like. They set the tone of the place, they get their boots cleaned and they dish out the stick. You can call it stick, banter, whatever you like, but I have never experienced anything to compare with it.

You think teenage schoolkids can be cruel? You haven't heard anything as harsh and unforgiving as the stick directed at the young lads at a football club. You have to be able to take it, and you have to be able to give it out, or you end up going under. Football has changed since I was growing up. Now the academy system makes for a much different introduction to football. I was part of one of the last generations to go through it in the traditional way.

As I got older at Tottenham – and I was there in those crucial years of 14 to 19 – I learned what it was to be a professional footballer. I saw the different personalities in the dressing room, the relationship between players and managers and the strong bond that can be developed in a good team. There is something unique in the spirit of a group of young lads trying to make their way in the game and trying to do their growing up along the way.

It was a cruel system, always has been. Some kids get dropped at

14, some at 16, some get professional deals but still never make it. It gets serious when you are offered your first YTS – Youth Training Scheme – contract. That was a very big deal, much more significant than the associated schoolboy forms we signed at 14. The age of 16 was a major cut-off point for young players, the hurdle that so many promising footballers failed to clear.

By 1996, the Youth Training Schemes run by clubs had long since replaced the old style apprenticeships and have now been replaced by the academy scholars system. A YTS contract was football's version of the government scheme then in place for 16-year-old school leavers learning skills in the workplace. You were affiliated to a club while they decided in those two or three years whether to offer you a professional contract. A bit more studying was available if you wanted to do it, but in general, there was football, crap pay and a lot of cleaning the first team's boots.

I was told of the decision on my future just before I went with Tottenham's Under-16s to the Northern Ireland Milk Cup, a prestigious international youth-team tournament. A few of us who were one year below that age group had been selected to go with the older lads – Ledley, Nicky Hunt, Narada Bernard, Gavin Kelly, the goalkeeper from West Middlesex Colts, and me.

A few days before the trip we were at White Hart Lane and Bob Arber, one of the youth-team managers, called us into the kit room. He said, 'You boys coming on the trip to Ireland are getting YTS.' That was it. I had made the cut with a year to spare. I was excited, relieved even. Ledley looked pretty calm about the whole thing. Maybe he already had a pro deal sorted out by then. He was that good. At last, I could think of myself as, if not a professional footballer, then a full-time footballer at the very least.

The trip to Northern Ireland was an enlightening introduction to what life would be like living and working as a YTS boy. I was one of the youngest and quickly discovered how sharp you had to be just to defend yourself when the banter started. Before the football even began, the whole team decided to get their heads shaved. Well, put it this way, the older lads decided we were having skinhead cuts and I was never going to get away with not having it done.

One by one we all sat down in a chair and had our hair shaved off by our team-mates. When they had finished with me there was no getting away from it, I looked like a refugee from some terrible conflict – nothing but bones topped off with a haircut that made me look like a prisoner of war.

We travelled around Northern Ireland playing in different stadiums, and although I was on the bench for much of it, the tournament was the first time I had played in front of decent crowds. We had a strong team and my moment of glory came in the quarter-finals at Cricket Park in Ballymoney. We were 1–0 down to the youth team of Brondby from Denmark and, on as a substitute, I scored the equaliser before we won on penalties.

I marked the goal with a ridiculous celebration. I don't know what made me do it – the fact that I had proved myself among a group of older players, or that I had secured my YTS, or that I was experiencing the thrill of playing for Tottenham among the best young players from around the world, or perhaps a combination of all of them. Anyway, I ran off across the pitch like an idiot with this daft skinhead haircut and dived on the floor. All the lads piled on top of me.

Despite also playing a year above his age group, Ledley featured in all the games, including the final at Coleraine Showgrounds, where we beat the youth team from Blackburn Rovers 1–0. What stands out in my memory is not so much the game but the celebrations in the evening. There is something so sweet about the aftermath of a good win, even sweeter when you are young and starting out on a career with your mates around you.

The sense of victory was not the only intoxication for us that night. At the party after the final we all got a bit pissed. It was one of the first times I had drunk a few beers and, dressed in my tracksuit with my medal around my neck, I was feeling pretty pleased with myself by the end of the night. Bob Arber was our manager but his assistant Stan White, a physio and kitman at Tottenham, was given the job of rounding up us boys. He hadn't taken any clothes apart from his tracksuit and moulded football boots and had some trouble getting about the nightclub dancefloor in his studs, ordering us all back on to the bus.

The messing about didn't end there. I might have thought that scoring a goal for the team, mucking in with the haircuts and the night out was my inroduction to Tottenham completed but the boys had one little surprise left in store for me. I don't know how they managed to slip into the chalet that Ledley and I were staying in – or maybe they had an accomplice – but when I woke up in the morning after to prepare for my flight home from Northern Ireland I found I had been the victim of one more initiation ritual.

Someone had pissed in my suitcase. All my gear was covered. It was another one of those pranks that the younger lads in the team were likely to suffer. I questioned Ledley. Had he heard the lads planning this sabotage? The future captain of Tottenham just shrugged. There was no point confronting anyone, this was life as one of the kids at a club. I suppose you know you've made it when you're the one pissing in suitcases instead of having it done to you. I was faced with a problem – a suitcase full of clothes that stank of piss. What to do? I turned it over in my head for a while. Run them under the tap? Try to get them bagged up with the kitman's stuff? Sod it, I thought, zip it up and take it home to Mum.

As well as those youth-team tournaments, I got to see what the competition was like around the country at the trials for the Football Association's school of excellence at Lilleshall, now shut. No one ever really explained exactly what getting a place at Lilleshall involved. Was this a trial to play for England? I was dimly aware that it was 'an honour' to be accepted but I didn't see much evidence of that in the organisation.

This was supposed to the system that picked out the élite school-boy footballers but in reality the trials were a shambles. I was asked to play ten minutes on the left wing, ten minutes in centre-midfield and ten minutes up front. Midfield? Left wing? Hadn't I just told them that I was a striker? And the person judging me was a schoolteacher with a clipboard on the touchline making the decision on how good I was.

I was already at Tottenham and, having seen the Lilleshall set-up, I really wasn't bothered about it. I know it still annoys Steven Gerrard that he wasn't selected, and any centre of excellence that couldn't see Stevie was among the best in the country must have had problems. I enjoyed staying at Bisham Abbey for a week and meeting other lads, including Stevie and Francis Jeffers, even if the football experience was a strange one.

At the time, Scott Parker was regarded as the top man. As 15-year-olds we were all seriously impressed that Scott had, at the age of 13, filmed the McDonald's advert that was on the telly during the 1994 World Cup finals. He was 'Jimmy', the kid playing keepy-uppy in his back garden who resists his mum's offer of a McDonald's dinner to carry on practising. At the Lilleshall trials, us lads from Spurs were nudging each other and pointing out 'Jimmy'. He was the star and breezed through the selection process. They never asked me back.

The following year my GCSE results were respectable – five grades between A and C and an E in French. During the French exam it really dawned on me. I was a few days from leaving Drayton Manor. I was 16 years old and the summer stretched out in front of me. Most importantly, I was about to become a footballer full-time. It wasn't much of an incentive to keep my mind on French. I was struggling horrendously with the paper, anyway.

When I think of the journey I had to do in the early days just to get to training – the same one I'd discovered for myself two years earlier when my dad abandoned me – it tells me just how enthusiastic I was for my new life. There were no tears now, though, despite having to get up at six in the morning. I caught the tube from Ealing Broadway with Gavin Kelly. We would meet the rest of the boys at White Hart Lane and eat a quick bacon sarnie in the café before a bus would take us to the training ground in Chigwell. Still living at home, I had to travel the breadth of London before I got a ball at my feet. It didn't matter. I loved life at Tottenham.

I was able to ditch the train when I got myself what I thought would be the smartest set of wheels outside of the first-team car park. Mum and Dad remember my lime green Volkswagen Polo as 'the Bogey' – which was the nickname it acquired in our house because of its similarity in colour to the contents of a handkerchief after a big sneeze. I just remember the crushing sense of disappointment that the car I had banked on to boost my credibility with the rest of the lads became such a standing joke. Surely, I had thought, I couldn't go wrong with this little motor?

I would like to say that Mum and Dad helped me out when it came to paying £6,000 for the Bogey, but in reality they bought it for me. I was on £47 a week and the only part of the Bogey I could afford were the new alloys on the wheels that I convinced myself were the finishing touches to a seriously smart car. As I squeezed behind the wheel for the first time, there was little doubt in my mind. OK, so it was a bit of a tight squeeze getting my legs folded in behind the dashboard. And yes, my knees did come up close to the steering wheel. But in this car I truly believed that I was the main man.

The first doubts crept in when I hit the North Circular, to collect my mates for training. First up was Gavin in Ealing, followed by Narada in Stonebridge. Both of them immediately expressed serious concerns about the choice of colour and the likelihood, or not, of the car emerging from the Spurs Lodge training ground unscathed. When we picked up Ross Fitzsimon at Brent Cross, he even took some persuading just to get into it.

As we headed west to Chigwell, with my confidence a little dented, we pulled up at some traffic lights just as a mint-new Mercedes nosed in alongside us in the next lane. The window slid down to reveal John Scales, at the time a first-choice centre-half at Tottenham who lived in Wimbledon. He looked in disbelief at my new car.

'What. The Fuck. Is that?' Scales asked over the hum of his Merc's engine.

That was it. The rest of the lads in the car were laughing their heads off. Scales was so incredulous about the Bogey and its lurid green paint that several times he slowed down to let us catch up. I would try to roar off at traffic lights, which he would let me do, before cruising past me as the Bogey struggled up through the gears. The car was targeted mercilessly at the training ground but I maintain to this day that it was a good car – just, with hindsight, an atrocious colour.

Things have changed at club academies now. They do not seem such raw, intimidating places as they did even ten years ago. When I was a teenager, the piss-taking had no rules, no limits and really, up to a point, the managers and coaches encouraged it. They thought it was part of your education, and I suppose most of them had been through it themselves, like some strange kind of initiation rite. I wouldn't have changed life because we had such a good laugh, but I suppose I was one of the lucky ones. I survived.

Chris Marshall, a goalkeeper, used to be taunted relentlessly. He would drive an old Volkswagen Beetle to training every day, an even more obvious target than the Bogey, and every day there would be mud or flour spread all over it or apples in his exhaust pipe. Every day. It was a form of bullying really. At times it was funny, but it could overstep the mark. The worst thing Chris did was to get his mum to come in to say, 'This is too much,' to the staff. The poor guy just couldn't handle it but once his mum had visited – and all the boys found out about that – he got it even worse.

Another lad, Kieran Duffy, had an incredibly strong Irish accent. That was his only offence. Everyone seized upon it and just pretended they couldn't understand a word he was saying. He got so much stick that after the first year of YTS he didn't come back. There was more to making it in football than having the talent. You had to be a strong character as well.

As a trainee I wouldn't dare speak up to someone in the first team or even the reserves because I knew I would get shot down. I kept my head down and got on with it, although no one ever completely escaped the banter. I was responsible for cleaning the boots of Spurs' tough midfielder David Howells and, later, the brilliant French winger David Ginola in the season he won the PFA player of the year award, 1998–99.

To this day I don't know what happened to Howells' boots one frosty winter morning when they had been specifically entrusted to my care. As the time ticked down to first-team training I searched for them frantically but they were gone, nowhere to be found. I was panicking. Someone had stitched me up horribly and to make matters worse, Howells turned up late for training. He was raging.

'Where the fuck are my boots?' he shouted at me. 'I need my fucking boots NOW.'

What could I say? They were gone, long gone. Probably in the boot of someone's car, stuffed at the bottom of a kitbag, locked in a locker. I'd been done, utterly done, and I was going to have to take my medicine.

'I'm so sorry,' I said, gulping helplessly, 'but I really don't have a clue where your boots are.'

The beauty of the situation for the perpetrators of this crime was that Howells had no other boots at the training ground, and so he ran out for training that morning not only late, and in a very bad mood, but wearing a pair of standard running trainers. For his lateness and his inappropriate footwear he was excluded from training and told to jog round the pitches while my team-mates delighted in my misery at the huge bollocking he'd given me.

We never had much money in those days. As schoolboys we'd be given £3 expenses daily and I lost a lot of that flicking coins up against the wall before training. Closest coin to the wall takes all. I never quite worked out why the east London lads always seemed to win. As penniless YTS boys we judged the first-team pros on how much money they gave us as a Christmas tip. Ginola was generous. He gave me £60, which was not as much as Les Ferdinand handed over. He would tip his boot boy £100. Les, all us young lads agreed, was the top man.

Of all the laughs we had at Tottenham, nothing will ever touch the 'eggyboff' days. Eggyboff. Not a word you will find in the *Oxford English Dictionary*. Well, not yet anyway. I have witnessed just the mere mention of that word reduce a room full of serious professional footballers to badly behaved schoolboys. I know that, should any of my former team-mates read this book, they will find it hard to suppress a smile at the mention of eggyboff. The game of eggyboff, the legend of eggyboff, started at Tottenham and it has a lot to answer for.

The basis of the game was that no one wanted to be branded as eggyboff. If you were eggyboff, you were the outcast, the outsider, the rejected, the ridiculed, the pariah. 'Don't fucking talk to him,' we'd say to one another, 'he's eggyboff.'

It's a simple game and I reckon I might be partly responsible for its spread, particularly during my days in the England Under-21s when we played in the European Championship in Switzerland in the summer of 2002. From there, the lads took it back to their respective clubs and the legend of eggyboff spread.

The game only works properly in the confines of a squad of players, thrown together and living according to their own strict set of rules. You have to have the power of peer pressure to make it work. Eggyboff was very straightforward. Someone would set the challenge and then we would wait to see whose nerve broke first.

'First one to speak is eggyboff.'

'Next one to move is eggyboff.'

'First one out the door is eggyboff.'

Childish stuff, but you have to understand the hothouse, intensive atmosphere of the trainees' changing rooms at a professional club. We were all sportsmen, all natural competitors and no one wanted to lose. So when the eggyboff challenge was, for instance, not to leave the room or not to move and we were supposed to be going out for training, or even to play a match, it could not be ignored. It would prepare the ground for some serious tests of willpower.

Under our rules, only the person who had called the eggyboff could cancel it and often we found ourselves begging the person in question to put us out of our misery. For example, we would be changing for a morning training session at Spurs' training ground and the coach would order us out. Then, out of the blue, someone would call it. 'Eggyboff, first one out the door.' The die was cast, the challenge was set. We would all sit there and prepare for the battle. No one was going out the door.

A few of the lads would go to the window to watch the coach laying out the cones for training. After a minute or so he would look around and realise that none of us had come out. He would lose his temper and come stomping back on the long walk around the pitches towards our changing room. 'For fuck's sake take it back,' we would beg whoever had called the eggyboff.

It seemed that I was always the one to get the blame from the coach, regardless of whether I was guilty or not. He would burst back into the room.

'What the fuck is going on? Crouchy, what the fuck are you doing?'

'Sorry boss, just doing my laces. I'll be two seconds.'

I would start to rise up from my seat as he turned and went back out the door. Then as soon as he'd gone, I'd sit down again and we would plead once more with the perpetrator to end the eggyboff. Often there would be no backing down until finally the coach would be so raging that the eggyboff would have to be taken back to avoid complete meltdown.

The most hardcore of the lot was 'Eggyboff, first one to move' and never more so than the occasion it was uttered at the start of a youth-team game at Tottenham. We were in formation ready for the opposition to kick-off and someone shouted, 'Eggyboff, first one to move.' There were coaches on the touchline, a whole team lined up against us and parents and scouts watching. I was OK because, as a striker on the halfway line, I could just about get away with standing still. For the rest of them, there was a difficult decision to make.

You would be underestimating the power of eggyboff to think that once called it would simply be ignored. The whistle went to start the game. This was diehard. The lads did not move a muscle. The opposition kicked off, the ball went back to the midfielder on the edge of the centre-circle, he carried it forward and, to his gradual amazement, was met with no resistance at all. On the touchline, our manager was going mad.

It just escalated. Our closest midfielder to the bloke with the ball failed to close him down, then the next one stayed stock still. And the next one. They were just standing there like statues until finally the guy reached the edge of the area and Alton Thelwell relented by putting in a last-ditch tackle that saved us from conceding a goal. The relief was incredible but after the game it didn't save Alton, who went on to play for Tottenham's first team. It didn't matter that he rescued us from going a goal down.

'Don't touch him,' we said. 'He's eggyboff. Don't even go near him.'

The manager did try to talk to us about it, to find out what was going through our teenage minds, but he never got much out of us. However mad this might seem, it was part of what made us a team. It was part of what drew us together. Eggyboff got so bad that the coaching staff banned it. They never did find out what we called it, they just referred to it as 'that fucking stupid game'. They were right about that one.

I was known as 'Splinter' or 'Sticks' in those days because there still wasn't much weight on me. It was the experience of playing and working with such a tight-knit group that had the greatest effect upon me. We were together for the whole day. I would be up at the training ground for 7.30 a.m. and we wouldn't leave until 7 p.m. because we were doing jobs until it was dark. It was a pretty traditional apprenticeship and I loved my time there.

The first match I played in to be televised, on *Sky Sports*, was the final of the FA Premier Youth League against Arsenal in May 1998. Ashley Cole played in the first leg at White Hart Lane, which we lost

2–0. I scored the only goal in the second leg and it was a proper live broadcast – commentators, graphics, the works. When you are starting to make your way as a footballer, moments like those prove so memorable.

In my spare time, I would hang out with Ledley, who still lived at home in Bow, in east London, and we'd play snooker at the Mile End club. His mother Beverley was an amazing woman. She brought up six kids on her own and she was very kind to me. Ledley was pushing on quickly. He got a pro contract before I did, and trained with the first team before I did. On the few occasions I was roped in, just to make up the numbers, I felt that I froze.

By then, Gerry was gone, sacked in 1997 and replaced by Christian Gross, who lasted a year only. His influence barely reached the young professionals at my level – I had signed my first pro deal at the club just after my 18th birthday in 1999, after playing for the England Under-18s. Still, I wasn't making much of an impression in the first-team training sessions that I was invited to join. I was really nervous, too nervous. In my first training session on the bottom pitch at the training ground, my touch went. Everything went. It was a bit of a nightmare.

There were a few big names at the club then, including Les Ferdinand, Tim Sherwood, Sol Campbell, Steffen Iversen, Chris Armstrong and Darren Anderton. Their world seemed very distant. When I trained with the first team I struggled, and when the youth team played no one seemed to be paying attention. I tried to cling to every encouragement I could. When I scored with a scissor-kick – my speciality – in a youth-team match against Chelsea, a last-minute equaliser from the edge of the area, it picked me up for weeks.

As you move up through the ranks at a club you inevitably meet those on their way down. Players fall foul of the manager, they lose their pace, they lose their fitness. Many of them are killing time waiting to be moved on to another club, or seeing out their existing deal. That's a weird kind of twilight for any career, ending up binned in the reserves. Reserve-team football is crap. No one cares, there's no edge and most first-teamers are only there to get a bit of fitness back after time out through injury.

Ruel Fox was a classy little winger bought from Newcastle. He'd had a good career but by the time I met him, he didn't want to be at Tottenham any longer. George Graham had taken over and binned him immediately, so he was training with the reserves every day. He was still a great player. You could tell that from his touches. The problem was that his heart didn't seem to be in it any more.

One of Foxy's favourite targets was David Pleat, then Tottenham's director of football. When I say target I mean that literally. Foxy would see Pleat walking round the training pitch and ping balls at his head. I was never sure what Foxy was so upset about, apart from being in the reserves. I think he wanted Pleat to pay up his contract so he could leave. He certainly made us all laugh.

I had grown up believing your attitude had to be spot on. Suddenly I was meeting players who, for one reason or another, just didn't seem bothered. In the reserves, players from the two ends of the spectrum meet – those on their way up and those on the way down – and it makes for a strange kind of team.

Tottenham had a big squad, which meant many good players were left on the margins – Fox, Paolo Tramezzani and Moussa Saib among them. None of them seemed too worried but I was most amazed by the refusal of Jose Dominguez, a Portugal international, to do much that the coaches told him. He would go out the night before reserve games and spend the time before kick-off having a snooze on the benches in the changing room. The coach, Theo Foley, would tell him that he had to go out and warm up but Jose wasn't fussed about that.

'I don't want to,' he would say. 'I'm just going to have a little sleep here.'

It didn't make any difference. Dominguez was still brilliant. He was still the best player on the pitch.

I turned 19 in January 2000 and, although I had been selected for the England Under-18s the previous year, it became increasingly obvious I wasn't anywhere near the first team at Tottenham. David Pleat clearly didn't fancy me as a player. George Graham didn't rate me much, either. Pat Holland and Chris Hughton, the coaches, encouraged me and I have a lot to thank those two for. But when I got word that Pleat was planning to farm me out to Dulwich Hamlet, a non-league team of part-timers, I started to get concerned.

It was a difficult time for me. The club wanted me to go to Dulwich Hamlet for their own reasons. I disagreed with them. It can be an uncertain time for a young footballer when the club that has nurtured you seems to be using you as a bargaining chip. You're on your own. In that situation any word of encouragement from a senior pro means a great deal, and I will never forget that Les Ferdinand stuck up for me.

Anyone in football will tell you what a top bloke Les Ferdinand is. As a young pro I noticed that, while all the other senior players just chucked their training kit on the floor, Les would fold his up and put it in the bag for the kitman. Les treated people at Tottenham with respect – cleaners, cooks, even unknown young players like me.

I had mentioned to Les that Pleat wanted me to go to Dulwich Hamlet. We were in the changing rooms and Pleat walked past Les, who was, at the time, deep in conversation on his mobile phone. When he caught sight of Pleat I remember hearing Les murmur into the phone, 'Stay there, babe, hang on a second.' Then he looked up and shouted, 'Oi, Dave, what you farming Crouchy out to Dulwich for?'

Pleat was caught on the hop. Les was one of the senior players and the rest of the dressing room had turned to listen.

'Oh, I think he needs it, Les,' said Pleat. 'I think he needs to get out there and play.'

Les wasn't having that. 'Crouchy's fucking better than that by the way,' he retorted.

Clearly flustered, Pleat started laying out his reasons for sending me to Dulwich but Les wasn't listening any longer – he was back on the phone to his lady. 'Sorry about that, babe,' he was saying. 'Anyway, what time are we meeting?'

Les scooped up his bag, strolled out the door and climbed into his Porsche, which was parked in the car park outside. I thought *one day I want to be like that*. Professional football as I had imagined it still seemed a long way off, especially when I was heading to Dulwich Hamlet in the Ryman Premier League.

8

DULWICH, SWEDEN
AND HOME AGAIN

Dave McEwen. I don't know where he is now, I don't even know if he's still playing football, but he was the reason I finally left Tottenham. Don't get me wrong. I don't blame the bloke. He was just trying to push on in his career and had clearly been banging in the goals at Dulwich Hamlet. But when you're part of the sweetener in a deal to bring in a non-league striker, you don't need telling twice that your club don't want you.

It was very hard for me to take at the time. Tottenham had scouted McEwen when he was playing in the Ryman Premier League, which is one division below the Conference and five levels beneath the Premiership. Pleat clearly had some idea in his head that he could find a little gem playing amateur football and turn him into a Premiership player. Let's be honest – that doesn't happen too often in modern football.

McEwen was a student who came to Tottenham at the start of 2000. I trained with him a few times. He was a decent player, fast and stocky, impressive enough for Spurs to take a chance on him, although he later followed me out to Queens Park Rangers. Dulwich had not been able to get a fee for him because he had played for them on a non-contract basis so, to soften the blow, Pleat said that they could borrow one of our strikers until the end of the season.

They were offered a few players, including Paul McVeigh, now at Burnley. Eventually, Dave Garland, the Dulwich Hamlet manager, came to watch a Tottenham reserve match at St Albans and picked me. I was called in by Pleat to learn the bad news.

'We're going to sign Dave McEwen,' he said. 'I think you should go on loan to Dulwich. Get some experience down there, you'll be playing every week.'

I was seriously pissed off. I didn't think that Dulwich was exactly the best way of getting first-team experience. I was happy to go on loan – go anywhere – as long as it was a league club. Someone had mentioned Leyton Orient. But I was clearly being moved about to suit Tottenham's needs rather than my own development. They owed Dulwich a favour and would pay my wages. I would even continue to train at Tottenham and just go to south London on a Saturday to play.

I had nothing but the greatest respect for Dulwich and the guys there, who worked full-time and trained in the evening, but that didn't mean it was the right place for me. Pleat didn't give me an option. I said, 'I'm better than that. I don't want to go down there.' He kept saying that I needed the experience and it would be good for me. I had no reputation, no real clout at the club, and Pleat, as the director of football, was eager to be seen to get things done. I was going to Dulwich. There was no choice.

I didn't get on with Pleat that well. Perhaps he thought I had potential but if he did, why send me to the Ryman Premier League? I wasn't unrealistic. I knew I wasn't ready for the first team and I didn't expect the manager to take a gamble on me at that point. What if I had frozen? When I finally joined QPR, at least there was less focus on me in the Championship. Make big mistakes in the Premiership and you may never recover.

There's a simple assumption that when a footballer drops down a few levels he can immediately dominate games, but it's not like tennis or golf. In a team you are reliant on the ability of your team-mates to bring you into the game, to give you a pass or to anticipate a pass. The tackles are tough, especially when you're a kid on loan from Tottenham, and, no matter how much ability you think you have, it can be difficult to stand out.

When I walked into the changing rooms at the Champion Hill Stadium in Dulwich on 4 March 2000 for my debut against Billericay Town, the Dulwich captain and goalkeeper Les Cleevely took one look at my size 12 feet and asked me if I wore football boots or cardboard boxes. That broke the tension straight away and we all had a laugh. Let's be honest, I was used to far worse stick from the lads at Tottenham.

I scored with a glancing header but we lost 2–1. In fact, we lost four of the six matches I played at Dulwich, although I felt I acquitted myself well in the club's famous pink and blue shirt. I certainly didn't feel like a big-time footballer and I definitely never acted like one. I got on with playing and I think my team-mates respected me for that.

Sadly, I can't say that they were golden days. During my short spell there, Billericay, Hampton and Richmond Borough, Carshalton Athletic and Harrow Borough all beat us. We drew with Heybridge Swifts and, in my last game, against Aylesbury United, we finally got a win, 3–0. I was kicked around a lot but I didn't let that upset me. When the ball was at my feet I knew that I stood out.

None of the Dulwich players were stand-offish, even though I had walked straight into the first XI without featuring in a single training session. The manager introduced me as 'our new signing from Tottenham' and I certainly felt a bit of added pressure coming from a big club. They were great lads who accepted me straight away. I like to think people realised I was first and foremost a decent bloke and that I worked hard.

I trained all week at Tottenham and then my dad would drive me across London to play for Dulwich at the weekend, and I was always in the starting XI. It was a bizarre experience really – interesting to say the least – and, having been through it, I wouldn't change it. My mates from Ealing would come across town to watch me play and, after matches, Dad would be invited into the boardroom by the club's chairman Martin Eede. At Dulwich they were a lovely bunch of people – unpretentious, real football-lovers, and very proud of their club.

Those games toughened me up. I might have been better served playing on loan at a league club but you soon learn to look after yourself when you're being marked by a centre-half who earns his living as a bricklayer. I probably felt more prepared as a footballer, and ready to take up the battle for a place in the first team at Tottenham. Pleat, however, had other ideas for me.

He had been busy in the transfer market again, this time bringing a 16-year-old Swedish kid called Jon Jonssen to Spurs for £250,000. Once again, a few conditions were attached. Jonssen had come from a club in southern Sweden, IFK Hässleholm. Never heard of it? Not surprising. Even by the fairly laid-back standards of Sweden the town is regarded as a sleepy kind of place. It's the Swedish equivalent of Crewe or Swindon. That means it's famous – which is perhaps not the right word – for being a railway hub. Even most Swedes don't know where it is.

With the promise of loan players in the Jonssen deal, IFK Hässleholm were on the look-out for a full-back and their manager, Cony Olsen, liked the look of Alton Thelwell. To make it easier for Alton to settle in Sweden, Tottenham suggested that Hässleholm take another young player as well. That extra young player was seen as a little present for the Swedes. No prizes for guessing who got the job.

I had just finished my stint at Dulwich Hamlet and the prospect of potentially missing out on my eagerly anticipated summer holiday didn't exactly fill me with glee. The lads at Spurs were taking the piss about me getting kicked up in the air by a load of part-timers in the third tier of Swedish football while they relaxed on the beach. But sod it, I was up for sampling something new and at least at Hässleholm I'd be getting a regular game. Alton and I were struggling to be selected for the reserve side at Tottenham because so many good players – Les Ferdinand, Chris Armstrong, Steffen Iversen, Rory Allen – couldn't get in the first team and were dropping down a level to play. Besides, I had found out that the Swedes were part-timers and trained in the evening, which meant that for the first time in years I would be entitled to a lie-in.

Alton and I were met at the airport and taken to a two-bedroomed flat the club had found for us in an area of the city called Ljungdala. We asked the taxi driver on the way from the airport what Ljungdala was like and he told us that in English it was called 'the ghetto', which wasn't the most encouraging news. I have to say that in all the time we spent there, it seemed absolutely fine to me. We were instructed by the club to train on our own in the mornings, although I can't say that was particularly high on our agenda. I spent most mornings in bed.

The Swedes were very friendly, and most of all they didn't seem too bothered by the fact that I was 6ft 7in. tall. I didn't get all the normal crap – 'What's the weather like up there?' and all that rubbish. I can take a joke as well as anyone but when you've heard that nonsense ten thousand times before, you appreciate it if people just keep their thoughts to themselves. None of the team kit at Hässleholm fitted me but they didn't make much fuss. They just got me another one.

One aspect of our new team-mates completely threw me, though. I noticed it after our first training session as I looked around the dressing room.

'Alton,' I whispered, 'why are the lads here all so ugly?'

You couldn't deny it. They all seemed to have a protruding upper lip, that curled up higher than their teeth. We could have been at an audition for 'The League of Gentlemen'. What was going on here? Had inbreeding struck Hässleholm? Were all the locals the victims of some terrible deformity?

The reason, we quickly realised, was quite different. The Swedish boys were all taking a tobacco called 'snus', which is rolled into a pellet and squashed in behind the top lip. At Hässleholm the players loved it. Before games, after games, during half-time, the little tins of snus would be passed around and the lads would be shoving it into their mouths as quickly as they could.

I'm told it's not nearly as harmful as smoking cigarettes but it hardly seemed like the usual thing for a serious sportsman to be taking. All the Scandinavian players I have met through my career laugh when I mention snus, and some of them still take it. Antii Niemi, the goalkeeper at Southampton when I was playing there, would constantly have snus under his top lip when he wasn't playing. It might not be that bad for your health but it makes you look horrific. I tried snus once and it came close to making me throw up.

The men in Hässleholm may have a problem with their top lips but there is absolutely nothing wrong with the women there. In fact, they proved hard for Alton to resist. We were having a brilliant time until he got himself a Swedish girlfriend. I hammered him every day about his new lady but to little avail. Who was I going to knock about with now when I wanted to go out? He was loved-up and suddenly I didn't have anyone with whom to kill the time between training and matches. He was all for staying in with his girlfriend. I wasn't happy. What was I going to do?

As Alton became increasingly domesticated with his better half, I got to know some of the other foreign lads in the team. There was

Bernard Makufi, my fellow striker, who was a Zambian international, and I made friends with Ahwed Estefanos, from Eritrea. We went out for meals and ate the local dish, 'Planksteak', which was pretty much as it sounded – a lump of steak served on a plank of wood, surrounded by mashed potatoes and doused in béarnaise sauce. Absolutely delicious. It became my staple diet in Sweden.

I played eight games in Sweden and scored four goals. I suppose these days a lot of 19-year-olds are going to university, or travelling on a gap year and gaining experience of life. That month away was the first time I had lived abroad for any length of time, and it contributed to my development. I was among a lot of young guys, the Africans especially, who were trying to earn a living in football at whatever level they could. Life is not easy when you know the next contract is the difference between having a job or not, or keeping your work permit or having to return home. As trainees at Tottenham, we had been insulated from the pressure of having to play for a living.

When England played against Sweden in the World Cup finals of 2006, a few newspapers got in contact with IFK Hässleholm to find out what I had done in my time there. I don't blame them. I suppose it's an interesting angle on the story. The chairman there said that I wasn't much good at heading the ball and had been more interested in drinking beer. I thought that was unfair, but I have always done my best to fit in at whatever level I have played. There we were, 19 years old, playing one or two games a week and stuck in a town that even the Swedes thought was boring. No complaints from us but we had to find something to do. There was just the one lively bar in town and that was, ironically, an English-themed pub called the Red Lion. You really do find them wherever you go. Yes, Alton and I did end up in there a bit and we did have fun, but when the games came round, we took them seriously. I loved playing regularly, even if Hässle-holm's players were mainly students and the level wasn't great. We never gave less than everything. I certainly came back a lot more confident from the experience. I was playing every week and loving it.

The chairman at Hässleholm couldn't have thought that we were that bad because Alton and I were at the centre of a minor diplomatic incident of the club's making. When it came time for us to leave, Hässleholm's season was still in full swing. They didn't want us to go, so they wouldn't give us our passports back. We were stuck there and it took Chris Hughton to come out to Sweden to sort it out and get us back home.

Back at Tottenham, more than ever, it was clear that David Pleat didn't fancy me as a player. I had been given a professional contract although I still felt such a long way off the first team. You didn't have to spend too long analysing the facts to understand that being loaned out to Dulwich Hamlet and IFK Hässleholm in return for, respectively, a non-league footballer and a teenager meant that I was not exactly regarded as Tottenham's next great centre-forward. Gradually, I came to realise what many young hopefuls have to accept. I just came to feel that I didn't want to be there any more.

In the summer of 2000, I made up my mind that it was time to get out. Dad and I agreed that I desperately needed to be playing first-team football and help was at hand from a familiar source. Gerry Francis and Des Bulpin were back at Queens Park Rangers. Des had always championed my cause before the two of them were forced out at Tottenham, and he was on the phone to Dad that summer, inviting me to accompany the team on their pre-season tour of Devon to give Gerry a chance to decide whether he wanted to give me a contract.

The tale of my transfer back to QPR, five years after I moved the other way, is an old-fashioned transfer, which took all Gerry's considerable skills. I've been transferred a few times since then and I learned a lot about changing clubs in that first move to QPR. It was a strange experience from the start.

On the QPR tour of Devon I ended up rooming with Leon Jeanne. A few years later he gained notoriety by selling his story of being a cocaine addict to the *Sun*.

Just my luck to get him as a room-mate.

Leon was a strange guy, a great player but one of those who just seemed destined to wreck his own career. He had been at Arsenal originally. All the big clubs had been after him as a kid. Unfortunately, he had very little interest in the rules that Gerry had laid down. The first night we were away he told me I'd have to make myself scarce because he had a girl coming round to the hotel room. I had been with QPR for one day and this was the last thing I needed.

I thought about arguing with him but I was on trial, and desperate to make the right impression, so I took myself off to find a floor to sleep on. The QPR lads seemed a friendly bunch, and I knew some of them from the occasional night out in Ealing. Gerry found out about Leon's visitor, they had a massive row and Leon left the hotel. He never came back for another six months. I later found out that was pretty much par for the course as far as he was concerned. He could have been a top player, but he just went off the rails.

I scored in a friendly against Tiverton Town and then, when we came back, played really well in a friendly against Brentford at Griffin Park. At the end of the match, the QPR fans were singing 'Sign him up' every time I touched the ball. It was the first time I had ever been singled out by the crowd like that, for anything, and I loved it. I desperately wanted to sign for QPR. The only problem was that the club had no money whatsoever in the transfer fund.

How were we going to get this transfer done? How was I going to get out of Tottenham when QPR had no serious money to buy me? Step forward Gerry Francis, one of the smartest transfer operators in football. Des had assured Dad that Gerry wanted me. In fact, Des had been in contact with Dad all the time I had been in Devon and, according to him, there was only one barrier to the deal being completed. Gerry – and Des could not emphasise this enough – did not like football agents.

When I say Gerry didn't like agents, I mean he really hated them, to the extent that he wouldn't even deal with one. Gerry himself assured us that it was totally out of the question. I had been signed up with Stellar Group, Jonathan Barnett and David Manasseh's management company, since I was a kid. Ledley and I had both signed up but, much as I respected their professional help, Dad and I weren't about to blow my chance to get some first-team football by insisting they get involved. Of course, Gerry knew this and Dad and I accepted that my agents would be kept out of it.

As I was walking off the pitch at Griffin Park after the Brentford friendly, with Gerry's arm around my shoulders, the QPR vice-chairman Nick Blackburn had button-holed Dad in the directors' box.

'We're having a meeting,' Nick said. 'See you under the stand in ten minutes.'

Ten minutes later and Dad was under the main stand at Griffin Park with Gerry and Nick. Dad and I had both agreed that we would accept pretty much anything for first-team football.

Once he had agreed there were to be no agents, Gerry laid out his plans for dealing with Tottenham. Somehow he had convinced Pleat to sell me for £60,000, which, even for a kid with no first-team experience, was a real steal. The trouble was that only Pleat had approved the transfer and we were worried whether the manager George Graham and his assistant Chris Hughton would also be willing to let me go for that kind of money, when they returned from their pre-season tour in a couple of days' time. We had to do it before they got back.

'We do it tomorrow, early morning. Come to the ground and we'll have the contract ready,' Gerry told Dad.

That was about the extent of the negotiations for my salary, and the next day the two of us went down to Loftus Road to sign the contract. The money was so crap that the club secretary, Sheila Marson, joked that she'd like to frame the contract and put it on her office wall. It was possibly the worst deal a player had ever done in the recent history of QPR – a couple of hundred quid a week and I'd signed on for three years. I don't think I even glanced at the salary when I put my signature on it. That's how much I wanted to play first-team football.

I got the impression that some among the Tottenham coaching staff were not too happy when they discovered that I had been sold for a measly £60,000. Something along the lines of, 'Why the fuck did you let him go that cheaply?' I think that may have been the part that Gerry, as a former Tottenham manager, enjoyed the most.

In the end, Tottenham didn't do too badly out of me. Pleat had also negotiated an appearance-based payment system, whereby they were paid according to how many games I played, up to 30 matches, which brought them in another £106,000. They were also entitled to 20 per cent of any sell-on fee above the £60,000 that QPR had paid for me.

So that was it. I left the club that had been home for five years. The day after I signed for QPR I was told to report to the Bromyard Leisure Centre where, all those years ago, I had joined Brentford's centre of excellence, under-age, and had to escape though the hole in the fence every time the man from the FA turned up. Now I was too tall to get through the hole in the fence, and life had changed completely in the space of a summer. I was out of Tottenham and ready to make my mark as a professional footballer.

9

MADE AT LOFTUS ROAD

At Queens Park Rangers that season, we tried everything to make it work. Every Tuesday was 'Terror Tuesday', when Gerry Francis would make us run our bollocks off – shuttle runs from the edge of one penalty box to the other, then to the halfway line, on to the first box and back to the middle. Over and over again. We had meetings. We argued. We made up. We went for bonding sessions in the pub. We tried everything to save our season from relegation.

My first season as a professional footballer was strange in a lot of ways. Rangers' problems were bad on and off the field. Gerry resigned in February and under new manager Ian Holloway we lost the battle and dropped down into what is now League One. The team was not working, a lot of the older players got frustrated and the fans were going through hell. The supporters even had to fight against a proposed merger of the club with Wimbledon, who were still in south London at the time.

Of course I was pissed off that we weren't winning. I could sense the tension around the ground and felt for the supporters because so many of my mates were QPR fans. But there was no point hiding from the fact that I was finally doing what I had always wanted to do. I was a first-team regular at last and I was scoring goals. I loved that part of it.

It had not been easy, though. It took me a few games to find my feet as a professional footballer. The first one that sticks in my mind was in August at the Hawthorns, a couple of weeks after my debut for QPR. We lost 2–1 to West Bromwich Albion but that isn't what I remember most about it. I had started getting abuse from the crowd as I warmed up on the touchline. It wasn't pleasant and I hadn't yet learned how to block it out or ignore it. Even before I came on I could already feel the crowd getting on top of me.

I needed a decent touch, a good pass, a good shot – anything to calm my nerves. But I was all over the place. Then someone made a run down the right wing and cut it back to me. I had reached the edge of the area when I got the ball, with only one defender and the goalkeeper between me and the goal. All I had to do was curl this one in the top corner. Instead, I shanked the life out of the shot.

The ball had got stuck between my feet, nothing more than that. It happens. It was bad luck plus a bit of nerves but it really got to me. There was an ironic cheer from the crowd and I have to say that I felt embarrassed. I honestly felt the crowd were laughing at me, like I was a joke. That was about as much as I did in that game. The next day I found a newspaper that my dad had tried to keep hidden from me. For the West Brom game it had those player ratings out of ten that come with helpful little comments attached. I can still remember the one next to my name – 'Crouch. 4/10. Not good enough for this level.'

Was I good enough for this level? Of course I fucking was. I hadn't gone through all those years at Spurs, all that practice, to give up now. But I have to admit that there were times after that West Brom game when I allowed myself to doubt it. I got binned for a couple of games by Gerry. I don't blame him. It wasn't turning into a great season for us and my professional career hadn't exactly got off to a flier, but things were about to change. Gillingham at home on a Wednesday night – 13 September 2000 – not exactly a major date in British sporting history but it was an evening I'll never forget.

Gerry picked Chris Kiwomya and Sammy Koejoe up front that night. I was on the bench, still feeling sorry for myself about what happened at West Brom. How much did I want to play that day? Not much and certainly not when I climbed out of the dugout to warm up. This time the abuse was coming from my own fans, or at least one fan in particular. 'Crouch, you're shit,' he shouted at me. Just this one bloke, abusing me. 'Crouch, you lanky twat.' What was this bloke's problem? I tried to ignore him, I tried to block it out, but I could actually see him. He was standing there in the east paddock lower stand, the seats to the players' left as they come out the tunnel at Loftus Road. In my mind now, I can't remember his face any more, just his voice shouting, 'Don't fucking bring Crouch on. What's he gonna do? He's shit.'

I know what fans are like – I've stood in enough crowds at football matches – and I laugh to myself when I recount it now. At the time, though, my head was spinning. Where had this geezer seen me play? I'd played at Loftus Road just three times in my professional career. Had he seen me against Birmingham on the first day of the season? Had he been at the Hawthorns? Had he been to the pre-season friendly against Brentford at Griffin Park? The crowd had sung 'Sign him up' when I played at Brentford. Gerry had put his arm around me on the pitch at the end of that game. I'd played well against Brentford.

We were 2–0 down with about half an hour left of the game, and my head was all over the place. This fan was still shouting but he wasn't having any influence on Gerry. Steve Morrow's number was up and he was trudging towards the touchline. This was it. Professional football. Sink or swim. *Got to get it right tonight, Crouchy.* I knew that I had to turn things around and I had to do it now.

Something happened as I crossed the line and ran on to the pitch, something small but important – there was a round of applause for me from the home fans. It wasn't massive but sometimes fans don't realise what a little bit of encouragement can do for a player. I had a couple of good touches and suddenly I really felt up for it. I felt confident. I was going to turn this game around and ram it back down the throat of the bloke in the east paddock lower. Richard Langley put in a corner, I chested it down and the ball bounced in front of me. This was it, moment of destiny. I shaped to hit it and my right foot, which was ready to smack the ball, slipped backwards. In that split second, I swear on my life I heard the reaction of the crowd. No lie. Not an exaggeration. I actually heard a groan from the crowd. A long 'Ahhhhh' of disappointment.

Then I lashed a half-volley into the top corner. I couldn't believe it. My first professional goal and we were back in the game at 2–1. I had lost my footing for a second and maybe that was what made me decide to hit the ball as soon as possible, and when I hit it, the ball flew so sweetly. The crowd were up. I didn't really do much celebrating, I never had a celebration planned. When you've scored, but your team is losing, the goalscorer is expected to grab the ball out of the net, no-nonsense style, and run back up the pitch. You know the way I mean, with that expression that says, 'It's not about me, it's about us getting the equaliser.'

So that's what I did when I scored against Gillingham, although really I couldn't have given a toss about the score at that precise moment. I was so happy I wanted to jump in the crowd. A lot of people, friends and family who were at the game, said to me afterwards how clever I had been, how clever it was the way I had dummied it before shooting. I went along with it for a bit but I had to come clean in the end. 'Yeah, it looked clever,' I said, 'but actually I slipped.'

I was on fire. I felt on top of the world. A diagonal cross came over, I got up and headed it down for Kiwomya to put the equaliser in for

2–2. They gave me the man-of-the-match award after the game and I had been on the pitch for just 36 minutes. Andy Hessenthaler, Gillingham's player-manager, said they 'couldn't handle' me. Gerry told the newspaper reporters that I reminded him of Niall Quinn.

When I got home the night after the game I rang my mates Greg and Herms. I wanted a night out to mark the occasion of my first goal as a professional footballer. We went to our local pub but somehow it didn't feel like it was the right place for such a big night. Then I remembered that my agent's uncle had a stake in the Café de Paris, which I'd heard was a bit of a celebrity place in town, so I rang him up to see if he could get us in.

'Come on lads,' I announced. 'We've hit the big time now. We're going to the Café de Paris.'

That was the plan, and we were heading into the West End. One goal against Gillingham and suddenly I thought I was the top man. When we got there we felt so out of place among that flash crowd that we stood in a corner for an hour, had a few beers and went back to Ealing. I didn't care, I'd scored against Gillingham. I was on cloud nine. I felt like a real footballer at last.

I kept my place in the team and with a few goals under my belt, I started to feel like an established professional. I scored 12 goals that season and cleaned up when it came to the end-of-season awards. The fans made me their player of the year and so did the club. My career had taken off at last but my greatest regret was that I couldn't prevent the club from going down.

It was a hard season and all the lads had tried their socks off. On some Tuesdays, after all that running, club captain Karl Ready would round us up and we would walk over to Jono's pub on the Uxbridge Road for a few pints. It's just around the corner from the training ground – not the kind of Irish pub that would strike you as a flash, high-class bar, just a normal little west London boozer.

I have to admit that I have always enjoyed that part of the culture of English football, the team going out to bond over a few beers. It may sound primitive, but drinking with your team-mates every now and again, socialising, having a laugh, makes a big difference. You can't do it all the time and, as professionals, you wouldn't want to, but every so often it helps to build a bond that cannot be forged simply on the training ground.

We didn't go overboard, we weren't in the pub every week and we always trained hard. We knew how serious the situation was at QPR. The trips to Jono's were a way of letting off steam together and a chance to talk about how we could put things right. I was wide-eyed about the whole experience. I had been around the bars of Ealing as a teenager with my mates, now I was hanging out with the local football team.

The Jono's Tuesday session I remember the best involved a player called Paul Murray, a great character who made us laugh a lot. 'Muzza' was only a little fella, very flexible though, and in the pub he could get a bit rowdy. He was from Carlisle and he would often be shouting the odds in his strong Cumbrian accent. On this occasion, however, Muzza took it too far, which was a mistake because in Jono's they didn't tolerate you messing about, no matter whom you played for.

Muzza was thrown out of the pub and told in no uncertain terms that he was now banned. He didn't get much support from his team-mates. We were all cracking up with laughter as Muzza's protests were waved away by the bloke on the door. Pretty soon he found himself out on the Uxbridge Road pavement.

In fact, we were still laughing about it when one of Karl Ready's mates came into the bar with a big sports bag slung over his shoulder about 15 minutes later. He went to the bar and made a big deal of ordering two pints of lager. Some of the lads started to giggle in anticipation – they must have seen this one before.

Ready's mate picked up one of the pints, looked around to check that none of the bar staff were watching, and stooped down to unzip his bag. We all leaned over to look inside. In there, with his legs and arms folded impossibly tight, his neck bent at a crazy angle, was Muzza. His hand reached out to accept the pint and he took it back in for a triumphant sip.

'They're never going to ban Muzza,' he squeaked from inside the bag.

You had to hand it to Muzza. The little fella would go to great lengths to get back on a session with the boys. We stayed in Jono's for another hour, passing pints to Muzza in the bag, then zipped it up and carried him out.

The spirit was good at QPR, but as a team we just weren't clicking, and those Jono's sessions didn't always bring the boys closer together. At the Christmas do, Paul Furlong cracked a joke about Chris Kiwomya's new shoes, beer got thrown and there was a bit of a ruck. Tensions often surface at a football club and they tend to get worse when results are going badly.

As well as the bad results, we picked up a lot of injuries. In the space of a few months I went from being fifth-choice striker to first as player after player went down with knocks. Furlong got injured, so did Kiwomya and Sammy Koejoe. Swedish striker Rob Steiner was so badly hurt he had to retire at the age of 27. At one point I was the only fit forward in the squad, and when I got my chances to shine, I did well. From an early stage we knew it was going to be a difficult season. I was determined that whatever happened, no one could accuse me of not fighting my corner for QPR.

Three days after my make-or-break game with Gillingham, we lost 4–2 away at Barnsley having been 3–0 down at half-time. As we walked towards the tunnel after the first half, our own fans were lobbing programmes at us, and this was only mid-September. We weren't in any doubt about how bad the situation had become or how upset our fans were.

It didn't stop me. I scored seven goals before the New Year and, privately, I thought that, despite the team's problems, the fans were taking to me. I was grateful for that because it was a difficult time to be a QPR fan.

On the pitch our injury problems defied belief. Richard Langley and our England Under-21 player Clarke Carlisle both ruptured cruciate ligaments within ten minutes of each other in a 2–0 home defeat by our west London rivals Fulham on 31 January. One cruciate a season is bad luck. Two in a game can feel like a curse. The cruciate injury is the one footballers dread – you can expect nine months to a year out if you rupture that ligament. Could it get any worse? It could, and did. Karl Ready was one of six players who broke a leg.

It was not just the league form that was making life difficult for Gerry. We were also beaten 4–1 at home in the League Cup by Colchester United, a division below us, and went out 4–2 on aggregate. Those were the nights when I really learned what it was like to be in a struggling team, at a club that is running on little more than hope. There was no hiding from the fans' anger.

To get to the players' car park at Loftus Road you had to walk out of the stadium and through the fans. I noticed that Chris Kiwomya, a seasoned old pro, took his time getting changed that night, obviously hoping that the fans waiting outside would go home. They didn't. He got loads when he walked out there. 'You're taking the piss out of this club.' That sort of thing. It wasn't pretty.

There were some happy memories, too, especially my first taste of FA Cup football in the third round in January 2001 against Luton Town at Kenilworth Road. It was one of those mad FA Cup days, a brilliant cup-tie, when we found ourselves 2–0 down within 36 minutes. Then in the second half, I scored two to get us back to

2–2. They took the lead again and Gavin Peacock equalised with a last-minute penalty to get us a replay.

That day at Kenilworth Road was one I will never forget and mostly for the aftermath of my second goal. As I ran towards the QPR fans in the away end to celebrate I caught sight of my dad – at 6ft 5in. he's not that hard to spot. The QPR fans were going crazy because we had come back from two goals down and as I ran towards them I pointed up at my dad, who was leaping about with his arms in the air. The last I saw of him was when he lost his footing and tumbled down the steps.

Dad had got so excited at my equaliser that he had tripped up and gone flying down the stairs. Apparently, in the rush of supporters to get down to the front of the stand, my poor old dad got trampled underfoot. I think he went all the way down from Row Z, crushed under the feet of people stampeding to congratulate his son for scoring an equaliser in the FA Cup. Now that's unlucky.

I lost sight of him as I got close to the stand, amid the melee of QPR fans going mad. They had all pressed to the front and players and fans were celebrating together. All the team were piling in around me and I found myself staring into the sea of faces in the stand. Suddenly, there was Dad. His jacket was torn and his face was cut but somehow in the thick of it he had managed to climb back up to his feet. He said later he'd done his back in as well, but it had been worth it all. Back at Loftus Road, thirteen days later, we beat Luton 2–1.

Reaching the FA Cup fourth round gave us a plum home draw against Arsenal, who went all the way to the final that year and lost in the last minute to Liverpool. This was a big occasion, easily the biggest game of my career at that point, and everyone I knew wanted a ticket. The crowd at Loftus Road was the biggest for seven years and I was up against Arsenal's legendary Tony Adams. He was 34, recently retired from international football and still, it seemed to me, unstoppable.

What a reality-check that was. I was three days short of my 20th birthday and playing against the most famous defender in the country. Adams taught me that playing in the Premiership would be at a totally different level. I barely got a kick all game. Ashley Cole cleared a header of mine off the line and we held out for thirty minutes before caving in 6–0. Arsenal needed no help to beat us but we contributed two own goals, and a third from Sylvain Wiltord took a huge deflection. It was one of those games. It was one of those seasons.

The thrashing by Arsenal took its toll. I thought a lot about that game and how hard it had been to get away from a top-class centre-back such as Adams, with his power and positional sense. For a while, it had me convinced that the Championship would be my level forever. I hadn't had a kick for ninety minutes, he was a class above. How could I do the business against players like him week in, week out? Whatever praise came my way for the rest of that season at QPR, the memory of Adams and Arsenal kept my feet rooted on the ground.

With the goals came the first experience of fame, or something approaching fame anyway. My height, naturally, had caught the imagination of the national newspapers that took a passing interest in QPR's struggles. I was constantly described as QPR's 'beanpole striker' or the 'gangly marksman'. No points for originality, but in those days, being mentioned in the newspapers was still a novelty and I read them all. These days I tend to be a bit more selective.

Now and again I hear footballers say publicly that they don't read the sports pages of the newspapers at all. I can assure you they do. If you are being written about, good or bad, it's difficult to resist the temptation to see what people are saying. I love to read the good stuff but, as I've got older, I've found it's just easier not to look when I know that I'm going to cop a load of stick. I've had a bit of experience in that department. My first real brush with the newspapers taught me a great deal.

It was January 2001 and we had beaten West Bromwich Albion at home and knocked Luton Town out the FA Cup when Gerry told me he wanted me to do an interview with the *Sun*. I was never one to refuse the manager but I tried tentatively to explain that, all things being equal, I would rather not do this one. Gerry was positive about it though, and said it would be good for me, so I did although I was a bit bewildered as to why.

My experience in this case, however, taught me that young players can be vulnerable. It's not something I look back on with much fondness.

The *Sun* sent their reporter Andy Dillon to meet me. He's a friendly bloke and he had done his research. Dillon had picked up that my nickname at the club was 'Rodders', after the hapless Rodney Trotter character from the television show 'Only Fools And Horses'. Go to a game that season at Loftus Road and you couldn't fail to notice the chant the fans had for me: 'ONE RODNEY TROTTER! THERE'S ONLY ONE RODNEY TROTTER!'

The nickname started with the fans and then the players took it up as well. I was considered to be exceptionally laid-back, like Rodney Trotter, and, apparently, physically similar to Del Boy's on-screen brother. It turned out that the *Sun* saw the whole 'Rodders' angle as the way they wanted to go and, as a naïve teenager, I walked straight into it. At the time I suppose I thought it was funny. I look back now and think *What was I doing?*

I don't mind taking the piss out of myself but I really wish Gerry had told me that the photograph of me was going to be featured on the front of the *Sun*'s SuperGoals football supplement. I don't know where the newspaper got it from, but they brought a yellow Robin Reliant car painted in the famous Del Boy-style – 'Trotters Independent Trading: New York – Paris – Peckham'.

The pictures of me sitting in the car – my feet on the pavement – were taken outside Loftus Road with the high-rise estates of White City in the background to make it look like Del Boy's Peckham home turf. 'ONLY TALLS 'N' HORSES' was the headline, continuing lower down with the line 'RANGER RODDERS JUST LUVVLY JUBBLY'.

I was a big fan of 'Only Fools And Horses' but I didn't like it so much that I wanted to make an idiot of myself in honour of the programme in a national newspaper.

I had to laugh that one off, especially when the pictures were pinned to the dressing-room wall before the game away at Norwich. When I read the story, it was clear that Andy Dillon wasn't about to leave the Rodders theme to the pictures alone. 'Peter Crouch was chuffed to bits when his QPR team-mates told him he was blessed with the looks of a famous TV star,' he wrote. 'Unfortunately, he felt a right plonker as he twigged that his sniggering pals actually meant Rodney Trotter, Del Boy's dimwitted brother from "Only Fools And Horses".'

Thanks a lot. It seems that the pictures taken that day are destined to follow me around forever. They tend to get dusted off every time a profile piece is written, and in the build-up to the 2006 World Cup finals, there they were again. At the time, I actually copped more stick from my team-mates for the shoes I was wearing. I had bought them from Clarks shoe shop and thought they were pretty smooth. Looking back, they were horrific.

As a club, we were in the shit. Gerry called a lot of meetings, where he would pick out players and be very direct about what they were doing wrong. In the end, he just had enough. Gerry resigned on 16 February but he stayed on for another three games while the club found someone else.

I scored the second goal in a 2–0 win over Barnsley, we beat Gillingham 1–0 and just as it seemed as if Gerry's resignation had given us a bit of momentum, we lost 5–0 to Wimbledon in his last game in charge. Gerry was made director of football and the club appointed his friend, and former QPR player, Ian Holloway.

Ian was a real character. Since then he has become famous for his unique use of the English language, and I hear there has even been a book published of Holloway sayings. Sacked by Bristol Rovers four weeks earlier, Holloway introduced himself at QPR in his own style. What he wanted to say was that he had loved his experience of managing at Rovers so much that he wanted to get straight back in there.

'Once you're bitten in the neck you're a vampire and you can't wait to get back into management,' he said. 'I totally believe I can keep QPR up.'

Anyway, I think that's what he meant.

I loved working with Ian and I have the utmost respect for him. He's a brilliant bloke, and telling him I was leaving QPR was one of the saddest things I have had to do in my football career. At the end of the season, when a few clubs were bidding for me, Ian told me he wanted me to stay and that he was going to build his team around me. It was a pity that we never got to do that.

I would love to work for him again. He makes you enjoy training to the extent that in the morning you want to go in to work. He's a good coach and funny, too, one of the lads. Training was fun. He would be involved and we would do it with a smile on our faces. Ian would be laughing and joking, just like he does when he's being interviewed on television.

In those days, most away trips involved a new stadium and a new experience for me, and in a few cases, another test. That was certainly how I felt when we went to Gillingham in the last few games of Gerry's regime. I have played at their Priestfield ground twice since then, with Portsmouth and Norwich City, and the feeling is the same. I get the worst stick of all from the home supporters. For some strange reason they just seem to hate me there.

That QPR game at Gillingham in February 2001 is the only match of my professional career that my dad has had to leave before the end. The abuse they threw at me was so bad that Dad did not trust himself not to lash out at someone. He would certainly have liked to, but when you're a footballer, even when you're the father of a footballer, you have to keep your cool. Dad always reasoned that if I could handle the stick, he had to as well, and he didn't want to let me down by getting in trouble for whacking someone.

That day Dad went to the Gillingham game with his mate Andy and it was Andy who broke first. Andy went to get the teas at half-time and, according to Dad, couldn't help himself when he heard yet another Gillingham fan abusing me. There was a serious commotion, the police got involved and were videoing Andy like he was some kind of hardcore football hooligan. When Dad worked out that his mate was at the centre of the trouble, he was faced with a terrible dilemma. Should he wade in and do what his instincts were telling him to do? Or take the sensible option, grab Andy and get out of Priestfield before he lost his rag, too.

It was really hard for Dad when people had a go at me, especially in the early days. I may have been a professional footballer but I was still his son and he found it tough to handle. The two of us have talked about Tony Adams' father, Alex, who for many years couldn't bear to go to games to watch his son play because of the 'Donkey' abuse that he had to endure. Adams' father was a strong bloke but you can't take on a whole stand of people.

I accept that abuse is part of football, and the nature of the football crowd, but it can get really nasty for the families of players. What made it worse that night was that Gillingham had bizarrely put the players' families among the home fans. Dad still talks about it. I was getting the standard stuff, the catcalls of 'freak', but this time there was an extra edge to it, a different kind of fervour. The abuse was weird and concerted – intense.

Looking around at the faces of the home support at Gillingham, the irony was never lost on me that these people had the cheek to call me a 'freak'. Perhaps they should have taken a look at themselves first.

Dad remembers his first visit to that Medway town in Kent quite clearly. In the Gillingham pub where he went for a drink before the match, the locals were watching 'Supermarket Sweep' on television, and they were betting on it with cash. Outside, Dad said he saw a bloke draining oil from his car direct into a drain while his kid played with the family's Staffordshire bull terrier dog. If you've never had the pleasure of visiting Gillingham, I hope that puts you in the picture.

I found Priestfield a bizarre place. It was a shame that Dad had to leave so early because I set up the winning goal for Chris Kiwomya in the second half. In the first half, however, I admit that I struggled a bit. It wasn't just a few people giving me stick, it seemed to be the entire home support. *Why here? Why Gillingham?* It was affecting me. I couldn't stop thinking the worst. *I'm getting abused here. This is going to be difficult. I can't really cope with this.*

So I took hold of the situation. As I walked off at half-time, I forced myself to look at the people who were shouting at me. I forced myself to pick them out individually, to think about their lives and the factors that had brought them there on that Tuesday night to call me a 'freak'.

I picked out a father and his son, both of them screaming abuse at me between chewing mouthfuls of hot dogs. They clearly hadn't thought what they looked like to me. *You're calling me a freak? You lot look like the hill-billies in the film 'Deliverance'.* I stared back at them. *Surely you have better things to do than this?*

All this hatred, all this bile. I had to overcome it and I did it by confronting the abuse. *This is all they have in their lives.* That was the way I pictured it to get through. *These people have got nothing better to do in their lives than go to Gillingham and shout abuse at me for no reason and then go home and be happy with that.*

I could have been wrong, all those people might have had fulfilling careers, Priestfield might have been full of brain surgeons that night for all I knew. That didn't matter. My mind was set. I was going to face them all down.

These people are not worth me thinking about them. That was my way of dealing with it and it's been the way I've done it ever since. *They are not worthy of my thoughts.* It works well. *After getting a result here, I am going to get back on the bus, go home and have a totally different life from them.* Second half I came out happy in myself, set up a goal and we won.

That's the longer version of how I cope with the abuse. The simpler version can be boiled down to two words. *Fuck them.*

I would say I am a friendly, easy-going person but I am also very private. If something affects me, I would rather not tell anyone. I just get over it in my own way. I did that when I was young. I would rather keep it to myself and get over it. I didn't speak about the abuse to my team-mates that night at Gillingham. I concentrated on the crowd as I walked off at half-time and I dealt with it my way.

Ian Holloway was positive with us, but the damage to our season was already done. We lost seven of the 13 games for which he was in charge up to the end of the season and won just one. The last nail in the coffin came on 21 April when Delroy Facey scored in the last minute to give Huddersfield Town a 2–1 win over us at their place. QPR had not been out of the top two divisions since 1967 and it felt horrible to be part of the side that finally went down with two games left to play.

I didn't feature in the last QPR home game of the season, a 3–0 defeat by Stockport, because I was suspended. The first red card of my career had come on a horrible night against Crewe at Gresty Road. We went 2–0 up. I scored after 15 minutes and then set one up for Andy Thomson ten minutes before half-time. This would have been a massive win for us. We hadn't won in eight games and the tension got to us. It certainly got to me.

I had been booked for a tackle early on and then, before the hour, I stood up two yards in front of the ball when the opposition were trying to take a quick free-kick and picked up my second yellow card. I had been fired up and I had done something stupid. The walk to the tunnel was horrible, I felt terrible. Above all, I was angry.

I watched the rest of the match from inside the tunnel. We held out for 85 minutes before Dean Ashton pulled one back for them. Then we went to pieces. Karl Ready was sent off for pulling down Rob Hulse when he went through on goal and they scored from the free-kick in the last minute. When that hit the back of the net I turned and walked back down the tunnel to the changing rooms.

On my own in the changing rooms I was in tears. I get upset when things go wrong but it's rare for me to be emotional when others are around. I was really bad that day. I felt it was all down to me. QPR are my local team, most of my mates are fans and the club means a lot to me. It was a terrible feeling, knowing that we were almost certain to go down. From a personal point of view there was a lot to be proud about that season, but that day it felt like everything was my fault. I'd got caught up in the tension of it all. I felt it was my responsibility. My dad hadn't been able to make it to the game, on a Wednesday night. Alone in the dressing room, I called him on my mobile. 'Dad,' I said, 'I've fucked up.'

We were relegated and I was for sale. There was a fair bit of interest in me, most of which I found out about from the newspapers, like any other fan. I don't know how much was true. Sunderland, Middlesbrough and Charlton Athletic – all Premiership clubs – were mentioned but none of them ever made an approach. QPR had given permission for me to talk to other clubs. They desperately needed the money that my transfer would generate. In April 2001, the chairman Chris Wright had put the club into financial administration amid talk of debts of £14 million.

The ins and outs of football transfers are strange indeed. In any other business, I'm sure it would be more organised. In football it seems you have delays every step of the way. You have to wait for people to get back from holiday. You have to wait for papers to be signed. Deals don't get done until right at the last knocking, or at the point when people realise that if they don't act soon, it might not happen.

Burnley, Preston North End and Portsmouth asked to speak to me. I kept Ian Holloway informed because I didn't want anything to happen behind his back. I'd had a taste of Championship football and I didn't want to drop down a level. Stan Ternent, manager of Burnley, seemed the keenest and I met with him. I also saw David Moyes, who was then at Preston, but it was Graham Rix at Portsmouth who impressed me the most.

I had lunch with Graham in a restaurant in Port Solent, which is where I lived when I moved to Portsmouth. It's a new harbour development with restaurants, shops and bars, as well as the Spinnaker Tower, set around a marina. If Graham was trying to impress me, he succeeded. But it was the way that he talked about football that really caught my imagination.

I liked him straight away and I liked what he had to say. He had visions of me playing up front on my own, with Mark Burchill and Courtney Pitt just behind me – one up and two off. He told me that I would enjoy working at Portsmouth. He sold the ambition of the club to me. My mind was made up. Portsmouth had beaten relegation by one point that season but I believed in Graham, who had known me since he was a youth-team coach at Chelsea ten years earlier. And Portsmouth believed in me. The £1.25 million fee they offered for me that summer was a club record for them.

10

FRATTON PARK – EIGHT MONTHS AND 19 GOALS

I had made my choice and it should have been simple but, as always seems to happen with transfers, there was a problem over my move to Portsmouth. Burnley wanted me so badly they were ready to force the issue. Their chairman Barry Kilby was so determined to get his man that he was prepared to pay the £1.25 million transfer fee up front, instead of the usual practice of spreading payments. For a club in Queens Park Rangers' difficult financial situation, that was too good to turn down.

Ian Holloway called my dad and told him that the club desperately needed me to agree to go to Burnley. QPR had been relegated into the third tier of English football, they were in administration and they had already released around fifteen players from their contracts. Ian was blunt – without this money, the club could fold. It was a question of survival for QPR and Portsmouth were not willing to pay in cash.

QPR were turning the screw on us to accept the move to Burnley – who could blame them? Dad said to Ian that he would think about it. He also said that I was a young player and it was a lot to expect me to save my local club as well as make the right decisions about my career. But this was QPR and I was an Ealing boy. Dad and I agreed that we would have to do something to help them. We had a responsibility, and neither of us wanted to see a club we had grown so fond of go under.

I went up the M6 to meet the Burnley manager Stan Ternent with my agent Jonathan Barnett and I remember that journey because we went in his car – a Bentley. Jonathan – and his Bentley – were at the centre of Ashley Cole's Chelsea transfer saga, the story that has become one of the most famous in football. As the tale goes, Ashley and Jonathan went in the Bentley to meet Jose Mourinho in a flash Kensington hotel and the rest is history. My story wasn't quite so exciting. I got to ride in the famous Bentley but it wasn't to Kensington. We went to meet Stan Ternent in a motorway Little Chef.

In his autobiography Stan claimed that I didn't want to go to Burnley because of the race riots that broke out there that summer. That honestly wasn't the case. I was flattered by Stan's interest in me but Graham Rix's philosophy on football just struck a chord with me. Looking at Stan's book again, he seems a bit loose on the details of that transfer. First off, he said that we met in his house and that when we talked in his kitchen, he thought my wife wanted me to join Burnley. The truth was that we met in a service station off the M6 and, as far as I know, I've never been married. Stan seemed a nice bloke although the move was never for me.

Dad and I discussed it at my agent's office in Lancaster Gate and then we walked around the block about six times, discussing the options. We went back home to Ealing and sat up late into the night talking it over with Mum. That's become standard Crouch family practice when a big decision on a transfer has to be made. We call it the 'overnight test'. Make a decision. Go to bed. Then see if you still agree with it come the morning.

The next day, Dad rang up Milan Mandaric, chairman of Portsmouth. He explained the situation and told him that it was vital the transfer fee should be paid to QPR in cash rather than over the course of my contract, which is the norm in a lot of these deals. Dad said that I wanted to join Portsmouth but if they couldn't come up with the money, I would have no choice but to join Burnley.

Portsmouth came up with the money that helped bail out QPR in the short-term, and we were very grateful to Milan for paying the transfer fee in cash. They paid £1 million and the rest, about £250,000, in six instalments. Of course, a percentage had to go to Spurs as per that agreement, but the money was enough to keep QPR in business. Burnley's fans weren't happy. When I played at Turf Moor in November, the home fans booed me throughout the game for turning their club down. I responded by scoring one of the best goals of my career – that was another one of those lessons in dealing with a hostile crowd.

Within 12 months of leaving Tottenham without a senior game to my name, I was a million-pound footballer. My original transfer fee of £60,000 had proved, on top of the 12 goals, a very handy investment for QPR, and I moved to Portsmouth on the kind of contract that reflected my value as a goalscorer in the Championship. It was certainly worth a lot more than the one that they wanted to frame and put on the wall of the secretary's office at Loftus Road.

This was the last summer of the big spenders outside the Premier-ship, before the bubble burst and Carlton and Granada, the backers of ITV Digital, pulled out of the £178 million contract upon which so many clubs had come to rely. My deal at Portsmouth, negotiated with the help of my agent this time, was worth around £6,000 a week, which was a lot of money for a 20-year-old footballer breaking into the big time, but par for the course in the Championship then.

The transfer, the big fee, the rise in wages may have convinced me that I was in the big time at last, but when I got my first tour of the Portsmouth training ground, I realised that I was still some way off it. No wonder Graham Rix had suggested that we met at Port Solent when he persuaded me to sign. The facilities at the training ground in Fareham, just around the harbour from Portsmouth, were horrific. We changed in Portakabins and we played on pitches that were often in a terrible state.

Our Fareham training ground was part of the Royal Navy's HMS Collingwood base and, in keeping with the nautical theme, we often turned up to find the pitches were under water. The playing surface was responsible for a fair number of injuries and more than once was unusable. The Navy base's rugby team played on it and a lot of the time Graham would take us over to the David Lloyd gym in Port Solent for some work on the running machines because the pitch was so bad.

As for the training kit, we had to take that home and wash it ourselves, or for those of us new signings who had not yet found a house, there was the option of paying Kev 'the kitman' McCormack £60 a month to do it for us. Nice little earner Kev had going there, especially as all he did was hand it over to the girls in the laundry. Kev was something of a local legend at Portsmouth, a former amateur boxer, and he came in very useful when I moved into my new flat.

After training we would drive across the naval base and have our lunch sitting at the long mess hall benches with the Navy recruits. It was a strange contrast of professions. They would have to turn up to lunch wearing uniform and in strict formation. They literally came marching in before they sat down to eat. At the opposite end of the scale were us lot, Rag-arse Rovers, all wearing T-shirts and shorts in the summer months. They were there to learn maritime warfare, we just fancied a bit of pasta and a cup of tea. I don't think they thought much of us.

My Portsmouth career got off to a flier and I never looked back. In July we played a friendly at Fratton Park against a good Tottenham side that included Ledley King, and I scored both our goals with headers in a 5–2 defeat. I scored in every pre-season game we played and by the time the season started I felt that I was already settled and confident in the side.

After the Tottenham game I bumped into Glenn Hoddle, who was in charge of the club by then. 'We couldn't handle you today, Peter,' he said. 'Who made the decision to let you leave Tottenham?'

It was an unexpected conversation but great for my confidence. Glenn told me that I was just the kind of player they wanted at Tottenham, a tall centre-forward who could cause trouble for centre-backs. Glenn even spoke about me in his post-match interview with Sky. It was positive stuff and coming from him it meant a great deal to me. His assistant John Gorman said that if I ever decided to leave Portsmouth, Tottenham would be interested. Little more than a year earlier, they had let me leave for a basic fee of £60,000. It was an early lesson in how quickly your luck can change in football. But I had a new club and was determined to prove myself.

At Portsmouth, the club was dealt a terrible blow in August when our goalkeeper Aaron Flahavan was killed in a car accident in Bournemouth. I had known Aaron for just a short while – he had played in the game against Tottenham – but he had been warm and friendly towards me when I joined the club. As a local lad and a former trainee at the club, he had been there longer than anyone else and had made an effort to welcome me as the new signing. I can't say I knew him well, but I saw the impact his death had on my team-mates.

Shaun Derry called me to tell me the sad news and all the boys met up that day to talk about Aaron and pay their respects. He was their mate and they had lost him. The club retired the No. 1 shirt for the rest of the season.

They were terrible circumstances in which to lose a friend and a team-mate. At a football club in the summer, everyone is generally full of optimism and hope for the season ahead, and it changed the mood. Life has to go on. We played Wolves six days after Aaron's death on the first day of the season, but he was never far from our minds.

A huge number of people attended the funeral, including both the Southampton and Portsmouth teams. Before the first home game of the season, Aaron's mother Irene and his fiancée Naomi Favell laid a wreath in the goalmouth while the crowd sang 'Abide With Me'. The emotion in the ground was remarkable. You couldn't fail to be moved. It was such a sad start to the season.

Harry Redknapp had been introduced to the fans at the Tottenham friendly as the club's new director of football and he was a powerful figure at the club. With Harry in that position and Graham the manager, I don't think it was ever going to work. They are two characters who want to get involved in the football side of things and Graham knew that. I had great respect for Graham but this season was heading the same way as my previous year at QPR. The manager who signed me was eventually sacked.

Also just like at QPR, I was, in spite of the team's problems, playing well and enjoying my life. I bought my first flat by the marina at Port Solent. It was perfect, a two-bedroomed apartment close to where Courtney Pitt and Shaun Derry lived. 'Dezza', who is at Leeds United now, became a good mate of mine, and still is. Courtney was a former Chelsea trainee. I had to chauffeur him everywhere because he couldn't drive. Rix would call us 'The Three Musketeers' because we spent all our time together.

Courtney and I had arrived that summer, Dezza the previous year, and none of us knew the area. Our social circle consisted of just the three of us. We must have eaten in every single Port Solent restaurant, tried everything on every menu and found ourselves on first-name terms with every restaurant owner in the area. One night Dezza announced that we couldn't go on like this. He said we needed to start cooking for ourselves and so we gave that a go. My signature dish – chicken and pasta – went down well. Never mind the Musketeers, we were like a little family.

At Dezza's flat after a few beers, Andy Petterson spotted some golf clubs and suggested a little challenge. He dropped a golf ball in the middle of the room, opened up the French windows and told us all to stand back. This was balcony golf. Shank it or slice it and we were going through the French windows, or, worse, sending it rebounding like a bullet round the room. Catch it right and there would be a satisfying plop as it landed in the harbour. Fail to make the distance and there would be a rattle as it dropped in a yacht.

Once I'd bought my flat, I set about adding the furnishings. I bought myself a sofa, splashed out on one that would look good, and couldn't wait to get it into the front room when it arrived. I summoned Dezza and Courtney to help me lug it upstairs to my flat on the first floor. We were useless removal men – no good with the angles needed to get it up the stairs, no idea how to solve the problem. It wasn't going up.

I had a nice view of the water from my front room and a lovely sofa to sit on to look out on it. Unfortunately, the sofa was in the lobby downstairs on its end. Word went around the club of my domestic difficulties and I got a lot of stick, but I was also offered a solution – Kev the kitman said he reckoned he could sort it out for me.

I was doubtful but Kev's a big bloke. We used to watch videos of his boxing matches on the coach on the way to games and he was as strong as an ox. He came round to the flat to take a look at the problem, sized up my balcony and returned later with a ladder.

'I'm going to take it up another route,' he said.

'It's bloody heavy, mate,' I replied.

'I'll manage,' he said.

Kev told the other two lads to hold one end of a rope on the balcony. Then he leaned the ladder against the outside wall up to my balcony, and lifted the three-seater sofa on to his shoulder. Quite a crowd was gathering to witness this he-man feat. He put a foot on the bottom rung of the ladder, then a second on the next step and up he went. In the end, he climbed high enough so that, with one last effort, he could shove the sofa over the front of my balcony. From there we dragged it in through the sliding doors.

At last I felt I was getting value for money for the sixty quid I was giving him to do my kit every month.

I started the season with a goal against Wolves in a 2–2 draw and I felt confident. The £1.25 million transfer fee that Portsmouth paid for me may not seem much now for a club owned by Alexandre Gaydamak and famous for having some of the deepest pockets in the Premiership. At the time, however, it was a lot. It was no longer a club record when Graham paid around £1.8 million for the Japanese goalkeeper Yoshi Kawaguchi, but it came with its own pressure.

The atmosphere was tense. Quite a lot of players had been there a long time and they felt under pressure because Graham was a new manager and he was changing things. The club had finished just one point clear of relegation in what is now the Championship the previous season. I could sense that around the ground and the team some players were bitter about what was going on. I got on well with the new players whom Graham had signed but it took a while for the old guard to take to me. I got the sense from a few of them that they would quite happily have seen me fail. I came in as an expensive signing and I had a lot to prove. The older guard weren't in the team as often as they would have liked, and with them not playing, I was under pressure to perform. So it helped that I scored six goals in my first eight games and 19 by the time I left them at the end of March. With the goals I later scored at Aston Villa, I ended up with 21, which is still my best-ever return for a season.

Third game of the season was Colchester again in the first round of the League Cup – then the Worthington Cup – and, as the year before at QPR, the team from Essex were the source of great embarrassment. At Fratton Park I got the equaliser after they took the lead, and then Muzzy Izzet's brother Kemal scored the winner for them. For the second year in a row I had been dumped out of the League Cup by Colchester, who had finished 15th in the division below us. The fans weren't happy.

Fratton Park was similar to Loftus Road in that it was an old football stadium hemmed in by houses and, just as at QPR, you had to walk out of the stadium, through the fans, to get to the players' car park. The Pompey fans would lie in wait for us in order to voice their opinions on our performance and, like most football fans, they didn't shy away from criticism when they thought we deserved it.

It was with no great enthusiasm that we went on the walk of shame that night. I guess I was OK because I had scored twice in three games already, and the fans seemed to like me. As I came out, one fan said something to me along the lines of, 'Crouchy, what's going on? We should be beating Colchester. It's a fucking shambles.' I did my best to acknowledge him and show some sympathy while moving as quickly as possible in the direction of the car park.

Behind me, Neil Barrett wasn't quite so lucky. Neil was another former Chelsea trainee. We called him 'Fido' because he looked like the cartoon character from the 7Up drink adverts. 'Oi, Barrett!' I could hear one fan shout at him. 'You were fucking useless tonight, you were fucking hopeless!'

Every supporter is entitled to an opinion of course, but it does help if fans have a few of the facts at their disposal. Fido hadn't played against Colchester that night. He wasn't even on the bench, not that his disbelieving protests – 'I didn't even fucking play!' – had much effect on the disgruntled Pompey fans.

That moment stuck with me because it showed how much some people actually watch the game. Barrett hadn't played and yet some of those people at the match hadn't even noticed. From then on, I thought to myself, if someone has a go at me, I just have to remember that it's nothing more than the opinion of one person. Here was a fan slagging off a player who hadn't even played in the game in question. That's the level of the debate sometimes. That's the way you have to look at it.

There were times at Pompey, under Graham Rix, when we really clicked as a team. We won three league games in a row after the defeat by Colchester, and at the second of those, a 4–2 win at home to Grimsby Town on 27 August, it all fell into place. I scored two and so did my strike partner Mark Burchill, who had signed from Celtic, after being on loan to Ipswich Town, for £900,000 that summer. Burchy and I looked like a really good combination and then, within a month, he injured his cruciate ligaments in training and, after just six appearances, never played again that season.

That was the kind of season we were enduring, with injuries and terrible inconsistency. After the death of Aaron Flahavan, Rix picked Dave Beasant, 42 years old at the time, who was playing out of his skin in goal for us. Then, in November, the club signed Kawaguchi. He was a legend in Japan but had such a torrid time at Portsmouth that he almost lost his place in the Japan World Cup finals squad in the summer of 2002.

He didn't have the greatest of debuts, conceding his first goal 24 seconds into the match, away at Sheffield Wednesday. I scored two that game and we won 3–2. Against Grimsby in December, Kawaguchi had an absolutely terrible time. The ball was swirling around in the air and every time they put a cross in, he was just all over the place. I put us 1–0 up, and then he went flapping all over the place and we lost 3–1.

Yoshi was a lovely bloke, another one of the Port Solent crowd, although he did not speak a word of English. That fact made his appearance at the Christmas fancy dress party even more amazing. He got to the pub earlier than everyone else and when the rest of us arrived we found him sitting alone at a table drinking a beer – dressed as Big Ears from the Noddy books. Unbelievable. He must have been thinking, 'What am I doing at this club?' I don't know who had managed to tell him that he needed to wear a costume, I didn't expect him to have one. He even had a big pair of comedy ears.

As captain of Japan it can't have been easy for him coming into this new environment, training at a crappy Naval base. We always suspected Graham Rix was under pressure to pick him. There were loads of Japanese journalists at training every day, Japanese fans giving him presents. By the end of the season he was dropped, but he should have been out a lot earlier.

The Cups proved a disaster for us. The FA Cup turned out to be even more shaming than the game against Colchester United in the League Cup. We lost to Leyton Orient, who that season finished 18th in the fourth tier of English football, two divisions below us. It was an atrocious performance. We weren't just beaten, we were humiliated on third-round day with a 4–1 thrashing at Fratton Park. It came on the end of a run of five defeats out of six in the League and in the aftermath, Milan Mandaric sacked Graham's assistant Jim Duffy. Only Harry Redknapp's intervention saved Graham from going the same way.

After the match, as I headed for the car park with Mum and Dad, I was attacked by a Pompey supporter. There was a pretty unpleasant atmosphere outside the stadium and he was waiting on the street we had to walk down to get to our cars.

He was steaming drunk and had been shouting at the players one by one as they came out. I didn't see him until the last minute. He called me 'a fucking disgrace' and took a swing at me. Dad clocked the danger long before I did and stood between us. As soon as the fan swung a fist, and missed, Dad was straight in there. He didn't need asking twice. It hardly needed to be said that when you're the club's centre-forward, and wearing your match-day suit, it's not a great idea to be seen scrapping with the fans outside the stadium.

Dad is normally the model of restraint but this time he had a pretty good excuse. He rugby-tackled the fan to the ground and dragged him into the front garden of a house on Frogmore Road. As he pinned him to the floor, he calmly told me to take Mum and fetch the car. I reckoned Dad could take care of this one himself. In between the flowerbeds, the old man seemed to have a firm grip of my attacker. So I steered Mum off to the car.

When I came back, Dad had dusted himself down and was ready to leave. Whoever Pompey's Mr Angry was, he hadn't counted on having to take on Bruce Crouch. That wasn't the end of it, though. A couple of weeks later, I came out of the stadium to walk to the car park and the same bloke was there again.

'You were out of order,' I said. 'I didn't even see you coming.'

'I only wanted to speak to you,' he said, 'but I thought that big bloke you had with you from the club's security company was a right animal.'

I didn't tell him who my minder really was but it was good to know that I wasn't the only member of the Crouch family to leave a lasting impression at Portsmouth Football Club. In truth, I felt hurt at being singled out by the supporter in question. I felt my performances had been excellent. Up to that Leyton Orient game I had scored 15 goals in

25 matches. It was the same weird situation as at QPR – I seemed to be playing well but the team wasn't winning games.

In all, I scored 16 goals before Graham Rix was sacked at the end of February and I believe that I did my bit for the team. The pressure, however, was on Graham right from the start. We just struggled to put together any run of form. We beat Manchester City and Nottingham Forest but lost to Rotherham, Millwall, Crewe and Gillingham.

Towards the very end of Graham's time, we scored seven goals in two games and came out with just a point – we drew 4–4 with Barnsley and lost 4–3 away at Sheffield United – and his last game in charge was a 5–0 defeat by West Bromwich Albion. I defended him as much as I could that season when I was interviewed by the newspapers, but when the pressure became really intense, a few of the lads took it a bit further.

Between them, a few of the senior players decided to go to see the chairman to ask him not to sack Graham. A lot of us were close to him, he had brought me to the club and I enjoyed working with him, but I didn't want to be involved. Nevertheless, I was dragged along with the group to see the chairman.

It was like going to the headmaster's office. I was only there because I was one of the few in the team who was actually having a decent season and they thought my presence would give them a bit more clout. I didn't do much of the talking and Milan Mandaric didn't do much listening. Graham was out by the end of the month. I have great affection for Graham but I still don't believe the players should have anything to do with decisions over the manager.

Milan was a very hands-on chairman, definitely one who liked to be involved. He was not afraid of coming down to the changing rooms – or the 'locker rooms' as he called them – if he wasn't happy with the way things were going. He wasn't best pleased when he came to see us over the New Year period when we lost five in a row, including that FA Cup third-round game to Leyton Orient.

'You haven't won this month and if I was in any other job and you hadn't done anything this month, I would have fired you,' he said. 'So this month I'm not paying you. You haven't won so why should I?'

So he didn't. The lads were up in arms. Still, we didn't get paid for the month in question. The team threatened action from the players' union, the PFA, and everyone at the club was telling the chairman that he had to pay, but he held out for a few weeks before we got that month's money. A lot of the lads were seriously pissed off. I know that you can't do that kind of thing. I understand that if you sign a contract, you have to come up with the money, but privately, I had a bit of sympathy for him. When a team isn't getting results, I bet a lot of chairmen would like to do the same thing.

Milan had pulled off an unbelievable transfer at the start of the season. The former Croatia international Robert Prosinecki had joined on a free transfer, after a bit of trouble getting his work permit from the Home Office. What an amazing player. He'd had stints at Barcelona and Real Madrid, won a European Cup for Red Star Belgrade and was the only man in history to score for two different nations at a World Cup – Yugoslavia and Croatia. And he smoked about forty cigarettes a day.

He caned them. They were Marlboro Reds too, not for the faint-hearted. Prosinecki was Croatian but he had a Serb mother and had played his football for Serbia's most famous team, so he knew Milan, who was also Serb. He was a top, top player but very different from what we were used to. We were English lads playing for Portsmouth and suddenly we had this massively famous player among us. He didn't do much running to say the least – he couldn't run really – but he was a fantastic player.

I got on well with Prosinecki but he didn't see eye-to-eye with a lot of the lads and he didn't mind telling them. As we struggled towards the end of the season, a few of the players were constantly calling meetings to discuss what was wrong. I had the greatest respect for Linvoy Primus and Darren Moore, two of the senior players at Portsmouth, both religious men who did a lot of incredible charity work outside of football. They were leaders at the club and examples to young players such as myself. Dezza and Carl Tiler were involved in the meetings, too. Prosinecki, however, was not impressed. When he was told that the players were getting together for a meeting, he would dismiss it in that harsh Croatian accent.

'Why are we having these meetings?' he asked indignantly. 'This club! It's always meetings, meetings, meetings.'

He was right. It was a waste of time. Prosinecki would sit at the back with a look of complete disgust on his face, saying nothing and smoking lots.

'Come on, Robert, what do you think?' Tiler would ask. 'How can we put things right?'

'I don't want to talk in this stupid meeting,' Prosinecki would shoot back. 'You are all talking utter rubbish.'

The lads were just trying to discuss what we were doing wrong and where we could improve. I agreed with Prosinecki. To me, work on the training ground stood a chance of turning it around but I didn't see how talking about it was going to make much difference. As a team, we just weren't performing.

In the end, Portsmouth stayed up but it was at the cost of Graham Rix's job, which I was sad about. However, by the end of March I was on my way to another new club.

11

FIVE MILLION QUID?

I was in the lobby of a hotel in Portsmouth when the call came, just waiting around, enduring the dead time before a Saturday afternoon match. We had won two out of our last seven games. Harry Redknapp was slowly turning it around since taking on the manager's role after Graham Rix left.

As a footballer, you don't tend to get calls in the few hours before a game unless it's important. People leave you alone. They assume that you don't want to be disturbed, but that morning one of my agents, David Manasseh, called.

'Peter, I know you're playing this afternoon but I just thought you ought to know. Aston Villa have bid five million pounds for you. It's been accepted by Portsmouth. Just go out and play. We'll sort everything out.'

'Fucking hell,' I said. 'How much?'

After the call from Manasseh, I rang my dad immediately.

'I've just heard the news from David,' he said. 'We'll talk about it properly after the match.'

Then I saw Harry in the lobby.

'Boss, I hear there's been a bid from Villa.'

'Crouchy, it's a lot of money,' Harry said. 'I don't want to lose you but the board have accepted it. You need to speak to Villa now and see what you want to do. It's the Premiership. It's where you should be.'

And that was it – from sixty grand in August 2000 to five million and the Premiership within nineteen months. The goalless draw against Sheffield Wednesday was my last game for Pompey. I can't say it was my best. I charged around after the ball, trying desperately to give the fans one last goal. It was my last game at a club I loved playing for – and I'd scored 19 goals in 39 games – but my mind kept flicking back to the conversations I'd had before the match. Five million quid?

Before I could even think about Villa, I had another big challenge ahead. David Platt had picked me for his England Under-21s squad. The Under-21s were to play Italy at Bradford's Valley Parade ground on the Tuesday. This was recognition for the goals I had scored in the Championship and a chance to measure myself against established Premiership players, still biding their time in the Under-21s.

It was a whirlwind. I turned up to meet the squad for the first time, well aware that I would be doing the same with the Villa boys in a few days' time. The very strong group of players included Alan Smith, Jermain Defoe, Paul Robinson, Shaun Wright-Phillips and Scott Parker. At training I met the captain, Gareth Barry, who was to become a great friend at Villa.

'Are you signing then, mate?' he asked.

'Actually, I'm going to meet your boss later. What's he like?'

Graham Taylor must have called in a favour with Platt because I was allowed a bit of time off, and to take a Football Association car to a hotel to meet the Villa manager. Graham wanted to tell me how he saw me as a player, why he rated me and why I should join Villa. I suppose he wanted to look me in the eye and find out what he would be getting for his money.

I had known there was interest in me because there was plenty of it in the newspapers, which I followed with great interest but quite a bit of confusion. Exactly who was in the race to sign me? I was linked with a few clubs that had been interested last time but Villa caught my eye. When he was Watford manager, Graham had spoken to me in the tunnel at Vicarage Road in my first few months at Queens Park Rangers, and been very complimentary.

During the game against Crewe the previous week, I had caught sight of him in the main stand at Gresty Road. It's not the biggest stand and as I was looking for my dad my eye had fixed on the area where the coaches and scouts sat, and Graham was there. He had only taken over at Villa in early February after John Gregory left. Against Crewe I had scored in the 1–1 draw, and played well.

To come to talk to me Graham had caught a train from Watford into London and all the way back again to York. I met him in a hotel by the railway station. He was very keen on me as a player and had followed my progress, he told me, right from when I was in the youth teams at Tottenham. He had tried to sign me the season earlier when he was at Watford but the club hadn't been able to come up with the fee.

It was the first time I had spoken to him properly but what came across was how much he cared about football. I knew immediately that I could trust him. I know that he has taken a long time to shake off the treatment he was subjected to in the press after England failed to qualify for the 1994 World Cup finals, but he is a dignified man. He impressed me in that meeting as someone I would like to work for. Graham Taylor was – still is – a decent, kind, honest bloke. So I had no hesitation in saying that I would sign.

I was a little more confident than I had been for the first two transfers of my career, to Queens Park Rangers and Portsmouth, because now I had worked with some big-name managers. Gerry Francis, Graham Rix and Harry Redknapp were respected in the game. I wasn't daunted by the idea of meeting Graham Taylor and afterwards I felt that I had reached an important moment in my

Above left: Leaving the house, suited and booted, for my first day as a professional footballer with QPR.

Above right: I scored twice against Luton Town in this FA Cup third-round tie on 6 January 2001. The match ended 3–3 and Dad got trampled in the crush as the QPR fans celebrated!

Right: The game that changed everything. I set up Chris Kiwomya's equaliser against Gillingham, 13 September 2001. I had already scored once and my confidence was high.

Left: Patrick Vieira chases me down in an FA Cup fourth-round tie against Arsenal, 27 January 2001. We lost 6–0, but I got my first taste of top-level football.

Below: Why did I agree to do this? I was well and truly stitched-up by the *Sun* newspaper when they got me to pose as Rodney Trotter, January 2001.

I scored the winner for Portsmouth against Manchester City on 17 November 2001. Mum's side of the family are all City fans and weren't too happy.

Against Grimsby at Fratton Park on 27 August 2001, I got two.

Signing for Portsmouth in the summer of 2001. The haircut's changed since then.

My first Premiership goal, for Aston Villa against Newcastle on 2 April 2002, was immortalised in paint by the artist Brian West. My parents commissioned the picture as a present for me.

Above: Graham Taylor brought me to Villa. He's a great manager and a top man.

Right: Celebrating that first goal at Villa Park. It was only my second appearance for the club.

Below: On the stretch for Aston Villa against Charlton, 22 February 2002, during my difficult second season at the club.

Lining up to play for England Under-21s against Switzerland in the European Championship, 17 May 2002. We won 2–1.

With Jermain Defoe at the Hilton Hotel in Basel during the Under-21 European Championship. Did someone mention eggyboff?

The England Under-21 team to face Italy, 20 May 2002. We lost 2–1. Back row (*left to right*): Sean Davis, me, Zat Knight, Chris Riggott, Gareth Barry, Paul Robinson. Front row: Alan Smith, Luke Young, Paul Konchesky, David Dunn, David Prutton.

Left: With Darren Huckerby, signing on loan for Norwich City, 10 September 2003. The club gave me my championship-winner's medal the next season.

Above: Nigel Worthington, my manager at Norwich City, is a great bloke. I got my confidence back at Carrow Road.

Below left: Playing for Norwich against Millwall, 8 November 2003. I was enjoying football again after being frozen out at Aston Villa.

Below: The lovely Delia Smith and her husband Michael Wynne-Jones, the majority shareholders at Norwich, were very kind to my family.

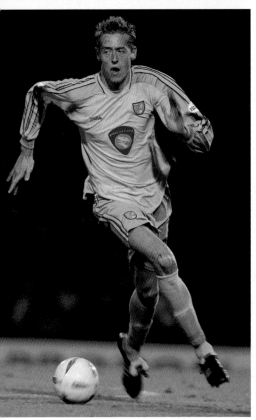

career. I felt I was ready to take a big step up and that it was all happening very quickly.

I came on as a substitute against Italy, and we drew 1–1. I felt comfortable in the training sessions, and knew I could play at that level. I must have done well because on two separate occasions Italian blokes came up to Dad after the game and asked what my situation was with Portsmouth. They were from AC Milan and Juventus and they were interested, too. The week just kept getting better.

Then the madness of a football transfer took over. After the game, Dad met me at Valley Parade and drove me south to The Belfry hotel, which is next to the famous golf course just around the corner from Aston Villa's training ground, Bodymoor Heath. The Belfry is a smart hotel and Villa had pulled out all the stops.

Dad and I turned up late that night to find the club had booked us into the smartest suite you could imagine. Champagne and strawberries were on ice, and our two beautiful big rooms had a view over the 18th hole. *Now this is life in the Premiership.* We took the bottle and sat out on the veranda. It was a bit chilly in the west Midlands in March but it was time for the Crouch family 'overnight test' for the third transfer of my career.

We talked for hours. Was it too early in my career? Villa were paying £4.5 million up front for me and a further £500,000 depending on whether they qualified for European football and how many games I played. Was the transfer fee going to put on pressure?

'Forget about that,' said Dad, 'that's the transfer market. That's Villa's decision to spend the money. There's nothing you can do about the fee. Take it as a compliment. The manager must really want you.'

When I woke up the next morning in my luxurious Belfry hotel room, I knew there was only one decision. I wanted to sign. We were collected by the club and chauffeur-driven down to Villa Park to complete negotiations and sign the contract. The red-brick Trinity Road stand loomed up ahead. With all respect to QPR, this was a bit different from meeting under the main stand at Griffin Park.

Dad and my agent went in to meet the great Doug Ellis, at the time Villa's legendary chairman. As it turned out, Dad didn't thank me for that. He was in there for what seemed like an eternity. I sat outside drinking cup after cup of coffee. I read the newspaper in reception back to front and finished the crossword. The Sky Sports News bulletins on the telly were rolling round for the fifth time. What the hell was 'Deadly' Doug talking to them about?

Absolutely everything, apparently. Dad had a kind of traumatised look on his face when Doug finally released him and the door to the boardroom swung open.

'Christ, Dad, what kept you?' I whispered to him.

'I've just had the man's life history,' he muttered back.

The ordeal wasn't quite over for Dad. He had to have dinner with the chairman in a restaurant in the stadium. I was the lucky one. I was heading down to the training ground to meet my new team-mates. When Dad and I met up later, he told me what he could remember of the conversation with the chairman. And there was plenty to remember.

Dad said the boardroom itself reminded him of the classic lair of a James Bond villain – a huge, long, shiny table, a big picture of Doug on the wall, and Doug himself sitting at the other end of the table. All that was missing was Doug swinging around in a swivel chair and welcoming Dad with the line, 'Ah, Mr Crouch, I've been expecting you.' You get the picture.

Doug was keen on talking about his favourite subject and that subject was Doug Ellis. He began by giving Dad the impression that he had invented the overhead kick while he was a rating in the Royal Navy. Remarkable. There was me thinking that the overhead kick had been invented by some Brazilian from the 1930s, or perhaps Pele. I assumed that the technique I saw performed so beautifully by Marco van Basten and Hugo Sanchez was the brilliant concept of one of the South American greats. Don't be silly. It was Doug, during a break from swabbing the decks on HMS *Ark Royal*.

'I did it and people said, "What's that?"' Doug recalled. 'And I said, "That's the overhead kick."'

Dad said the contract talks took about ten minutes. The rest was Doug talking about Doug and Aston Villa, but he did try a classic negotiating tactic with Dad to get a few quid off my wages.

'Mr Crouch, you seem like a sensible parent. I'm very worried about the money these young men are earning. I worry that it will affect their football. They may not be able to handle being so well paid at such a young age.'

'Don't worry, Mr Ellis,' Dad said. 'I'll be there to make sure Peter handles it.'

On and on Doug went. He began singing the praises of one of the Villa youth teams of the time, the side that went on to win the FA Youth Cup in 2002 and included players such as Liam Ridgwell and Gary Cahill. Doug pressed a buzzer and a list of the squad was brought in for him. He went through every single boy, describing his talents. Dad's hopes of getting back to the office in London that afternoon were quickly turning to dust.

At the training ground at Bodymoor Heath, I stood awkwardly by the changing rooms as the players came off, introducing myself and shaking hands. Lee Hendrie was the first, and we later became great mates. Dion Dublin and Steve Staunton were there, established names in the Premiership. I was nervous. They were welcoming.

I had the medical, signed the contract and that was it. Less than four days after I took the phone call in a hotel lobby in Portsmouth, I was an Aston Villa player.

I never got to say goodbye in person to the boys at Portsmouth. Dezza and Courtney rang to wish me well. I had scarcely been there ten months and I'm glad Portsmouth are back in the Premiership now, where they belong. On my first day off at Villa, I drove back down and picked up as much stuff as I could get in the car to see me through for a while. A few weeks later, Mum cleared out my flat in Port Solent and we handed the keys over to a letting agency. I had been very happy there but the morning I'd left for the game against Sheffield Wednesday, my life changed.

I've not been back. That's football. In less than two years I'd been all over the place – Dulwich, Sweden, QPR, Portsmouth and now Villa. No sooner had Kev the kitman chucked my sofa over my balcony in Port Solent than I was thinking about life in a new club, in a new city. But, most important of all, I was in the Premiership.

That first day I introduced myself to a few more of the Villa staff, shook some hands and made sure I knew what time training began the next day. Dad had gone back to London. It had been an incredible few days. I would get to see my team-mates close up in training the following day, but for now I wanted to be on my own to contemplate my Premiership debut. That would come away at the Reebok Stadium in three days' time.

The club had written into my contract that they would pay my accommodation fees for three months. It would take a while to get my bearings in Birmingham. I certainly didn't know where was nice to live, where was handy for the training ground or where most of the lads had settled. However, I thought the agreement with the club meant that I could only stay in the hotel. I never realised that they would have paid my rent for a flat or a house for the same amount of time. I thought it was either the hotel or find a place to buy.

Choosing between finding a new place and stopping in a luxurious hotel around the corner from the training ground seemed like a no-brainer. Did I want to spend the next few months trailing around after estate agents or sitting in my beautiful Belfry hotel suite looking at the view over the 18th with my feet up? I'd hit the jackpot with this place – or so I thought.

The concierge at the Belfry caught me as I was walking through the lobby. He looked a bit embarrassed. I think he'd had to do this before with Villa signings.

'Mr Crouch, about your room. You probably know that we've moved you to another one. I hope you find the new place to your liking.'

To my liking? There was nothing wrong with the first one. This didn't sound good. And when I turned the key in the door of my new room, my fears were confirmed. I would have found it more to my liking if there had been any remaining room once me and my bag were in there. The room was so small it was a joke. I don't know where they were keeping the brooms at that hotel once I was sleeping in their cupboard. They might as well have given me a wardrobe. To get to the toilet from my bed I had to stand on my bag.

You had to hand it to Doug Ellis. If he wasn't going to save money on the contract, he would save it elsewhere. I had gone from the best suite in the place to the broom cupboard the moment I had signed on the dotted line. The concierge came up to show me to my new room and I slung my bag on the bed in disbelief. There wasn't anywhere else to put it with both of us in there. He looked up at me sympathetically. I looked back at him despairingly. I'd been well and truly stitched up.

Most players would have walked out and told the club to sort it. These days I wouldn't put up with it, either. Then, I was 21, eager to impress and not sure if this was the norm or not. I was new in the

Premiership. I didn't want to turn up to training on the first day and start whinging about the size of my hotel room. Whoever I told, I thought it might get back to the manager. So I kept quiet.

Within hours my stuff was all over the place. I'm quite messy and moving it seemed like a hassle. I had a system – stuff thrown here, stuff thrown there, shoes under here. My dad came at the weekend and thought I was joking when I opened the door. He said I should complain. I didn't. I spent three months in that pokey little room. Villa have got themselves sorted since then. They have a brilliant player liaison officer, Lorna McClelland, who tells the new signings what they are entitled to and the best way of getting a new place.

I could sympathise with Alan Partridge in that series where he tragically lived alone in a motorway travel tavern. Most nights I ate alone in the piano bar, eating carvery dinners. I stayed so long I was on first-name terms with all the staff by the time I left. Even the pianist got to know me so well that on quiet nights he would shout over to me as I ate, 'Crouchy, any requests?'

I was lucky because I made great mates at Villa. I still speak to Lee Hendrie and Gareth Barry a lot, and when I finally moved out of the Belfry I went to live in Solihull, where those boys settled. The more I got to know them, the more I wanted to live over that way. It was one of the best decisions of my life. Lee is from Birmingham and Gareth had been there five years by then, so they both had a big group of mates. They accepted me and took me in, and I keep in contact with a lot of people around there. I had a great time, and I never really wanted to leave.

We lost on my debut, 3–2 away at Bolton. I was given the full ninety minutes and I felt my touch was good enough, but it was a bad result against a newly promoted team struggling to survive in the Premiership. I had played against Bolton the previous year for Queens Park Rangers. It was a bad one to lose. But I had shown enough to stay in the team. The game was faster and harder than what I was used to but I knew I could play at this level as soon as I had the ball at my feet.

The big one was my home debut, against a Newcastle team captained by Alan Shearer and managed by Sir Bobby Robson. I really knew that I had arrived when I saw the name of the former England captain in the programme. There were 36,597 people in Villa Park that night and they saw Shearer score the 199th goal of his Premiership career, and the first of mine.

The game was played on a Tuesday night, and my dad got away from work early to come to watch – no chance of him missing this one. For me it was another one of those matches, like Gillingham at home for QPR – a turning point. Time to lay down a marker. Prove yourself. Get out there and show them that you can play at this level, that you belong.

Newcastle played three at the back that night, including Nikos Dabizas. He had joked before the game that he was going 'to take a ladder' to Villa Park so he could mark me at corners. What a funny man. The ladder wouldn't have been much use to him that night when I nipped in ahead of him and stuck a diving header in the far corner. That one was down to sheer technique, the result of hours of early morning practice heading Dad's crosses at Hanwell Town.

I have seen the goal a thousand times on video. We went 1–0 down to Shearer's goal in the third minute. In the 26th, Gareth Barry whipped in a cross from the left and I ran from a position in line with the back post to the middle of the goal and launched myself at it. I glanced it across Shay Given and into the far corner. I don't know what Dabizas was doing. He seems to be diving, literally diving, arms outstretched, as I make contact with the ball.

It was one of my proudest moments. Mum and Dad commissioned a painting of the goal and gave it to me for my birthday. The Villa fans took to me. I played the last six games of that Premiership season, finishing with a trip back to the stadium I knew so well. Stamford Bridge was the place I first dreamed of being a professional footballer, where I watched games as a ball-boy, and it gave me the perfect end to an incredible season.

That day was emotional for me because two years earlier I had been on loan at Dulwich Hamlet, playing in front of 200-odd people and worrying about my future. It was emotional for Dad, too. Lots of his mates from the days when he travelled around watching Chelsea had got in touch to give him their congratulations. He met up with a few of them for a drink before the game, as he had done before hundreds of Chelsea games, but this one was different. This time he was going to watch his son play at Stamford Bridge.

Before that day Dad had never sat in the away supporters' enclosure, which, at that time, was behind the dugouts. It was a sunny May day and he and Mum were near to the tunnel as I came out. I had come a long way in a short space of time. This was everything I had worked for, everything I had hoped for during all those years as a trainee. I was establishing myself in the first team of a Premiership side.

I had been growing in confidence at Villa and on that day against Chelsea I really proved I was ready for this level. My touch was good, I won everything in the air and Darius Vassell and I were linking up well. I scored after twenty minutes. Steve Stone struck a corner from the left and I got in front of Mario Melchiot. I didn't catch it that sweetly but I headed it down hard enough and it bounced up past Carlo Cudicini and in.

We won 3–1 that day and while it was Darius who got all the headlines – he was off to the World Cup that summer – I had one very special moment to take away with me from the season. As I came back to the halfway line after my goal I spotted Mum and Dad in the stands behind the dugouts and blew them a kiss. My dad's not one for tears in public but Mum said he was as close as ever at that moment.

That May, the England team that went to the Uefa Under-21 European Championship in Switzerland went with as much hope and expectation as the senior team took to the World Cup in Japan. It fell apart just the same. We didn't even make it out of the group stages.

My memories of those few weeks divide up very clearly. I had great fun with the boys, including Gareth Barry, Alan Smith, Jermain Defoe, Sean Davis, Paul Robinson and David Dunn. The football I enjoyed much less. Manager David Platt picked me for the first game and I scored against Switzerland in a 2–1 win. Then he played me up front on my own against Italy, with Dunn playing just off me. It didn't work and he hauled me off at half-time.

I was fuming. The formation kept changing under Platt and I had done my best to make this one work. It had gone well in the first game with me alongside Defoe, but this new system didn't come off. When I got subbed it felt like I was being hung out to dry by Platt. Massimo Maccarone got a couple for Italy, we lost the game and I was dropped for the last match against Portugal. With another line-up change, we lost 3–1 and were out.

That was the football. We did our best to adapt to the new formations and it didn't work. The lads were brilliant, the spirit was good and we all got along well, considering that the Under-21 squad changes a lot from match to match. I had played just twice for them before Switzerland – the second was against Portugal in April – but they seemed like a good bunch. So I thought I'd introduce them to the legend of eggyboff.

The boys loved it and before long we were locked in the kind of mind games we used to play in my days at Tottenham. We had a routine of visiting the stadiums we were playing in the day before matches. We did it before the Italy game in Basel. Everyone came, Platt and his backroom staff too, and they wandered out on to the pitch while we sat down or stood around the dugouts. It was a beautiful, warm evening and the players were just chatting. Then Sean Davis called it on.

'First one to move is eggyboff.'

Right, I thought, let's see what these boys are made of.

Pretty stern stuff as it turned out. Platt and his staff came back off the pitch and walked past us. They wandered down the touchline and back out of the stadium. Not a muscle moved among the lads. Everyone was stock still.

After a minute or so there was some laughter and nervous giggles. The manager must have been on the team coach by then, waiting for us. The staff had an idea of what was going on but, as at Tottenham, they weren't completely sure what we were up to. A few more minutes passed.

'The gaffer has got to be biting now,' someone said.

Suddenly Paul Westwood, the FA security man on the trip, came stomping back into the stadium with his two-way radio crackling. He was a funny bloke, anxious in the way security people can be in football. He stood in front of us – a whole squad of England players, in tracksuits, unmoving.

'Come on lads, we're leaving now.'

No one moved.

'Seriously lads, everyone on the coach. You've got to move NOW.'

No one stirred. So poor old Paul – and I felt for him – got on the two-way radio.

'Gaffer, they're not moving.'

Through the static I could hear Platt's voice. 'Well get them moving.'

'I can't. They won't do it. They're all stood here looking at me. They're fucking playing silly buggers.'

This went on for another ten minutes until Sean Davis was finally persuaded to call off the eggyboff. When we got back to the bus, Platt took it quite well. He didn't say too much. The next time it happened, though, he wasn't happy.

In the September of that year we played Yugoslavia at Bolton. On the coach to training someone called it.

'Eggyboff, first one off the coach.'

And that was it. Platt and his coaching staff got off and none of the lads moved. Not a muscle. Platt was so pissed off he sent Les Reed, one of the coaches, back on to the bus to hand the bibs out there. Les was on there just pretending we were out on the training pitch, walking up and down the aisle dishing out bibs and giving us instructions for training. The power of eggyboff had everyone under its spell.

Joleon Lescott snapped first. 'I'm not having this,' he said, and walked off. Lescott was eggyboff. The rest of us were free to go.

We got a bollocking from Platt for it.

'I don't mind you having your fun but we're here to fucking well work today. This is training. It's all right for you to piss around when we're in Switzerland the day before the game but we're training today.'

That was eggyboff for you. It could strike at any moment.

12

BINNED BY O'LEARY

I want to be clear about my time at Aston Villa – I never wanted to leave. I had two full seasons there, plus those seven games at the end of 2001–02, with a loan to Norwich City thrown in. Yes, I had some hard times but I was happy there. I was playing well by the end of it and I had a great relationship with the fans. I left because I had to. I left because of the manager, David O'Leary.

O'Leary binned me but he never had the guts to tell me to my face. It was always a case of 'You're in my plans' or 'You've got a role to play here' or 'We need you'. I began seriously to doubt that towards the end of 2003–04 when my reward for scoring important goals was a place on the bench for the next game. When I finally got wind of the fact that he was bringing in Carlton Cole that summer, I knew that it was time to go.

Before I found out he was after Carlton, I believed O'Leary when he told me there was a place for me at Villa. I wanted to stay and fight for it. I knew I could do it. I took the manager at his word, and eventually I had to have it spelled out to me by my dad and Jonathan Barnett. Jonathan represented Carlton, too, so he knew of Villa's interest. O'Leary was telling me I was his main man and all the time he was trying to get Carlton in without me knowing. And he thought I wouldn't find out? Before then, I couldn't see what people were telling me – that I had to leave to save my career.

Now my time at Villa is often regarded by others as a failure – too much too early for a striker who had not even played two seasons in the Championship. I don't believe that. When I came back from being on loan at Norwich in December 2003, I was full of confidence and ready to score goals. I had a great life in Solihull, great mates at the club and I would have stayed if O'Leary had shown some faith in me and given me a run of games in the team.

These days when Liverpool play Villa, I still get a great reception from my former club's fans. They know that through the difficult times and the injuries I did my best to live up to the price tag, and that I could have done more given the chance. Despite the problems, I remember my time there with fondness. It was my introduction to life as a Premiership striker.

In the summer of 2002, all that hurt was still a long way away. I had finished the season as Villa's new striker with two goals to my name already, I had been part of the England Under-21 team at the European Championship and life looked good. The move to Villa had hiked my wages up, so I suggested to my mates from Ealing that we go on holiday.

It turned into a brilliant summer. With my signing-on fee I paid for our hotels and flights for fifteen days on the west coast of America – five days in Las Vegas, five in Los Angeles and five in San Francisco. Right up until I played in the World Cup in 2006 I could wander about in those cities without getting much hassle. It was the anonymity that America gave me that I loved about the place as much as anything.

I had been away with the boys before, on a disastrous holiday to Ayia Napa a few years earlier. Herms, Greg and I joined up with Ledley King and some of the trainees at Tottenham. It wasn't our scene at all. In fact, the Ealing boys hated it so much that we hired mopeds – the really crap ones with baskets on the front that the locals rode – and got away to parts of the island that weren't full of British holidaymakers.

I know footballers are supposed to love places like Ayia Napa and Magaluf, but I don't and neither do my Ealing mates. I suppose we should have known before we went what it would be like. Everyone was steaming drunk and wearing football shirts in the boiling midday heat. The clubs and bars were shaking to the sound of hardcore garage music. That's not for me. Ever since that holiday, we've always gone somewhere different.

I came back from America fully recharged and ready to make my name as a Villa player. I had scored 21 goals the previous season and I was full of confidence. The problem was that I got off to a slow start. At Queens Park Rangers and Portsmouth, even though the team had been struggling, I had got into my stride pretty quickly and started scoring goals early on. But in the Premiership that August of 2002, I quickly found out that patience for a striker is very short indeed.

I did all right in the Intertoto Cup, although we were out by August, beaten in the second round 2–0 at home to Lille and knocked out 3–1 on aggregate. Graham Taylor had kept faith in me through those two ties, home and away, but I needed my first goal of the season. I was 21 years old and very eager to impress, perhaps over-eager. I was anxious about scoring that goal, about the transfer fee, about showing everyone that I belonged in the Premiership.

It got to me a bit. In the end, it got to me a lot. I can see that now, looking back. I thought I had done well in the first two games but we lost them both, at home to Liverpool on the first day of the season and then away at Tottenham. We should have beaten Tottenham. I played well and had a couple of chances, but Kasey Keller was unbeatable that day. Jamie Redknapp scored with a volley that turned out to be the winner. Graham subbed me at half-time for Marcus Allback.

A few of the newspapers mentioned that I had been a Tottenham player barely two years earlier. It would have been great to go there and show them what they were missing but I was more concerned about my first goal of the season. I didn't think I was playing badly. I just needed a goal to settle my nerves. If I had got one in those first two games, I think it would have settled me. If I had put one away against Liverpool, if Keller hadn't been so sharp . . . Success and failure. It's the finest of lines in football.

Our third Premiership game of the season was against Manchester City at home, and Graham stuck with me. I was grateful for that. I had wanted to get off to a flier and now I was starting to get anxious. In that City game I had a couple of one-on-one chances to beat Peter Schmeichel and I should have done better, but it was one of those frustrating days. All the good things I had done at the end of the previous season felt a long way away. Scoring that first goal of the season was becoming a big thing. When you miss a chance, you can hear the murmurs in the crowd. I wasn't used to it. I wasn't used to playing in this big old stadium, and I wasn't used to the high profile of being an expensive striker. The expectancy was greater than I had known before. That was what got on top of me, that and my eagerness to impress. It all started to affect my confidence.

The newspapers didn't look great the day after the Manchester City game. Graham was under pressure to back me and he did. 'Don't worry – Crouch will come good' was the headline in the *Birmingham Mail*. Graham said that the time to worry was when I wasn't getting chances or wasn't trying to score. 'Peter will score goals. The worry will be if you suddenly see him stop having any efforts.' But he could see that the pressure was starting to take its toll on me.

Funnily enough, I've since found out that Graham was close to dropping me for the next game, away to Bolton, because of an incident with Schmeichel, who had left Villa earlier that season and was playing out of his skin. I don't remember it but, apparently, he'd come for a cross with serious intent, threatening to flatten anyone who got in his way. I suppose I couldn't see much chance of getting to it, pulled out and the Holte End crowd groaned. Much later, Graham said that he became worried that the crowd's response would have a serious effect on me. He wasn't angry with my actions on the pitch. In fact, he agreed with them. The ball wasn't really there to be won and with Schmeichel being so big he's the sort of bloke who could have done me an injury.

Graham gave me one more chance against Bolton at the Reebok Stadium and when I made it eight games in a row without a goal, in our third 1–0 defeat of the season, that was it. Four games into the season I was dropped for the home game against Charlton.

I don't remember the incident against City at all. That's life I suppose. I remember the chances, I remember some unrest in the crowd, but not the brush with Schmeichel. There were four other strikers at the club – Juan Pablo Angel, Darius Vassell, Dion Dublin and Marcus Allback. Darius and I had been the pairing of choice that far but I suppose Graham had to change it. 'The thing with Peter is that he hasn't bucked his responsibility,' he said in an interview before the Charlton game. The team won 2–0 and I was not selected for the derby with Birmingham City. Villa were beaten 3–0 and I was back in the side for the next game, against Everton.

We won 3–2 and that was when the season really did change for me. I didn't start another game for Villa for five months. Everton came back from two goals down before Dion Dublin, on as a substitute, scored the winner for us on 85 minutes. Dion had come on for me four minutes earlier and he never looked back. He ended the season, aged 34, with 14 goals, the club's top goalscorer, and I couldn't budge him from the team. After that, the only starts I had that season came when Dion was suspended.

These days when I miss a chance, I react differently. People might get annoyed, I might hear the crowd grumble, but it's water off a duck's back. I know that next time I'll score. That mentality helped me through the run of eighteen games at the start of my Liverpool career when I didn't score a goal. But as a young, relatively inexperienced player, it's different. When you are playing for the first time at Villa Park against Liverpool, or at Old Trafford, these are big games. Now I see it with young lads who come into Premiership games aged 18 or 19. Footballers are expected to be able to cope, to deal with the pressure, but not all of them do. Some of them are overawed and, at Villa, that happened to me.

It can simply be the occasion that gets to you. I had watched the players I was up against on the television for years and suddenly I was thrust in there among them. When things didn't go well, I had to learn to deal with it. I had to have strength of character to come back from it. Graham may think he should have left me in the team, but when I look back on it now, it was probably the right decision to take me out.

Dion was very supportive of me, but the way he was playing I just couldn't get into the team. To make matters worse, I picked up an ankle injury in a reserve game against Everton in late November. I wanted to impress as quickly as possible to get back in the first team, but by the time I was fit again, Dion was established, and I played just five more games for Villa that season.

It was David Weir who did me in that reserve game. The two of us had been having a bit of a go. I caught him with an elbow – completely unintentionally – and I knew he wasn't happy about it. I picked up the ball on the halfway line a few minutes later, turned and he clattered me from behind. The pain in my ankle took my breath away. It was complete agony. I hadn't felt pain like it since I missed the high-jump mat at Drayton Manor.

I can't complain. I've been so lucky with injuries in my career. In fact, this one is still the worst, and it came at such a bad time. I was at a low point, trying to get back into the team, and at least show how willing I was in reserve-team games and training. I've got nothing against Weir and respect him as a defender. I just refused to believe that I couldn't carry on.

The anterior and interior ankle ligaments were damaged, but I dragged myself up on to my feet and put a bit of weight back on the bad ankle. Pain shot up my leg. *Grit your teeth.* I limped back into position. Walking was hard and running was killing me but I couldn't bear to go off. I had missed enough football already. Mustapha Hadji, the Moroccan international who was at Villa at the time, jogged over to me. He could see the pain on my face. I'll never forget what he said.

'Crouchy, it's not the World Cup final. Get yourself off.'

He was right of course. It was the Bescot Stadium in Walsall on a Tuesday night with 400 people watching. That didn't matter to me. What mattered was that for the last four Villa first-team games I had either been left on the bench or missed out on the squad altogether. It was 26 November and I didn't play again for Villa until 18 January.

You cope with a different challenge each time you join a new club. At Queens Park Rangers it was my first season as a professional, at Portsmouth it was being a record signing. At Villa, in the Premiership, it was completely different. A lot of famous players were there, with big reputations and a history of success in the game. Schmeichel was still at the club when I joined, although I can't say I was sorry to see him go. Paul Merson, Steve Staunton and Steve Stone were there, and I was nervous around them, although they were good to me. They did their best to put me at ease.

Merson made the greatest impression on me. He was a big character around the place, an absolute demon trainer and one of the best players I have ever seen. He used to take over the training sessions if he didn't think the drills were right, or the session wasn't up to his standards. Graham Taylor's assistant John Deehan would be left in no doubt if Merse wasn't happy.

'Nah, Deehsy,' Merse would say, 'this is shit. We're gonna do it this way instead.'

And if Merse didn't think his team-mates were putting in the effort or contributing to a good session, he would walk off the pitch. No arguments. No compromise. Straight off. Training meant a lot to him, and he had to see commitment from everyone. He was coming towards the end of his career at Villa but he was still a fantastic player with loads of ability.

At the opposite end of the scale was Bosko Balaban. His name has become a byword in the Premiership for bad foreign signings. John Gregory, Graham's predecessor, had paid something like £6 million for him and he barely played while I was there. He had a reputation for getting a few goals at Dynamo Zagreb but when Graham gave him a run out, he looked really poor. Around the training ground he was carrying a few pounds and was soon dropped. He trained with the kids and disappeared for months. It amazes me to hear that he is still playing with Bruges in Belgium.

The 2002–03 season was not going well for Villa. The defeat by Birmingham hurt us, we lost at home to Southampton, Sunderland beat us, and as it got worse, Graham Taylor decided to bring in someone to look at us – sports psychologists, or 'psychos' as the lads called them. They are a relatively new part of English football. Foreign players and coaches seem to be quicker than us to use these people. We are a bit stuck in our ways. Let's be honest, in England we are not the quickest when it comes to embracing new ideas and, after training, footballers just want to shoot off home, so it didn't go down too well from the start. But seeing the psychos was compulsory.

I don't know if the lads took it too seriously in the first meeting, when the psychos talked a lot about adopting a positive frame of mind. I have always preferred to deal with things in my own head, and I will probably always be that way, but I thought that if Graham wanted us to do this, I should give it a go. Anyway, we had no choice.

The guy gave me a sheet of paper and asked me to write down my targets for that year – the one-year plan – and another longer term set of targets, my five-year plan. The early targets were to get back into the Villa team, to start playing well and to score goals again. The five-year plan was to play for England and become an established player. 'You will achieve these goals,' the psycho kept saying to me in a very earnest way. 'You will achieve these goals.' He certainly didn't have any problems getting in a positive state of mind himself. I just agreed with him.

The funny thing is, I did achieve those goals. I have looked for that sheet of paper with the five-year plan on it, but it must have got lost in the moves I have made since then. I did play a bit more regularly at Villa when I came back from being on loan to Norwich City the following December, and I did go on to play for England and establish myself. The psychos may not be quite my cup of tea but, for some players, they do seem to work.

Meanwhile, I went to see Graham in his office a few times to ask him if I was going to play again, to tell him how frustrated I was. He was quite honest with me. 'What can I do?' was his response. Dion was playing well and scoring goals. I didn't really have an argument. Graham took it the right way. You could speak to him about the playing side of things and he wouldn't hold it against you.

In the reserves I became worried that I wasn't being noticed. I had a problem with Juan Pablo Angel. He's a good bloke, we got on well off the pitch, but on it I didn't think he was exactly the ideal strike partner. Basically, Angel was a goal-hanger. I would be working my bollocks off running down the channels, closing down defenders and making a nuisance of myself to the opposition. And Juan would stroll around in the box, score a couple of goals and get all the glory. It pissed me off. I mentioned it to Graham. He told me not to worry – he had noticed the difference between the two of us.

While coping with injury and struggling to get in the team was tough, life in Birmingham was great. I had a flat next door to Clinton Morrison, who played up front for Villa's deadly rivals Birmingham City – he scored the first in that humiliating 3–0 defeat at St Andrews in September, when Peter Enckelman let Olof Mellberg's throw-in roll under his foot. I can't say I spoke to Clinton too much about football. When we passed each other in the hall, the last thing we wanted to do was discuss the rivalry everyone else in the city was talking about.

I had some great nights out with Lee Hendrie, Gareth Barry and their mates in town. 'Henders' seems to have a reputation around the game as a troublemaker but people don't know him properly. He's been a great friend to me and did as much as anyone to help me settle at the club. I can still remember Henders' mate Tony, on an icy night in the city centre, catching hold of the back of a bus and skating all the way down Broad Street on the snow. It was the West Midlands equivalent of water-skiing – they called it 'bus-skiing' – but I thought it would be unprofessional to have a go myself.

It was not a happy end to the season. We lost at home to Birmingham City, finished 16th and, in the five games I played in the New Year I did not score once. Only two of those games were starts, the first against Charlton in February, when I missed a good chance one-on-one with Dean Kiely. There was no chance of a proper run in the team for me and our season was going from bad to worse.

Four days after the last game of the season, Graham resigned as manager. He left with dignity, but made it clear that he found it difficult working with the chairman. Ellis was picked out as the villain of the piece, getting slated by fans and ex-players in the media. It was him they wanted to go. Ellis was copping the blame. He needed to take the heat off by appointing a new manager and the man who came in was not exactly a novice to Premiership football.

I thought O'Leary was OK at first. We were interested to see what he did, what changes he would make. He said he wanted to shake the whole thing up. In fact, he talked a lot – especially in the press – although I never really felt he wanted to speak to me. The optimism I felt about his arrival ran out very quickly indeed.

Under Graham, even when I wasn't in the team I felt I could deal with it. He explained to me that other players were doing well and I couldn't really argue with that. But under O'Leary, I was just depressed. No matter what I did, in training or in reserve-team games, it seemed to make no difference. Now I think that he had made up his mind about me before he took the job. When O'Leary arrived, I was binned from the beginning.

Thirteen minutes is all the first-team football O'Leary gave me to prove myself before I went out on loan to Norwich in September 2003. I came on as a sub in the first game of the season, away to Portsmouth, and wasn't even on the bench for the next three games. He kept saying he didn't want me to go on loan, but what option did I have? I was so frustrated with the total lack of opportunities that when my agent said he could get me out on loan, I didn't have any hesitation in agreeing.

Norwich were the team I fancied from those offered. They were signing Darren Huckerby on loan from Manchester City and Kevin Harper from Portsmouth to try to push for automatic promotion into the Premiership. I asked O'Leary if I could go and he told me once again that I had a part to play at Villa. I told him that if that was the case, why hadn't he played me for two months? By September, aged 22, I was heading for the fourth club of my career.

13

HUCKS, HARPS AND DELIA – A NORWICH REVOLUTION

The Norwich City chairman Roger Munby is in the same line of work as my dad and they bumped into each other around the time things got difficult for me with David O'Leary at Aston Villa. Roger is in charge of a market-research company and had come to Dad's office for a meeting. Someone mentioned he was the chairman of Norwich.

'You don't happen to need a centre-forward, do you?' Dad asked him. Roger thought about it. Actually, he said, that was exactly what Norwich needed.

Nigel Worthington's Midlands scout had been looking at me for a while and Norwich were considering a loan. When they found out that I was unhappy at Villa and looking for a fresh chance to show what I could do, they made their move. I was relieved to get away from O'Leary, and for the chance of first-team football. The loan was set at three months and O'Leary told me, and the newspapers, that he still believed I had a role to play at Villa. And I believed him.

I had three great months at Norwich. I have great respect for Nigel Worthington. Delia Smith and her husband Michael Wynn-Jones were very kind to me, and my family, and I got my love for football back. In the fifteen games I played for Norwich, I scored four goals, and the old confidence came flooding back. I could do this. I could score goals. And along the way I like to think I played my part in

Norwich winning the Championship that year and going back up to the Premiership.

I joined Norwich officially on 4 September 2003, the Friday before an international weekend. Once again, I had a new life in a new city with a new club. Every one of my transfers has been different but some things never change. You find yourself in a place you don't know, among people you've only just met. Loans are even stranger. All my stuff was in Solihull. I'd packed only what I needed when setting off on that long, long drive into the heart of East Anglia.

In the nicest possible way, Norwich is a strange old place. Some of the people I met there called it the 'Far East' and I could see what they meant. Out in East Anglia, you feel like you're a long way from anywhere. The three loan signings whom Nigel had brought in – Darren Huckerby, Kevin Harper and me – were all put up in the Dunston Hall Hotel, a big old country house just south of Norwich.

Out in the sticks, living in a hotel off the A140, I really did feel like Alan Partridge. For three months, life was almost exactly the same as it had been at the Belfry hotel eighteen months earlier, just in a different part of the country. I was in the hotel's carvery restaurant every night, on nodding terms with all the waiters. I was sitting in my room in the afternoons wondering what on earth I was going to do to pass the time of day. Dunston Hall had one advantage over the Belfry hotel, though. At least they gave me a room that was big enough for more than two people to stand up in at any one time.

I wasn't bothered about going back to the Championship because I had such great memories of playing in it, banging in goals for Portsmouth. When I joined Villa that stopped. I wasn't even playing every game. I'd got used to the idea of playing all the time and scoring goals and now, at Norwich, I was back in the team and I loved it.

The fans at Norwich were great to me. I scored on my debut, against Burnley, and they were behind me from the very start. I couldn't have hoped for a better first game. I gave Burnley's centre-halves Andy Todd and David May a tough time that afternoon and when they got in a mix-up just before the hour, I seized my chance and drilled the ball into the back of the net. What a beautiful feeling. It was my first goal in senior football since I had scored for Villa against Chelsea at Stamford Bridge almost exactly sixteen months earlier. The fans in Carrow Road were on their feet. I was playing well and I felt great. I'm a striker, I live to score goals and at last I was at a club that was giving me the chance to do it.

When my number went up with twenty minutes left, the whole ground stood up to clap me off. We won 2–0 and suddenly all of Norwich was buzzing with excitement about what they could do that season with Hucks, Harps and me in the team. We didn't disappoint them. Our next game was away at Gillingham, the club whose fans had given me so much stick in my first two seasons in football. I got the same old rubbish from their supporters but I barely noticed them this time. Then, 23 minutes from time, Harps put a cross in the box and I stuck it in the back of the net – 2–1, game over. Thanks for the three points, Gillingham. I didn't hear much from their fans after that and I went so mad celebrating the goal that the ref booked me.

We were up and running. In the games I played at Norwich, we won nine and lost just once. I wasn't there to see the Championship-winning season through to the very end but when I played at Carrow Road the next season, for Southampton, Norwich presented me with a winner's medal all the same. That was a nice touch. It was their way of thanking me for the impact I'd had on their season.

Back at Villa, even O'Leary noticed that I scored two in my first two games. He said something to the local newspapers about how he believed my confidence had been very low when he arrived. I read that with interest. It might have been low when he arrived, but not as low as it was when he didn't even pick me on the bench for three games.

My third goal for Norwich was against West Ham in October when we battered them at Upton Park but came away with a point only. West Ham were also in the promotion places and our performance showed we meant business. My football career was back on track, and people were taking notice of me again. The club were pleased with me, and I was in the team every week. Football-wise, it was perfect. My only problem was finding something to do when I wasn't playing or training.

It can be lonely, living in a hotel, miles from anywhere. Nowadays, a bit older and bit more experienced, I would kick up more of a fuss. I'd get myself a house or a flat and organise my time better. When I was younger, I didn't want to piss anyone off by complaining, so I thought I'd just get on with it. But get on with what? That was the question I asked myself most of the time in Dunston Hall. There in the Norfolk countryside, I had a lot of time on my hands and absolutely nothing to do.

People in Norwich were friendly and I knew Paul McVeigh from my time at Tottenham. Phil Mulryne, the former Manchester United trainee, knew someone who owned a pub and we would go there occasionally, if we had time off, but most of the week I was on my own. I would get so bored some afternoons that I would just get in the car and drive around Norwich. I wasn't going anywhere in particular, just around the city, and then I'd come back for dinner – table for one in the hotel carvery.

I got it into my head one afternoon that Great Yarmouth would be a good place to visit. It didn't seem too far on the map, and sounded like a nice seaside town. A walk along the seafront seemed a pleasant prospect. I was tired of wandering around Dunston Hall and you can't spend your life in Norwich city centre, so why not try somewhere else? I have to say that my Great Yarmouth day trip was one of the most depressing experiences of my life. It wasn't quite the English seaside paradise I had hoped it might be. In fact, it wasn't anything like that. It was raining for a start, the wind was whipping in from the sea and the few locals who were hanging about looked as miserable as sin. I pulled up near the seafront, turned off the ignition and gazed at the rain beating down and the grey clouds above. Bollocks to that, I thought, turned the engine on again and drove straight back to the hotel.

However, there were many good things about Norwich. It may have a reputation for being a bit of a boring place but the people are great. The club itself is very homely and much of that is because of Delia Smith and Michael Wynn-Jones. Delia might be the club's majority shareholder and one of the most famous television cooks of all time, but she is also one of the friendliest people I have ever met. She was great to my parents the whole time I was there. She chatted to everyone in the stand before games and she signed a cookbook for my mum, who is a massive Delia fan. Mum's met a few famous people since I became a player – Steven Gerrard, David Beckham and so on – but I think Delia is the one she was most chuffed to meet.

Probably the most colourful character was the fan known as the Norwich City fairy – a bloke dressed up in tutu, tights, Norwich City shirt and hat, carrying a wand. He even refers to himself as 'the Norwich fairy'. Most players run into him at some point. He wears all the fairy gear but he's basically your average normal hairy bloke. He used to wait near the door that the players used to enter the stadium, and he gave me a bit of a shock the first time I saw him.

'Orroight Crouchy, me old mate,' he would growl as I walked past.

'Alright, Norwich fairy,' I would reply.

Training was intense at Norwich, and Nigel would often get stuck in as well. As the manager, he was relaxed enough to allow some banter around the training ground. We would have a special yellow jersey for whomever we decided was the worst on the day. At the end of a session, we'd play a five-a-side game, and afterwards, the winning side would vote for the player they thought was the worst. A lot of stitch-ups went on. You did one thing wrong and every one was on you. One misplaced pass, one dodgy shot and everyone would be on your case, shouting, 'He's a contender, he's a contender.' As a striker, you're always in the firing line – score a couple of goals and you're fine, but any shots go wide and you're a contender. Unfortunately, I won the yellow jersey a couple of times – totally unjustly I might add.

The story that got everyone talking in Norwich was the one about my shorts. I asked the club to get me some larger ones, and this was big news. They were even talking about selling Crouch-sized shorts in the club shop. I'm 6ft 7in. – not everything fits me. People still seem to be really surprised about that.

To be honest, the shorts at Norwich were terrible – small and tight. It took me back to my days of schoolboy football when I would turn up to play for a representative team and the kit was too small. These Norwich shorts were going to make me look like John Barnes in the 1980s again, and I wasn't having that. I wouldn't wear kit that made me look silly when I was a kid and I won't wear it now. It would put me off my game. As a player, you have to be comfortable in your kit because little annoyances can get in your head and affect you. Everything has to be perfect. If my shirt is not right, if my socks aren't right, it's a problem for me. At Liverpool in 2005–06, the shorts weren't right, too short again, so I had to get some new pairs made. I don't make any apologies for it. You've got ninety minutes to get it right on the pitch. The preparation has to be spot-on, right down to the smallest of details, and if those details aren't right, I don't feel comfortable.

It's a routine, something you grow up with, in training as well as matches. If my boots don't feel right, I have to change them. These worries about kit and boots creep in more when you are not doing so well. You go back over things in your head, trying to find something not quite right with your preparation, and, more often than not, you convince yourself that some small thing you didn't do can change the way you're playing.

I like my shorts just above the knee, not halfway up my thigh, and I'm not the only one who is picky. The England lads who played at West Ham tell me Paolo Di Canio used to wear 'large boys' size shorts because he liked them small. Joe Cole turns up the waistband of his shorts to make them shorter. A lot of the lads are the same – if things aren't right, they believe it affects their game. I have always been a long-sleeved shirt man. I pull the shirt out of my shorts and 'half' tuck it back in. It has something to do with the fact that when I was a kid you could never get replica shirts in long-sleeved versions and I thought long sleeves looked better. My dad got me a long-sleeved white Marseille home shirt, which I loved, so when I started playing professionally at Queens Park Rangers, I opted for long sleeves.

Once you start out wearing a certain type of shirt, or your shorts this way and your socks that way, you don't change. I wore long-sleeves for the World Cup, even though it was roasting hot. Anything that has got me somewhere, I'm not going to change. When I was younger, I was extremely superstitious before games. So much so that I had to tell myself to stop, and cut out a lot of those little routines. There are some England players who have strict super-stitions. For instance, one of us can't let the ball touch his foot before a game. All the lads will be mucking about with the footballs in the changing room and if one comes near him, he will step over it. It's a strange one. I would have been doing something similar if I had not curbed the superstitions as a kid. I think I would probably still be wearing the same pair of boots I had when I was 17, so thank God I talked myself out of that one.

Norwich did everything they could to make me feel at home and were desperate for me to sign, but with the kind of money involved, it just wasn't an option for them. O'Leary wasn't interested in extending the loan period, so Norwich had to make a choice. Trying to keep Hucks and me became the talk around the club, and eventually they raised the £750,000 needed to buy Hucks from Manchester City. I would have loved to stay. There didn't seem to be much for me back at Villa and we were flying in the Championship.

All the time I was at Norwich, I never once got a phone call from O'Leary or any of his staff. I just cracked on with the job at Norwich, but it did play on my mind.

We beat Walsall at the start of November and afterwards everyone started talking about winning the League. It was one of my best games for Norwich. We went up to the Bescot Stadium and scored three goals in the space of 12 minutes to win 3–1. I scored the last one, but I also remember the game for the second red card of my career. I had already been booked when, like an idiot, I squared up to Paul Ritchie in injury time at the end of the game. He grabbed me and I kneed him in the stomach – stupid really, and an obvious red card for a second yellow. Thinking about it on the way home, it reminded me of the Crewe game when I was sent off for QPR. Then, like the red card against Walsall, I had been completely caught up in what I was doing. It happens when I'm playing well.

My last game for Norwich was on 6 December, against Millwall at the New Den, and if it was Millwall, it meant another run-in with their notorious hardman in defence, Kevin Muscat. He's probably the worst I have played against, a nasty, nasty player. Thankfully, he's back playing in Australia now, which still isn't quite far enough away for me. A couple of times I'd say he tried to elbow me in the face as he ran past. I thought he was an idiot. His approach to games was to try to unnerve you, and although it never worked with me, I could see how it might with some players. He played at Millwall for two years and, no surprise, got sent off against Norwich for lashing out at Darren Huckerby.

Mum and Dad came to pick me up from Millwall to help me take my stuff back to Solihull. Dad and I had been through an interesting experience at the Den a few seasons earlier when I was playing there for Portsmouth. The whole Portsmouth squad were locked in the dressing room for about an hour and a half after the end of the game because both sets of fans were rioting outside. The stewards told us it wasn't safe for us to leave because of all the fighting outside.

I started to worry about Dad. He had been brave enough to come down to the Den and stand with the Portsmouth fans. I called him on his mobile and when he answered all I could hear were police sirens and people shouting in the background.

'You all right, Dad?' I shouted above the noise. 'Where are you?'

'I'm running, Pete,' he puffed. 'I've got four Millwall fans chasing me. They think I'm a Pompey fan.'

I laughed. I knew he'd be all right, although it turned out that he had to leg it all the way through an estate somewhere in Bermondsey to get away from the blokes who were chasing after him. Millwall came back to Fratton Park later that season and started another riot. People think that the players don't notice what goes on in the stands but we noticed that day at Portsmouth. With 85 minutes played, all the fans in the Millwall end left the ground. We were playing with no away fans watching, and suddenly all the police rushed to the corner flag on the opposite side. The Millwall fans had walked around the outside of the ground and were trying to get in the Portsmouth end. It was surreal. They were trying to kick the doors down to get in and the cops were trying to stop them while we played out the last few minutes of a 3–0 home win.

It was a pity I couldn't end my time at Norwich with a win but I felt I could look back with pride on what I had done there. My confidence was sky high when I went back to Aston Villa and I was desperate to give it another crack. I was looking forward to the challenge. O'Leary had kept saying that he wanted me back and that was good enough for me. I was sure that I was going to be part of his plans again.

I should have seen the signs. For the first game back, against Wolves, I was on the bench and didn't get on, but I did get seven minutes as a sub in a 2–1 win over Chelsea in the Carling Cup. I was confident. I came on and played really well and the fans were buzzing when I got the ball. I had done quite a few bits and pieces, and knocking out Chelsea, who were by then under Roman Abramovich's ownership, was a big factor. The night after that game I felt good. I thought the moment had come for me.

I was badly wrong. I didn't play a minute for the next four games after the Chelsea match. For the first two, against Blackburn and Leeds, I wasn't even on the bench. It was January before I got on again, a minute as a sub at the end against Portsmouth, then out of the squad for the next game against Liverpool. Then four minutes against Arsenal and out again for the first leg of the 5–2 Carling Cup semi-final defeat by Bolton. A pattern was emerging here. O'Leary would give me a taste of first-team football and then chuck me out of the squad altogether.

The worst times in those early weeks back at Villa were when I wasn't even picked for the first-team squad. Lee Hendrie and Gareth Barry were great. They would say to me that O'Leary was wrong, they'd take the piss out of him, they'd tell me I should be in the team. I appreciated it but the worst part was still being sent off to train with the reserves on the day before matches. I would be warming up with the first-team lads and have to suffer the indignity of being told to go to join the reserves instead.

Roy Aitken, O'Leary's assistant, would come to tell me. I had to walk off the first-team pitch and go to another part of the training ground, feeling so angry and frustrated. Over my shoulder I could hear Gareth shout at Roy, 'It's a fucking joke he has to train with them.'

At times like that I just felt like giving up on Villa. *I've had enough. I'm getting changed and going home. Just getting out of here. The manager obviously doesn't want me.* But, and this may sound stupid, I had too much respect for the reserve-team manager at Villa, Kevin MacDonald. It wasn't Kevin's fault that O'Leary didn't fancy me as a player. Kevin was a good manager and I would often get a good session with the boys in the reserves. I would channel my anger and frustration there. For a long time, I just got on with things.

People asked me why I didn't have it out with O'Leary, why I didn't lose my rag. It's always been in my nature to work hard rather than scream and shout and spit out the dummy. I was totally fed up, but I stuck with the way that had always brought me success. I wanted to prove him wrong. Most managers would have seen that and thought I deserved a chance to play. I didn't think that he would have to play me because I was working hard, just that I deserved to be playing when other lads weren't doing so well. Yet I was on top of my game and still not being given a chance. That's when you start to think that you will have to leave.

Then I played in the 2–0 win over Bolton in the Carling Cup semi-final second leg – not enough to overturn the deficit but I did well enough for O'Leary to keep me on for the whole game. I stayed in the team and scored two goals away in a 5–0 thrashing of Leicester City. That really was a great day for me. The first goal was a header at the back post, where a boot in the face from Jamie Scowcroft knocked me out cold for a few seconds. I woke up to the sound of Villa fans celebrating my first goal for the club in almost twenty months.

I was dizzy and my eye was black by the end of the afternoon but there was no way I was coming off. I was playing for Villa, doing what I loved. The second goal came from a Mark Delaney cross from the right. I turned and hit a low shot past Ian Walker. He had already had a scrap with a Leicester fan who had come on to the pitch to confront him.

I had got my place because Juan Pablo Angel and Stefan Moore were injured, but I had played well and I thought that was it for me. I finally believed I had earned my place in the Villa side beyond any doubt. So for the next game, against Leeds, O'Leary dropped me.

I couldn't believe it. I reasoned that even if he had made up his mind about me at the start, now things were different. I was firing for Villa – it was obvious. Yet I went from two goals against Leicester, to four minutes as a sub against Leeds, to two consecutive games sitting on the bench. It was clear that whatever O'Leary said, I wasn't in his plans. I was playing well and still not getting in the team and I didn't know where I stood.

I got three consecutive starts in April and scored against Bolton in the Premiership. I also scored a last-minute winner against Middlesbrough on 24 April, but that was when news drifted through to me about Carlton Cole coming to the club, and it became clear to me that I didn't really have a future there. All my worst fears about O'Leary were coming true.

O'Leary talked to other players in the squad and told them things he wanted to do, but he never had that sort of conversation with me. He just wasn't really interested in me. Whereas other lads would go to talk to him, I never felt that he wanted me to do the same. Gareth was my best mate at Villa and he would always be talking to O'Leary about tactics and where the manager saw him playing. It was the same with Juan Pablo Angel. With me, O'Leary didn't seem to care. He just let me get on with it. He would say, 'You're playing,' and I'd go out and do it. I didn't feel like I had a relationship with him, certainly not in the way I had with Nigel Worthington, Graham Taylor, Graham Rix or Gerry Francis. I could speak to those people. With O'Leary, I never felt that I could.

He had his reasons, I suppose, but he was never open about them with me in the way that Graham Taylor had been the season before when I hadn't been getting in the team. It was demoralising because, ultimately, your career is in the manager's hands. It's up to him whether he plays you or not. At first I told myself all I could do was work hard and do the best I could. Then when I was doing that, and playing better than the other strikers in the team, he still didn't pick me.

People say to me now that I must hate O'Leary for the way he messed me around at Villa. I think he was totally unfair with me but I don't hate him. This is football, a game of opinions, and in my opinion he was wrong. My mum doesn't agree. Every time he's on telly she gives him the V-sign from her sofa in Ealing.

I believe the way I was treated was totally unjust, but I try to remember it like this – my career at Villa finished because of one man's opinion, not because I was playing badly. There's no point having a burning hatred for O'Leary when it's obvious to me that I have proved him wrong. If you had asked me immediately after I left Villa, I would have hammered him, but now I just don't care about him.

I would watch O'Leary's performances in press conferences with interest. He played it sweet in front of the press, always pretending to be humble, but if you read between the lines, what he was actually saying was, 'Aren't I doing so well with what I've got?' His favourite line was, 'We haven't got that much money. I can't go out and spend but I'm so proud of the lads.' I heard that over and over again from him.

I'm sure there was also an element of O'Leary seeing me as his predecessor's player. He could always say to the board, or Doug Ellis, 'He's not my player.' Fair enough, that goes on in football when one manager inherits a squad of players from another, and I accept that just because Graham thought I was his kind of player there was no reason O'Leary should think the same. But all I wanted was a bit of honesty from him about my future, not the same old patter about being 'in his plans' when I knew for a fact that he wanted to sign Carlton Cole. That's where I really lost respect for O'Leary. Football is a difficult business to keep a secret in. I knew that Carlton was on his way to Villa on loan from Chelsea – my dad and Jonathan Barnett were in absolutely no doubt about it. I couldn't believe it at first, or wouldn't believe it. O'Leary was telling me he wanted me, and didn't mention anything about signing Carlton. Looking back, I guess I was naïve.

Dad and Jonathan were blunt – they thought that O'Leary was taking the mick out of me. With respect to Carlton, I didn't believe that he offered Villa anything that I couldn't give them.

'I think O'Leary's bullshitting you,' Dad said. 'You've got to go.'

I was fuming. I didn't need telling twice. The news about Carlton was the final straw. No more listening to the usual from O'Leary, no more listening to him telling me that I was in his plans only to find out I was back on the bench for the weekend. I needed to find a team that would appreciate me as a player. I had loved so much of my time at Villa, but now I was ready to leave.

14

HARRY AND THE SAINTS

Rupert Lowe threw down a copy of the local newspaper on the table in front of me. The back-page headline on the *Southampton Echo* read 'St Mary's faithful furious over 6ft 7in. ex-Pompey man's link'. My nine months at Portsmouth in 2001–02 made me, in the eyes of some at Southampton, a 'skate', a former player for the hated team in blue from down the coast.

'Can you cope with this?' the Southampton chairman asked me.

Southampton were my route out of Aston Villa. I believed I could get my Premiership career back on track there, but as a former Pompey player, it wasn't going to be simple. Until you've played or watched football on the south coast, you don't appreciate the bitterness of the rivalry between the Southampton and Portsmouth fans. It's one of the fiercest I have known, not dissimilar to the hatred between Liverpool and Manchester United fans.

I was 23, I had been at five different clubs and, at the last one, the manager had betrayed my trust. I had been abused by fans and gone from a £5 million move to the anonymity of the reserves at Aston Villa. I already knew a fair bit about the highs and lows of football. Could I cope with a few disgruntled Southampton fans? Of course I could. With all due respect to local feeling, it was the last thing on my mind. I just wanted to play football again, and the sooner the better.

Southampton had finally made a move for me in July of 2004. They got me for £2 million at a time when the future of their striker

James Beattie was the subject of a lot of speculation. He was in demand, and a move to Newcastle was apparently in the offing, although he didn't leave – for Everton – until January 2005. My arrival at the club was seen as a sign that the Saints' favourite striker would soon be on his way, and the fans weren't happy about it.

My Pompey connection didn't help, but a lot of Southampton fans seemed to be more annoyed that the club were signing a player who, as they thought, wasn't good enough for Aston Villa. For me, it was the same story all over again – new club, new fans, time to prove myself again. Two and a half years after my move from Portsmouth to Villa, did I care about fans giving me stick? Let them get on with it. I just wanted to get out on the pitch and show everyone I was a Premiership striker.

In the end, the 2004–05 season was the making of me, and showed that, in football, you can go from despair to triumph very quickly indeed – in my case, roughly six months. It didn't get off to a good start, though, with a succession of three managers in the first four months, the second of whom, Steve Wigley, just didn't seem to want to play me at all. I went from the depression of playing reserve-team football at Southampton in November to my England debut against Colombia on a steaming hot afternoon in New Jersey in May.

Who was actually behind the decision to bring me to South-ampton? I was never really sure. Paul Sturrock was the manager when I signed, and I know that his assistant Kevin Summerfield rated me, but I reckon that Rupert Lowe was the driving force behind getting me to the club. Sturrock said some nice things about me in the press after I joined, but that didn't convince me that I was his player. Pretty soon it wasn't going to make much difference anyway. Two games into the season, Sturrock was gone.

I scored a couple of goals in an 8–0 win on a pre-season trip to Sweden, and made my St Mary's debut as a substitute in a friendly against Italian team Chievo on 7 August. It wasn't the warmest of welcomes from a few of the Saints fans. As I came on I could hear boos ringing out around the ground, clearly because of my Pompey past. It wouldn't be the last time my own side's supporters booed me. Fourteen months later, I got the same from the England fans at Old Trafford.

At St Mary's that day, I really didn't give a toss what those people thought. If they believed that playing for Portsmouth three years earlier meant that somehow I wasn't committed to the cause, they obviously weren't too smart. Presumably, they were the same supporters who begged me not to leave at the end of the season after I banged in 16 goals for their team. When I was younger, the booing would have got to me. Since then I'd had a lot worse than this. Those long nights at Priestfield had taught me to block things out, and by the time I pulled on a Southampton jersey I was an absolute master at ignoring the abuse.

The boos caused quite an uproar among Southampton fans, most of whom were outraged that a new player had been treated like that. One bloke wrote to the *Southampton Echo* to say that he had been accused of being a Pompey fan when he told some of his fellow supporters to lay off me. Could there be a worse insult in that part of the world? I listened to a fierce debate on the radio on the way home from that game, over what the fans thought about me, and I knew I'd be OK. All that mattered was playing well and I could guarantee to do that if I was given the chance.

Sturrock put me on the bench for the first match of the season, a return to Villa Park. I would have loved to score the winner against O'Leary, but instead, I got 22 minutes as a substitute, and we lost 2–0. After that, I read in the papers that Sturrock had one game to save his job. I couldn't believe it. One game left? The season had hardly begun. I wasn't selected for the team that beat Blackburn 3–2, but even though we won, it wasn't enough to save the manager and he was sacked after just thirteen games in charge.

I felt sorry for Sturrock. I don't think he was right for Southampton, and it didn't go well for him, but all that was said about him not having the respect of the players wasn't true. It just seemed to me that the stories about him losing the dressing room got to him. He seemed to know that people were undermining him.

Saying goodbye to a manager who had signed me was not exactly a new experience. Sturrock's departure was the latest in a worrying trend. At Queens Park Rangers, Portsmouth and Aston Villa, the manager who had signed me lasted no longer than a season. I had barely got to know Sturrock, although I thought I knew something about his successor, Steve Wigley. He had been David Platt's assistant with the England Under-21s and I was under the impression that he quite liked me as a player. Time would tell.

I scored my first Southampton goal when I came on as a substitute in Wigley's first game in charge, a 2–1 defeat at home by Bolton. We didn't win until his eleventh game and by then it was probably too late to save his job – not that I was given much of a chance. I didn't start the next five games after Bolton, and then, when Beattie broke his toe against Manchester City, I came on for him and injured my knee. Wigley was down to the bare bones of his squad, and the pressure was on.

During those first four months of the season, I worked hard in training to dislodge the partnership of Beattie and Kevin Phillips but didn't seem to make any impression on the manager, and then I missed another five games with the knee injury. By the time I was fit again, Wigley didn't seem interested in picking me. I was on the bench for the 5–2 Carling Cup thrashing by Watford, from a division below us. I sat on the bench again when we beat Portsmouth 2–1 on

13 November, our second Premiership win of the season. Inside I felt desperate.

Wigley had picked Dexter Blackstock for the Portsmouth game. He was an academy kid – Wigley had run the academy before he got the manager's job – who had come in during the injury crisis when Beattie, Phillips, Marian Pahars and I had all been injured. Blackstock was a trier and he got a goal against Portsmouth, but I could not believe that he was getting picked ahead of me. I was a sub against Norwich and we lost. I was a sub against Crystal Palace the next week as well. Wigley was playing Blackstock, a rookie, and telling him just to go out and do a job, totally undermining my ability. I could take it, just about, when Wigley picked Beattie and Phillips before me – at least they were proven players – but I found it hard to accept when he took a chance on a kid, presumably because he felt I couldn't deliver. I thought he was taking the piss out of me and I started seriously to question whether I had made the right move. It seemed obvious to me that I could offer more than Blackstock could. Southampton were in trouble with just two wins all season and relegation a serious possibility, and still Wigley didn't want to know me.

It was David O'Leary all over again. In my head, I turned over the reasons why I made the move in the first place. Surely, if I was going to be frozen out, it might as well have been at Villa, where I was happy and settled in Solihull, rather than at Southampton, where I was living in a rented flat and sitting on the bench of a struggling club. I fretted that I had made a terrible mistake and should have stayed at Villa in spite of O'Leary, and fought for my place. I had come to Southampton for one thing – to play football – and I wasn't doing it. I was angry and unhappy.

I thought it got beyond a joke when we went to Old Trafford to play Manchester United at the start of December. Wigley picked Beattie and Phillips in attack, and when Beattie came off with an injury after

22 minutes, I thought my chance had come but the manager gave Blackstock the nod. I didn't get a sniff of the action, and we lost 3–0. This was Old Trafford, a proper Premiership stadium, where I should be playing, and I felt a million miles away from the team. That was the final straw.

I had been to see Wigley a few times in the weeks before then – nothing aggressive or confrontational. I'm not the type. I just told him that I thought he should pick me because I could offer more than those who were playing. I said I thought he was treating me unfairly and, if I had the chance, I would prove to him that I was a good player. It obviously wasn't having much effect but I decided to give it one last go after the defeat at Old Trafford. We'd been hopeless. Blackstock had been near enough left on his own up front. Everyone could see it hadn't worked.

Wigley listened to what I had to say. He was under a lot of pressure, the papers were full of talk that he was on his way out the club and what he said to me that afternoon in his office amazed me. Wigley admitted that he had made a few mistakes with the team and that he should have picked me after all. I was stunned. For months I had been trying to make my point in training and in the little time I had spent on the pitch. Made mistakes? I'd been trying to tell him that for ages. I will never forget the last thing he said to me in that conversation – 'Crouchy, on Saturday, you're playing.' Two days later, Wigley was sacked.

I don't take any pleasure in anyone losing their job, but this is football and the irony of the situation wasn't lost on me. Since Wigley had taken over in late August he had given me just one single start – away at Northampton in the Carling Cup. Now, in December, in the week he finally told me I would be getting my first-ever Premiership start for Southampton, he got the sack. My future was up in the air once again. It would all depend on what the new manager thought of me, and in Harry Redknapp I struck gold. My season was about to come good.

Harry joined Southampton from Portsmouth in December 2004 amid howls of controversy. One year later he would top that by leaving Southampton and going back to Portsmouth. When it comes to big moves, nothing seems to faze Harry. Back then I couldn't have cared less what club he had been managing before he came to Southampton, or how he got there. All I cared about was whether he was going to pick me.

It was good news. For the first time since I left Norwich I felt I had a manager who rated me. O'Leary, Sturrock and Wigley had all binned me. Harry changed all that. He came to introduce himself to the lads and made a little quip, something like, 'Crouchy, you'll have to introduce me to those here I don't know.' It was just a little thing but it meant so much to me. I felt involved in a way that I hadn't felt before, and the best was yet to come. In our first training session Harry pulled Kevin Phillips and me aside for a chat.

'From now on, you two are my main men up front,' he said. 'I know what you can do, you're both goalscorers and you'll be the two who will get us out of this mess.'

I was buzzing. The confidence came flowing back. Just one simple conversation was all it took. No messing around, no tinkering with the team. Footballers thrive on confidence, having the belief of the manager and knowing that they will be in the team. My career changed forever at the Marchwood training ground. I went on a goalscoring run that took me all the way into the England team and I owe a lot of that to Harry Redknapp.

When it came to big decisions, Harry never messed around. He sold Beattie to Everton that January for £6 million, and it was clear from the start that he didn't think much of some of the players he had inherited. It was a weird side. Jelle Van Damme and Yoann Folly barely got a look-in after Harry arrived. To me, it had always been obvious that Kevin Phillips and I would work well together. I don't know why Wigley hadn't seen that. Harry made the decision straight away and I scored twice in our first two games.

There's a lot more to Harry Redknapp, the friendly Cockney bloke, than you see on the television. You don't mess with Harry. In our training session before his first game in charge, against Middlesbrough, we played against a shadow XI that included the youngsters Theo Walcott and Nathan Dyer. He had already told us what the team would be on the Saturday. Dyer was terrorising full-back Darren Kenton, who was having an absolute horror show. He couldn't get near Dyer and Harry wasn't happy.

'You better fucking sort yourself out or you can forget about playing,' Harry shouted at Kenton.

Harry was ruthless, and he had a temper. Calum Davenport came in on loan from Tottenham and didn't do well. Big things had been expected of him but he struggled, which Harry found hard to accept. Harry was fuming, screaming at Calum in the dressing room after the game, telling him he had let us down. The rest of the room was silent, watching in awe as Harry bollocked him. I was sat next to Jamie Redknapp, who had come in from Tottenham to join his dad. Jamie just shrugged.

'I've seen that temper for the last thirty years,' he said. 'And when it goes, it goes.'

Harry never used to say too much at training but when he did lose his temper, he wouldn't hold back, especially if he felt he wasn't getting what he wanted from us. Once, in shooting practice, we started taking the mick, trying to chip the goalkeeper instead of striking the ball properly. Harry was over to us like a shot. 'Do it fucking properly or we're not doing it at all,' he shouted, and we did it properly. Getting on the wrong side of Harry was not advisable.

People call Harry a wheeler-dealer. I think that sells him short. Yes, he's done a lot of business in the transfer market but only because he's had to. He's never had bundles of money to spend on players – until he went back to Portsmouth – and he has certainly never worked at a club that can attract the biggest names. Wherever he has gone he has done a good job, and if you put him in charge of a really big club, he would be successful. Maybe I'm biased because he was so great for me but I truly believe that if he had been at Southampton from the start of the 2004–05 season, the club would never have been relegated.

Harry kept it simple. I was in his plans right from the start and when we were talking about how we were going to play in a certain game, I was a fixture. I played in almost every game under him, which was just what I needed – someone to have faith in me. Of all the managers I have played under, Harry is the one who knows me best. He knows how I play and what my strengths are. For a start, I like to get the ball to my feet quickly. I can link up with the midfield or the wingers and then get myself into the box. If we are in trouble, the team can hit diagonal balls to me and I can knock them down for others, or I can hold up play, bring others into the game and then hit the box and score. That was the way Harry played at Southampton and it got me 15 goals in 24 games.

We struggled at first, got a 5–1 thumping at Tottenham and were beaten away at Manchester City. I was starting to score a few goals, and the confidence of playing in the team every week was helping, but it wasn't until we played Liverpool at St Mary's on 22 January that we turned all that promise into a really good win. Liverpool came to us needing a win after copping a load of stick for getting beaten by

Burnley in the FA Cup third round. No one expected us to win that one but we did, 2–0, and that was the day that my ability caught the eye of Rafael Benitez.

Jamie Carragher – 'Carra' to the boys at Liverpool – still talks about that day. He remembers it for one thing above all – Mauricio Pellegrino had an absolutely torrid time. The big Argentine defender played thirteen games for Liverpool and his performance at St Mary's definitely wasn't one of the better ones. David Prutton ran him ragged, and I don't think he was exactly renowned for his pace. We got the first goal after just five minutes. Prutton robbed Pellegrino, played a one-two with me and scored. Against Sami Hyypia and Carra, I had one of my best games and headed our second goal from a Prutton cross.

Sami and I had a real war. I always found playing against Hyypia a proper challenge because he is such a tough defender, but I felt I got the better of him that day. I know it made an impression on Benitez. He was generous enough to mention me in the post-match press conference despite all the flak he was taking at the time. Alan Hansen said on 'Match of the Day' it was the worst Liverpool performance he had seen since he retired from football fourteen years earlier. Mind you, four months later the Liverpool boys won the European Cup.

Benitez had seen me before, but that match was when I made him sit up and take notice. From then on, he had someone scouting me, and Jamie Redknapp told me later that after the St Mary's game, Carra had rung him up to ask about me. When I signed for Liverpool, Benitez mentioned the game at St Mary's and that my style of play would be important for Liverpool, especially away from home.

Jamie Redknapp was a strong and lively personality in the dressing room, and a big influence on me. Anyone who knows Jamie will tell you what a top bloke he is and he certainly helped build up my confidence. As a former Liverpool captain and an England international, I looked up to him. When Jamie told me that I was a good player, and if I did this or that, I could be even better, I listened. He is a good talker, he loves football and, in the last season of his career, he had a lot of experience to pass on.

Although I rented a place in Ocean Village on the east side of Southampton, I also bought a place in Surrey, about an hour from the training ground. I had to get in quickly before Joe Cole did – the house is not far from Cobham, where Chelsea have their training ground. I have bought a few properties on my travels. I still have places in Port Solent and Solihull as investments, but the house in Surrey, which is only twenty minutes from my friends and family in Ealing, is where I will live when I finish playing.

A few of the Southampton players lived in that part of Surrey, and Jamie wasn't far away, so occasionally, just for a laugh, he would hire a mate of his, who was a chauffeur, to drive us into training. We used to get a load of stick from the lads when we turned up in the car park in a £250,000 Bentley, even if it was only for the day. All the way to training we would talk football, about what I could do to improve, and Jamie would tell me about the famous footballers he had played alongside, and how they had played the game. It was around then that Jamie talked about me playing for England. He encouraged me to aim for it and I thought that if he believed it was possible, perhaps I should too.

One week after we beat Liverpool, my first south-coast derby arrived, and the stakes could hardly have been higher. Not only had Harry recently changed sides, but it was the FA Cup fourth round. In comparison, those early-season boos from a few Saints fans seemed trivial. On the day, the Pompey fans barely bothered booing me. They were too busy dishing out stick to Harry and Nigel Quashie, who had followed him to Southampton, which suited me fine.

What a day it turned out to be. The two sets of fans were scrapping in a park near St Mary's before the game, there were nine yellow cards, two dodgy penalties and one sending off. Matt Oakley got the first goal for us, a real beauty struck from 25 yards. Three minutes later Claus Lundekvam barged into Diomansy Kamara and Pompey got a lucky penalty, which Yakubu scored. Later, Kamara got a second yellow and was sent off. They were down to ten men and would have probably taken a replay at Fratton Park when, in the last minute, a cross struck Matt Taylor's arm – or was it his shoulder? The debate among the fans carried on long after the final whistle but referee Steve Bennett judged that it hit Taylor's arm and pointed to the penalty spot. It was a south-coast derby, FA Cup-tie, score at 1–1, and we were in the last minute of the match at St Mary's. Penalty. *Fuck it, I'm having this.*

Why not? I had scored three in the last three games and I was full of confidence. I had played well and now I wanted to settle it once and for all. It had been an incredible day, the stick had been flying, the atmosphere thick with the passion of one of English football's greatest rivalries. No one was taking the ball off me. This was going in the back of the net.

Then I made the mistake of looking over to the bench. For some reason, Harry wanted Nigel Quashie to take it. The problem with that was Quashie wasn't on the pitch. He wasn't even on the bench. Harry was gesturing at me. 'NO Crouchy! NO! Not you!' he seemed to be saying.

But Harry was caught in two minds. He didn't want me to take the penalty but the more he thought I was going to do it anyway, the less he wanted to affect my confidence, so he stopped gesturing as I looked at him. I could tell he was nervous. I could tell that I didn't exactly have my manager's full confidence. *Oh fuck, what now?*

Harry was right. I had never taken a penalty for Southampton but by now it seemed too late to give the ball to someone else. Sometimes the mood just takes you when you are confident and playing well. You get caught up in the game. The occasion, the crowd, the noise, the pressure all seem to fade away. So it was just me, the ball and 12 yards of turf to the Portsmouth goalkeeper, Kostas Chalkias. I struck it clean and hard – 2–1 to the Saints.

The place went mad. The Saints fans were jumping around and screaming and shouting so much that I could hardly hear my team-mates as they crowded around me. Portsmouth and Southampton haven't played each other much over the last twenty years or so, but this one seemed to make up for it. Saints fans still mention this game to me, and even now, Harry says how sorry he was not to have shown a bit more confidence in me. It was only afterwards I thought how terrible it would have been if I had missed, with the manager not wanting me to take the penalty in the first place. Later, Harry admitted he had turned to his assistant, Jim Smith, as I picked up the ball and said, 'Fuck me, not Crouch.'

I didn't let him down, and my season was changing for the better. I left the stadium that day with a new chant playing pleasantly in my head over and over again:

'Ohhhhh Crouchy, Crouchy,
He used to be a skate but he's all right now.'

I think you could call that acceptance.

15

CROUCH FOR ENGLAND

Those times when the adrenaline kicks in, your confidence makes you believe you can do anything, but sometimes it can get you into trouble. Against Everton at St Mary's on 6 February 2005, I felt unstoppable. We were 2–1 up, I'd scored the first goal, and we were absolutely battering them. The crowd were up, especially as we had gone behind after four minutes to a goal from James Beattie, just a month after he left. I didn't feel any doubts. We had played so well and this was going to be a massively important victory for us. In injury time I picked up the ball on the halfway line, turned, beat two men and set off into the Everton half. Around me the noise got louder as the crowd urged me on. *I'm going for goal this time. No messing around. This is going in.*

I beat a third Everton man. I headed towards goal, just a bit wide to the right, but in a position to crack one across the goalkeeper and into the far corner. Why not? I'd already got past three players. If this one went in, they could give me the goal of the season award there and then. If you could have looked into my eyes at that moment, they would have been glazed as I imagined the glory, the trophy, the endless re-runs on Sky Sports of this one flying into the net. One last look up and I smacked it. *Go on you beauty, straight in the corner.*

Except I didn't catch it right – not even nearly right. A rough estimate would be that it took about eighteen bounces to reach the goalkeeper, Nigel Martyn. It was a daisy cutter.

Obviously, with hindsight, I should have gone for the corner flag, wasted a few more precious seconds and taken the pressure off the defence, but I was on a high. Martyn picked it up and booted it down the pitch. Olivier Bernard and Calum Davenport didn't get it right between the two of them and it broke loose to Marcus Bent. The angle was a tough one for him, but he caught it perfectly, just right, and his shot flew up into the roof of the net. Everton had done it, 2–2, an equaliser with about one second of the match left.

I looked at the floor. It was a head-in-hands moment. We'd blown it. I'd blown it. Sixty seconds earlier we'd been on for all three precious points and now we were down to one. The final whistle blew. I had scored but I knew deep down that I'd messed up for their goal.

Back in the changing room, Jamie Redknapp was not pleased.

'Crouchy, you should have taken it to the corner. What the fuck were you trying to do? We had them, 2–1. When are we gonna fucking learn? If we play like this, we're going down.'

I was hurt and angry so I gave it back.

'Fuck off, I had a chance. What am I supposed to do? I was through.'

I've been in loads of arguments like that after a match. All the frustration comes out in angry words, and fingers point in blame. It tends to happen more when clubs are struggling and relegation is a possibility. Harry Redknapp calmed us down a bit and I went off for a shower. I was just doing what strikers do, going for goal. I could have scored a 'worldy' – what footballers call a 'world-class goal' – but I hadn't, and it was killing me. I got changed and Jamie came over

'I'm sorry, mate,' I said, 'I should have taken it to the corner.'

'Don't worry,' he said. 'You've done so well for us this season. Those three points were important, though.'

I pissed off another famous name three weeks later, although I had no sympathy for Arsene Wenger. His Arsenal team had come to St Mary's certain that they were going to get a result. Freddie Ljungberg scored and David Prutton went mad and got himself sent off. Then Jens Lehmann flapped at a cross from Jamie and I nodded it in. Simple really. We drew the game 1–1. That was a point we never expected to get, but Wenger wasn't happy. 'I think they have a basketball player who can play with his head,' he said after the match.

That surprised me, coming from him. It was a cheap shot from a manager who had expected to come to one of the Premiership's strugglers and roll us over. If he had been honest, he would have said that I dominated Philippe Senderos and Kolo Toure in the air all game – a very different story from when I played against Tony Adams in the FA Cup four years earlier. Wenger is a top manager and the Arsenal boys, past and present, who play with England speak very highly of him. He's an intriguing character and I have always had a lot of regard for him. The way I look just makes me an easy target for any disgruntled manager.

Since then, Wenger has been great. When I scored a hat-trick against Arsenal in March 2007, he said that I was 'technically intelligent and hard to play against', which meant a lot. It was generous and set me thinking. If I could change the opinion of me held by a top football man such as Wenger, why has it been so hard to win other people over? I suppose it takes a big man to admit that he might have been wrong the first time.

Despite the occasional dig, I was really enjoying my football and scoring plenty of goals – two in an FA Cup replay against Brentford, the week after Arsenal, and another two against Middlesbrough the next month. In terms of the team's performance, though, it was back to the same old story. While I was playing well, the team were struggling. After beating Middlesbrough 3–1 at their place, we lost to Blackburn and Aston Villa, drew with Bolton and then, a hammer blow, got beaten 4–1 at Fratton Park by Pompey. I pulled out of that one in the warm-up, and got some stick from the boys for it.

Football club dressing rooms are the least sympathetic places, no matter what you have done to yourself. When I broke my nose playing for Liverpool against Sheffield United, I was immediately christened 'Hook nose' as the doc cleaned me up. Half an hour before kick-off against Pompey, I was barely able to run, but I had an idea what the shouts from the lads would be – 'He's shit himself going back to his old club,' 'He's bottled it.'

I had tried my best to be fit, even going with Jamie to see his private physio in central London the previous day. Pompey was a massive game for us and I said to Harry that I would be OK, but when I went out for the warm-up, I wasn't right. I hate pulling out of games. I hate it even more when it gives the lads ammunition to have a go.

Life on the brink in a struggling team makes for a fraught atmosphere, and we were forever messing things up in the last minute. It became our thing. The final twenty minutes of each game were a white-knuckle ride. We were haunted by the constant fear that we were going to chuck it all away with some stupid mistake. Against Middlesbrough at home we shipped two in the last two minutes. At Highbury, Robin Van Persie nicked a last-minute equaliser. Leon Osman got an 88th minute winner for Everton at Goodison Park. The worst was the visit of my old mates Aston Villa in April.

We were 2–0 up and we threw it away 3–2, and it had been going so well for me back at my old club. I had scored our second goal after 13 minutes and treated the Villa lads to my chicken celebration, in which I expertly mimicked a chicken by bending my arms and flapping my wings. It was a reference to Lee Hendrie's recent fancy-dress stag-do in Marbella when my chicken costume had narrowly edged out Henders's cow in the competition for the best outfit.

Slowly, I felt people were taking more notice of me – and not just for my chicken impressions. I was playing and scoring regularly and the tag of 'Villa reject' was used less and less. There was a lot of interest in Harry and whether he could save Southampton from relegation, and when Harry spoke, the newspapers listened. He came out with all sorts of comments and stories that the press lapped up. He even told them about the plastic toy angel that his wife Sandra had given him, which he kept in his pocket for good luck. So when he spoke after a 4–3 victory over Norwich City, a real thriller in which we had twice come from behind to win in the 88th minute, they listened. And his main subject was me and the England team.

'It might sound silly but I'd have Peter Crouch in the England squad because he's different,' Harry said. 'He'd be someone you could have on your bench for games in World Cups when you can't break teams down, when you can't play through them, when Rooney and Owen are not the answer. Suddenly, with fifteen minutes to go, you bring on a 6ft 7in. guy and hit a few balls in the box. He gives you such an option. He's got a great touch, his skill is superb and brings people into the game.'

The newspapers loved it and I began to think that the Redknapps might just have started a bit of a campaign. Jamie had first suggested me as an England player in March, and he had got a bit of stick for it. A 6ft 7in. striker who hadn't made the grade at Aston Villa? But Jamie stuck to his guns. He said it in interviews both on television and in newspapers and, as someone who had seventeen England caps, his opinion carried a lot of weight. The more influential newspaper journalists, the ones who cover England matches, never come to watch players in a struggling team, but when Jamie and then Harry spoke about me in terms of England, a lot of people sat up and took notice.

After Harry took over on 8 December 2004, I scored 15 goals for Southampton, and I still feel that if I had played the first half of the season, I would have done the same. I was desperate to keep the goalscoring up and save Southampton from relegation. Sadly, the penalty I scored against fellow strugglers Crystal Palace on 7 May turned out to be my last goal for the club. Later in the game, I got myself sent off for a dust-up with their Uruguayan defender Gonzalo Sorondo.

What a stupid sending off. Sorondo went through me from behind and I swiped at him with a foot. There was a bit more shoving and I cracked him with an elbow. Sorondo didn't go down but around us it all kicked off. Graeme Le Saux came flying in from nowhere, then Palace's manager Iain Dowie got involved, and before you knew it the referee had to exert some control, so he sent both Sorondo and me off.

I felt much the same as I had after the red for Queens Park Rangers against Crewe four years earlier. We were in a relegation dogfight, playing another team fighting the drop, and I had got caught up in the moment and lost control. It hurt. I felt it was my fault.

In the changing-room area I sat down to watch the last thirty minutes of the game on television. Sorondo sat down next to me and shook my hand.

'Stupid all that, wasn't it?' I said.

He agreed. There was no bad feeling and we watched the rest of the game on television together. I wish that sometimes referees would take a step back and let the odd thing go. There was nothing malicious in our spat. We both knew we had been daft, but sometimes things can get out of hand in a split second. The worst part of it all was that I was suspended for the last game of the season. I tried to appeal. I even went with the chairman to see the Football Association in London but they turned us down.

So the infamous 'Judgement Day' arrived, 15 May 2005, when three teams out of Norwich, West Bromwich Albion, Crystal Palace and Southampton were destined to be relegated, based on how the results went. We had the easy option – all we had to do was beat Manchester United. There was some history between Harry and Sir Alex Ferguson. Harry's West Ham team had denied United the Premiership title at Upton Park exactly ten years earlier, even though they had nothing to play for. The rumour from among the United players was that, despite their friendship in the years since then, Fergie thought that he owed Harry one. He certainly got his own back.

We took the lead through a John O'Shea own goal but United came back with a vengeance, Darren Fletcher and Ruud van Nistelrooy scoring the goals. The news from elsewhere was not good. While Norwich were getting thumped at Fulham, Crystal Palace drew with Charlton – and West Brom stayed up by beating Portsmouth. I was in the stands, unable to do anything about it. I would have loved to score the winning goals against United to keep us up. I'd have done it for Harry, who looked broken-hearted at the end of the game. He had been through a crazy season and it had ended with relegation. It was the end of the line for Jamie Redknapp and Graeme Le Saux. For the fans, it was the end of twenty-seven years in the top division. A painful day.

When so many people you respect are hurting, it's hard to celebrate your personal achievements. Two days before the United game, I had some news that changed my life. I was at home in Surrey when a text message came through to my mobile from a number I had stored in my phone. It was from Anne Romilly, who had been one of the Football Association's administrators when I was in the England Under-21s. The message said that I had been selected for the senior England squad for the summer tour of America, and more information was to follow in the post. Was this a wind-up? It couldn't be – this was Anne's mobile number. This had to be for real. I was in.

Plenty of people have asked me how players find out whether they are in the England squad. The answer is simple – the FA send a text message. I don't know what I was expecting. Maybe a summons written on parchment and hand-delivered by a messenger on horseback. I didn't much care. I was so excited I forwarded the original text on to my dad, he forwarded it to his mates and pretty soon half of Ealing knew about it. I turned the telly on and there was my name on Sky Sports News, scrolling along the bottom of the screen against a yellow background – 'Peter Crouch named in England squad'. Crouch for England. It was official. All the way from Dulwich Hamlet to the Three Lions in the space of five years.

I couldn't wait to get out there, meet the team and get my first cap. When I told Jamie Redknapp he confessed that Sammy Lee, who was then one of the coaches with Sven-Goran Eriksson, had rung him up a few weeks earlier, asking whether he thought I was up to the job. Jamie had given me a glowing reference. Now I was really buzzing with excitement. England were due to play two matches, one against the American team in Chicago, and one against Colombia just over the water from New York in the Giants Stadium in New Jersey.

Texts and calls flooded in from family, friends and team-mates, including Charlton's Luke Young, who was an old mate from trainee days at Tottenham. He was also in the England squad for the first time, summoned when Gary Neville pulled out with an injury, and he said that he had one basic aim. It was a two-match tour, so we had to get two caps and that way, if we never played for England again, no one could ever throw in our faces that we were 'one-cap wonders'. He had a point. I'd seen it happen with Anthony Gardner, and with Michael Ricketts, Alan Thompson, Francis Jeffers, Gavin McCann, Michael Ball, even Chris Sutton back in 1998.

We flew to Chicago from Manchester, a young squad that included Kieran Richardson and Andy Johnson, an old mate from junior England teams. Steven Gerrard and Jamie Carragher weren't there – they had just won the European Cup in Istanbul. Michael Owen and David Beckham were joining up with us after the first game when the Spanish season finished. If you didn't know anyone in the squad, it would be easy to be overawed by the whole experience. Fortunately, I knew a few of the lads from the Under-21s, and that morning at Manchester airport, seeing those familiar faces – Andy Johnson, known as 'AJ', Jermain Defoe, Michael Carrick – allowed me to settle in quite easily.

I was very pleased to discover that there was a card school going among the England boys, because I've always been partial to a game of poker. I've seen stories about England teams gambling fortunes – £37,000 on the turn of a card – and I can assure you that I definitely wasn't playing for those stakes when we were in America, not on Southampton wages. The card school was a brilliant way of integrating new players into the squad. You could get to know your team-mates and have a laugh with them at the same time. We used to play for a bit of dough, but the newspapers blew it out of all proportion. The England card school has gone now and that's a real shame – we only played a few times before the World Cup in 2006. On my first few trips, Wayne Rooney, Mo – as Michael Owen is known among the lads – David James, Frank Lampard, Rio Ferdinand and I used to play, but that's been sacked now in favour of the PSP, the PlayStation portable. I prefer the cards. Beating Mo wasn't easy. He was the man when it came to cards and I found the games a really good way of getting to know him.

During that first trip with England I learned a lot about players I had only played against or read about in the newspapers. They seemed a good bunch. Sven was very much the quiet type who watched and analysed. He kept contact quite minimal in the build-up to matches. Steve McClaren, the main coach, and Sammy Lee would take training while Sven would watch the whole time. It was not better or worse for that – just different. I had come from playing under Harry Redknapp, who was on to us in a second if he wasn't getting what he wanted in training. A lot of managers I have played for have been hands-on. Sven was more of an observer – he watched training and that was that. He played it cool and calm.

He had something about him and had made a big name for himself in the game. I expected him to have a lot more to say because of it. The funny thing was that, traditionally, when a manager is reserved and stand-offish, his assistant gets on to everyone, but Sven's number two, Tord Grip, was even quieter than his boss. He stood on the sidelines and watched as well.

We trained at the Illinois Institute of Technology in Chicago, with not too much security or too many fans. It was a world away from what I later came to know about England training camps. The good news for me was that I was due to start the game against America at Soldier Field. This was the home of the Chicago Bears in the NFL, and some place to make an England debut. Then Sol Campbell munched my right ankle in training.

When you're about to make your England debut, just about the last person you want to stand on your ankle is big Sol. The ankle swelled up and despite my attempts to play down the pain when I went to see the physio, Gary Lewin, it was obvious I wasn't fit to play. I wasn't really fit to play in the second game against Colombia three days later either, but I wasn't coming all the way to America and going back home without a single England cap. Youngy got on as a sub in both games and was needling me about it – no danger of him being a one-cap wonder.

The team played well in the first game, and two goals from Kieran Richardson gave us a 2–1 win. Dad, Mum and Sarah had all come out for the Chicago game, expecting to see me make my England debut, and had flights home booked after that. Once I pulled out of the first game, Dad was never going to go home and miss my first match for England and, luckily for him, his boss lent him his house in New York.

It wasn't exactly the first-choice England team, but we won 3–2 and I was playing alongside Michael Owen – it didn't get any better than that. Michael scored a hat-trick and I made the second for him by taking a quick free-kick and threading the ball through the Colombian defence for him to run on to. The newspapers in England were full of 'Little and Large' forward line stories. Although I came off for Jermain Defoe with about twenty minutes left on the clock, the game had gone well for me, and it was not a bad way to end a season that had started with me on the bench among the reserves at Southampton.

I'd had to miss most of my annual summer holiday in America with my Ealing mates, but I was determined to catch the end of it, so I arranged with the FA to get a plane from New York to Las Vegas. That meant I had one extra night in New York while the rest of the team flew home. AJ was staying as well, and so were Becks, who was going to open a soccer school in Los Angeles, Sol Campbell and goalkeeper Robert Green. AJ and I were up for a night out and we weren't too bothered where we went. Any bar in Manhattan would do. As new boys in the England squad, it wasn't as if we knew the rest of the lads that well anyway. But then I bumped into Becks in the hotel lobby and he suggested we all go out together and, better yet, he said he was sorting out the venue for us. Brilliant. AJ and I agreed that anywhere that was good enough for Becks had to be good enough for us. We were happy to jump on the Beckham bandwagon and see where it took us.

It may seem obvious, but the thing about Becks is that he's just so famous. You're not sure quite how to approach him when you don't know him. He was very welcoming and friendly towards me, though, and after a bit I realised that he's a normal bloke. You can speak to him about anything, although I wouldn't say he was your stereotypical captain by any means. He's not a shouter or a screamer. Maybe the longer I was involved with England, the more I saw of that side of him, but earlier on he was just quite quiet. He carried out a lot of his captain's responsibilities on the pitch, leading by example when he played.

And he knew how to organise a top night out in New York. We hit a bar called Bungalow 8 on West 27th Street, which was very cool indeed. I was still on a massive high from making my England debut and the beers went down very smoothly. When I was playing in the reserves at Southampton in September, I never quite imagined I'd be rolling into a flashy New York bar with the England captain eight months later. Even in New York, everyone seemed to know who Becks was. He's that big a superstar. He sat in the corner, chilling out and looking extremely cool. I can't say the same for AJ or myself.

The season was officially over, we were England internationals at last, and we were up for a big night. Both of us played for teams that had fought a long hard season against relegation, and ultimately lost the battle, but now, at last, we had something to celebrate. I was on the dance floor throwing some shapes, and we were getting the drinks in. It was a night to remember – not that I do remember much of it. We were staying at a hotel by the airport and got a taxi back. I recall AJ saying that we were going to struggle to get up for our early flights and he was right there. I passed out on my bed fully clothed and slept right through my alarm call. When I did finally come round, my flight to Las Vegas had long since departed.

There was only one thing for it. I went to the airport and brazened it out. I told them they had definitely put me on the wrong flight, insisted on it. In the end, the airline relented and I got a flight to Las Vegas about five hours late. I met the Ealing boys and had five great days' holiday, reflecting on a brilliant season. The lads wanted to know what the England set-up was like, and about the different characters involved, and the beauty of it was that I could relax in virtual anonymity in Vegas. We had a proper blow-out there.

That was one of the last times I was able to knock about as an ordinary bloke. My difficulty these days is that I just can't hide or get away unnoticed. I suppose that's unavoidable when you're 6ft 7in. I go out in public with players who are much more famous than I am and they don't get recognised at all. I might as well have a big neon sign above my head flashing 'Peter Crouch – Liverpool and England'. If I'm honest, it has become a bit of a nightmare.

At first, the low level of fame was fine. When I got into the Queens Park Rangers team I was astonished the first time I was asked for an autograph. It was weird – exciting in a way. When I was a kid I was just the same. I would be awestruck by the sight of a famous footballer and I loved getting autographs. I know all the arguments about footballers and fame, that it's a small price to pay etc. I understand how it may look from the other side of the fence, but you have to understand how it affects my daily life, the ordinary things – popping down to the shops to get a sandwich, for instance, even in the quiet town in Cheshire where I live. If I want to go to the Trafford Centre, or into Liverpool to do a bit of shopping, I often weigh up the pros and cons and decide that I really can't be bothered, because it's going to be such a hassle. If this sounds unfriendly and ungrateful, it's not meant to, but people keep coming up, constantly. They just want to say hello or get a picture. I just want to buy a pair of shoes or a CD. It's got to the stage where I have to nip in and nip out quickly, before I get mobbed. It's only because I am so easily recognisable, and it's escalated recently.

Playing professional football is all I ever wanted to do and with football comes fame. I love the football, but I'm not so keen on the fame. If I didn't have it, I would be quite comfortable, probably more so. I just know that wherever I go these days – shop, restaurant, bar – people will be looking. You see that look. People try to be sly and quietly say to their mate, 'Oh look, it's him,' and you see their mate trying to look at you without you noticing. You just know it's all happening. As soon as I walk into a new place now, I look around to see who's where. It's a shame really but it comes with the territory. I can't complain. I'm happy with my life, but sometimes I just wish I wasn't quite so tall.

16

LIVERPOOL AT LAST

While we were in America, Andy Johnson and I discussed one topic above all others – we had to get out of our respective clubs. It was the only way we were going to have a prayer of getting into the World Cup squad the following summer. He was at Crystal Palace, I was at Southampton, and playing Championship football was not an option if you wanted to play for England. Besides, we would both generate good transfer fees for our clubs.

'I'm telling you, Crouchy, I'm gonna speak to the chairman as soon I get back,' AJ said. 'There's no way I'm going back to Crystal Palace next year.'

I was away at the start of August and out of touch with what was happening in England for a few days. As I came back through the airport, my attention was caught by a screen playing Sky Sports News, and what I saw makes me smile even now. There was AJ, the man who, two months earlier, was adamant that he was on his way out of Selhurst Park, modelling Crystal Palace's new kit. And standing next to him, with his arm round AJ's shoulders and a big smile on his face, was Simon Jordan, the Palace chairman.

I laughed at that one. AJ had a new five-year contract and a promise from the chairman. Apparently, he had Sven-Goran Eriksson's personal assurance that playing for England at the World Cup was not out of the question. Mr Jordan must be a very difficult man to refuse. As for me, I knew that, come what may, I had to leave Southampton, but it was easier said than done.

About a week after my England call-up, I'd had another staggering piece of news delivered to me in the front room of my house in Surrey, this time by Jonathan Barnett. He had insisted on coming round, although I didn't understand why he couldn't tell me over the phone. It became clear when he told me that Liverpool were interested in signing me, which was a total shock. Liverpool were the new European champions – for the fifth time – and the most successful British team in history. Their reputation and standing eclipsed every other side in the country. In his first season, their Spanish manager Rafael Benitez had not signed a single Englishman. And now he wanted me?

I had been through a few complicated transfers in my career, but none quite like the one that took me to Anfield. I loved playing for Southampton, I loved my life in Surrey, but I knew that Liverpool would come calling only once and this was an opportunity I could not turn down. Harry wanted me to stay so that he could build a new team around me. In the contract I had signed the previous summer, there was a condition that if we were relegated, my salary would be halved. Now Harry was saying that if I stayed, that condition would be struck out.

'I can fully understand why you want to leave, but I'm not going to make it easy for you,' Harry said. 'If I was you, I would want to go to Liverpool, but as the manager of this football club, I want to keep you.'

I understood that, but I also felt that, although Harry would make it difficult up to a point, if push came to shove, he would not stand in the way of me trying to make it as a player at the most famous club in the world. He'd been there before of course. When Jamie was 17 and playing for Harry at Bournemouth, Liverpool made him the most expensive teenager in English football at that time when they paid £350,000 for him. I comforted myself with the thought that, however tough Harry might sound, in the end he wouldn't stand in my way.

I spoke to Jamie about it, of course, although the poor bloke was in a really awkward position. He'd had a great time at Liverpool, he'd been captain, and he told me just what a fantastic club it was, but also, on his dad's behalf, he suggested that maybe I needed another year at Southampton before I was really ready for the big time. Deep down he knew full well that I had to go, and when I finally signed he was good about it.

'It's the greatest club in the world. You'll have a great time there,' Jamie said. 'You'll learn so much. It will be fantastic.' I know he was hurt for his dad, who was so anxious to keep me, but Jamie was very generous with his advice all the way.

Getting to Liverpool took almost the whole summer. A lot of people needed convincing, a lot of phone calls had to be made and a lot of meetings attended. At times it seemed as though it might not happen. Jonathan and I had a couple of meetings with Rupert Lowe in his house in the Cotswolds. We were honest with him. I was happy at Southampton, and if a Championship club had come in to make an offer for me, I would have stayed. But this was Liverpool – I had to go.

West Ham and Manchester City were also seriously interested in me. West Ham's manager, Alan Pardew, did more than anybody to try to persuade me to join. He was really keen, and on the phone to me all the time. He told me that I would be the team's number-one striker and he would build the side around me. It sounded like a great offer but in my heart I wanted to go to Liverpool. Funnily enough, Pardew lived near me in Surrey, despite Chadwell Heath, the West Ham training ground, being the opposite side of London. He told me that I could still live in Surrey if I signed for West Ham, and offered to give me a lift in to training in the mornings. That was kind of him but can you imagine the stick I would have got from the rest of the lads, turning up for training in the gaffer's car?

Stuart Pearce, the Manchester City manager, is an inspirational figure for any football fan of my generation and, of course, all my mum's side of the family are big City fans. When Dad told them that City liked me, I was on the receiving end of some serious pressure from the family around Macclesfield, all good-natured of course. Pardew and Pearce both seemed good blokes, but the decision was never in doubt.

It turned out to be another of those summers when I just wasn't sure where I was going to be come the start of the next season. At times I was worried that West Ham were much keener than Liverpool because Pardew was calling more. I was worried about the time the process of getting to Liverpool was taking. Was that normal? Did they really want me? It just seemed to be going on for so long. Since then, my team-mates have told me that's just the way it goes. It's not the quickest of processes.

I had a few long phone conversations with Jonathan when I was thinking that maybe it wasn't going to happen. I called Harry a couple of times to reiterate how much I wanted the move, and to say that I was not ungrateful for what Southampton, and Harry in particular, had done for me. I didn't want it to come across that I was jumping ship because they had gone down – that wasn't how it was. I wasn't exactly thrilled with the prospect of moving for the sixth time in my professional career, especially as I had started to get my house in Surrey just how I wanted it. But Liverpool were the European champions, and I had an England career to think about.

I tried to speak to Rupert Lowe too, but he seemed to be constantly on holiday. Anyway, that was what his secretary told me when I called him. He loves his grouse shooting and I'm told he's a dead shot too, it's a good job I didn't leave the transfer until the 'Glorious 12th' of August when the real blasting starts in earnest. I was pretty keen on having at least a weekend away that summer myself but I had to get the transfer deal sorted out first. The asking price was £7 million: some fee for a player who hadn't been considered good enough for Southampton a year earlier. The chairman's attitude seemed to be that if Liverpool were prepared to pay that, a deal could be done. Other than that, it wasn't really a concern for him.

By the time the transfer finally went through, I was back at Southampton for pre-season training, doing the hard running to stay in shape, even though I was hoping that I wasn't going to be there the next season. By then, the newspapers had got hold of the story and all the lads were asking me what was going to happen. I told them what I knew – I was still waiting for the call that would tell me the deal was done.

The call came on 19 July 2005. Dad and I got in the car and headed for my new club, as we had done so many times before. Queens Park Rangers, Portsmouth, Aston Villa, Norwich, Southampton – great clubs and some great times but none of them measured up to the place we were going now as we drove up the M6 towards Liverpool.

The club had booked us into the Sir Thomas Hotel in the city centre because the Radisson, where the new signings usually stay, was full. I was nervous coming down for breakfast the next morning. What do you wear when you're going to sign for Liverpool? I thought about putting on the suit – smart, but with the potential for piss-taking from the rest of the lads. So I settled for jeans and a shirt. I should have gone for the suit – after all, it was the biggest day of my career.

First, I went to Melwood, Liverpool's training ground in the West Derby area of the city, for my medical while the final contract documents were being prepared. As I walked across the car park

I could see Rafa Benitez walking towards the doors – the gaffer. I had never met him, although we had spoken briefly on the telephone. I felt a mild flush of panic – what should I do? Dash over and introduce myself? He looked round and saw me coming and I held out a hand to shake his. He looked at it but made no effort to respond. Now I really was worried. I looked at him and he gave me the nod.

'Inside,' he said under his breath. *Good start, Crouchy.* Once we got through the doors he smiled and shook my hand. 'There are photographers out there,' he said. 'Best to do it in private.'

The manager took me to the dressing rooms and I changed into my training gear for the medical, all the while looking round hopefully for a friendly face. The only one I knew at Liverpool was Steve Finnan – 'Finns'. I had met him socially a few times through Dezza, my Pompey mate, and we got on well. Joining a new football club is not much different from going to a new school. You just have to latch on to the person you know and hope he introduces you to the rest of the boys.

The Liverpool lads were off to Switzerland for their pre-season training camp that morning, so not many of them were there – Finns, Luis Garcia, Xabi Alonso and Josemi. It wasn't until I got out to Switzerland the following day that I met all the lads properly. So it was a quiet training ground on my first day and Dad and I were left with the club doctor, Mark Waller, whom I knew from the England Under-21s. He showed us round – Melwood is an incredible place. You can tell Liverpool are a top club just by looking at the pool and the gym.

Dad and I were in the canteen on our own, just taking it all in, when Frank McParland, the club's joint chief scout, wandered in for a chat.

'I remember you from that Under-19s game at Tottenham that Alan Sugar watched,' he said. 'There were two players on the pitch that day I knew were going to make it as professionals – Steven Gerrard and you.'

The famous game in question was a youth-team match between Tottenham and Liverpool at Spurs Lodge. Stevie had run the show that day. He was awesome, and after the match Alan Sugar, then the Tottenham chairman, had spoken to some of the Liverpool staff. Rumour has it he tried to sign him there and then for £2 million and, let's face it, at that price he would have been a bargain. It was nice of Frank to say that to me, and it helped put me at ease.

And so to Anfield. I hadn't been there that often, as a fan or a player, and I got a buzz just wandering round the outside. We found a little doorway and asked the security bloke if we could nip in for a peep at the pitch – my promised land, green and silent on a nice summer's day. This was where I would be judged as a footballer. I stood there for a minute with my hands in my pockets, just looking up at the rows of empty red seats on the Kop. It's hard to imagine all the famous afternoons and nights in a stadium's history when you're standing there before the season has even started. Keegan, Dalglish, Souness, Hansen, Rush, Barnes, Owen, Gerrard. Five European Cups. Eighteen league titles. In ten minutes' time I would be in the boardroom signing up to take part in this club's amazing history.

Dad and I walked round to the museum so I could take a look at what it really meant to be a Liverpool player. Silverware. Apart from that belated Championship-winning medal with Norwich City, I didn't have a single medal to my name. As we looked around the museum, we bumped into Bill Bygroves, the club chaplain and a lovely fella.

'Come on you two,' he said beckoning us through a door. 'There's something here you should see.'

I was looking at a picture on the wall when I heard Dad shout out.

'Fucking hell, Pete,' he said. 'It's the European Cup.'

There it was – the 'Big One', the trophy that Stevie, Carra and the lads had won in the most amazing game ever in Istanbul a few months earlier. Dad was beside himself with joy. Bill was already getting his camera out.

'Come on,' he said. 'Let's have a shot of you two together with the Cup.'

We've still got the picture of Dad and me holding up the European Cup, a handle each. Much to my horror, the photograph was hanging in the club museum for a while, a fact that Dad would point out with great pride to anyone who happened to be going up to Anfield. I felt a right doughnut. What were Stevie, Carra and the others going to think if they saw this? What would the fans think? I hadn't even signed for the club and there I was holding up the European Cup like I'd won the thing myself.

Apart from that moment, looking at the pitch, I tried not to think too hard about the history of the place. I'd take stock at the end of the season, but for now I wanted to get on with signing the contract and meeting the lads. The Anfield boardroom was impressive and everyone who needed to be there was there – Rick Parry, the chief executive, Bryce Morrison, the club secretary, Dad, Jonathan. *Show me the contract. I want to get this done.* I was told I would be wearing the No. 15 shirt, shook a few hands and that was it. Welcome to the club. I was a Liverpool player at last.

Rick came round to the car park with us, and I was on top of the world. I had officially arrived at the most successful football club in Britain. As we walked round the stadium a bus passed us on the road and a bloke shouted at me from the window, 'CROUCH YOU LANKY WANKER!'

There was a stunned silence for a second and then Rick said, very deadpan, 'Of course, we're not the only football club in this city.' We had a laugh about that.

I was told to pack a bag and Doc Waller and I were straight on a plane to Switzerland to catch up with the rest of the lads. By the time we got there, all the boys were out for a few drinks – their last treat before the hard work began for real. Since it was about 11 p.m. I decided to make a good impression and wait until the next morning to meet my team-mates, so I went to bed. I had already been warned this would be a tough old trip.

Bad Ragaz in Switzerland – just thinking about that place makes me feel tired. Under Benitez's assistant coach Pako Ayesteran, we worked very, very hard indeed – running, weights, the lot. It's a proper training camp, no buses. You ride your bike there, through the mountains, and then when you're done, you ride your bike back to the hotel. It was fully as hard as I expected – mentally tough as much as anything – but I loved it. There's not much to do apart from work hard, eat and sleep, and it was a great opportunity to get to know everyone. If we had been at the Melwood training ground, I'm sure that after the sessions everyone would have been shooting off home. When you're in Bad Ragaz, you have to talk to each other because there's nothing else to do.

And luckily for me, the Liverpool boys had a card school. The game was three-card brag and Pepe Reina, Luis Garcia, Didi Hamann, Steven Gerrard, Finns and I played a lot. I had an absolute stinker, and I suppose that helped me get to know the lads because they were all having a laugh at the nightmare I was having at cards. That's not the worst a new boy has ever done at cards, though. Jermaine Pennant took that title the next summer – he was absolutely atrocious – but as with the England team, playing cards was a great way to break the ice.

17

EIGHTEEN BLOODY GAMES

Even now, whenever I look at the list of games I played for Liverpool at the start of the 2005–06 season, I think the same thing – how did I go all those games without scoring? It was 18 matches in all, 15 of them starts, in a period of more than four months. When was I going to score my first goal for Liverpool? At one point this burning question started to consume my life and the burden grew heavier and heavier. It seemed to me it became a national obsession.

All through my career I have encountered difficult times, and it would be a lie to say that this wasn't one of the worst. By the time I joined Liverpool I thought I had made myself pretty immune to criticism, but the constant jokes, the digs from all sorts of people, well, they hurt. They hurt my dad, they hurt my family, and in the bleakest times I asked myself the same question I had asked a year earlier when I found myself cast into the reserves at Southampton by Steve Wigley. Had I made a mistake coming to this club? Was I out of my depth?

However, this time there was a big difference. In Rafael Benitez, I had a manager who backed me. The boss could not have been better to me during that barren run. He was great. He didn't have to say anything to me, and he didn't really. He kept doing the one thing that I needed him to do the most – he kept picking me. If he had pulled me aside and made a big deal of it, I would have got even more concerned. When the press asked him about my lack of goals, he would say, 'I don't need to speak to him because he knows what I think of him. We're winning games and he's playing well. That's enough for me, and I have no doubt he will score goals.'

That meant so much to me. He never complained about me or blamed me. Benitez kept the faith. The other great support were the Liverpool fans themselves. They never stopped encouraging, never stopped willing me to do the business when I was in the stadium or when they saw me out and about in the city. They're intelligent football people and they know when a player is giving his all, and doing everything to turn it around – they could see how much it meant to me. Watch the replay of my first goals at Anfield in December. When the ball went in, the place was rocking.

It didn't help that I had a tricky start at the club. Despite the fact that Liverpool had won the Champions League, Uefa had ordered them to qualify again because they finished fifth in the Premiership. The boys had already seen off Welsh team TNS before I joined. I started both games against the Lithuanian side Kaunas and, in the second, pulled my hamstring quite badly ten minutes into the second half. I was out for more than a month. I missed the first two Premiership games of the season – I wouldn't have been able to play in them anyway because I still had two games of my three-match suspension to serve for the red card against Crystal Palace at the end of the previous season – and I also missed the European Super Cup win over CSKA Moscow in Monaco.

Steven Gerrard was flying – he scored seven goals in the first four Champions League games – but our start to the Premiership season was not the best. We drew 0–0 with Middlesbrough and missed a load of chances against Sunderland at Anfield before Xabi Alonso settled it with a free-kick. I made my Premiership debut for Liverpool at White Hart Lane on 10 September and scored a perfectly good goal that was disallowed because I supposedly pushed my old mate Anthony Gardner in the process.

Three days later we went to Seville. The boys had already got through three rounds of Champions League qualifying to make the group stages. On my full Champions League debut, we took Real Betis apart. Florent Sinama-Pongolle got one inside 90 seconds and then I was part of the move for Luis Garcia's goal. I stroked a disguised pass into Bolo Zenden down the left and he crossed for Luis. Betis were supposed to be La Liga's up-and-coming side but they couldn't live with us in attack that day.

I honestly believed I was playing well but another reality about playing for the biggest club in the country was starting to hit home. At Southampton and Aston Villa it was normally enough to play well. OK, I wanted to score as much as any other striker but if I had created goals, played well and helped the team win, I felt I had done my job. At a club the size of Liverpool, those things are simply not enough. If you want to stay in the team, and get the plaudits, there is one requirement above all – you have got to score goals. And the games without goals were starting to add up for me.

In the Premiership we drew with Manchester United and Birmingham City – a game we should have won. In the Champions League our match with Chelsea, which was billed as the biggest of the round, ended 0–0 in a tense, tight match. The real disaster came four days later when Chelsea came back to Anfield for a Premiership match and beat us 4–1.

We beat Blackburn at home, then Anderlecht in the Champions League. Fulham beat us in the Premiership, Crystal Palace knocked us out the Carling Cup, and still no goals. Djibril Cisse was scoring, so was Fernando Morientes. We beat West Ham and then, in the victory over Anderlecht in Belgium, I got a chance at the near post from a cross from Stevie and put it just wide. Morientes nicked in front of me to get to a cross from Steve Finnan. The shot was saved and I couldn't wrap my foot around the rebound to put it in. The pressure was mounting. That made it thirteen games without a goal.

It didn't get any easier against Villa on 5 November. Bolo Zenden changed the game that day when he came on just before the hour. He put a cross over from the left, right on my head, and I headed it straight at Thomas Sorenson. I'd do better next time. That next time, Liam Ridgwell bundled me to the ground and Steven Gerrard stuck the penalty away five minutes from time. With a minute to go, a cross from the right just eluded me, Bolo picked it up on the left and stuck it back in. I lunged. This was it – it had to be. Four yards out. And then from nowhere, Olof Mellberg threw himself into the tackle, got the ball off my toe, it spilled to the edge of the area and Xabi Alonso drilled it in for the second goal.

That was the fourteenth game without a goal. After the match, I went back out into an empty Villa Park for a warm-down with Pako. It would have been brilliant to score the first one here, at a place where the fans still give me a good reception, against O'Leary. As I jogged round I heard my name being called from the press box in the main stand and looked up to see a friendly face. Graham Taylor is a summariser for BBC Radio Five Live these days and he was giving me a wave.

Sod it. I could do with a bit of encouragement. I finished running and climbed up into the stand to see Graham. He was his usual positive self. He put his arm round me and told me not to worry. He said the potential he had seen in me almost four years ago was still there and the goals would come. It was good to hear it from such a wise old football man, because by then the pressure was really starting to tell on me.

I had left the comfort and safety of Southampton, where I had scored goals, the fans loved me, and there was no real pressure. Good results against big teams were to be celebrated, and when we lost – well, that was what happened to small teams wasn't it? Playing at Portsmouth and Southampton had another advantage – I was the star of the show, the focal point of the team. The lads were geared to getting me early balls and I got on the end of crosses and passes in the box.

At Liverpool, of course, it was very different. There were so many different ways of playing and goals came from everywhere. Liverpool were full of real superstars, such as Stevie, who would be in most people's world XI, Cisse, Luis, Xabi and Morientes. It was much more of a team game and, to begin with, I couldn't get to grips with it. At corners, why was the ball not always aimed at me? I scored a lot of goals from corners, so why were we taking short corners when I was so used to the ball being played directly in to the box? At Southampton, all dead balls would revolve around me, while at Liverpool, they didn't, and it took time for me to adapt. I felt the expectations of playing for this famous club. There are no written rules. You learn as you go along. *You're in the big time now, Crouchy lad. Better shape up.* And the longer I went without scoring, the more anxious I became.

Dad came to just about every game and the longer my goalless run went on, the more upset he became, although he hid it from me at the time. The players' families were a great source of support for him, and none more than the Carraghers. If you follow Liverpool home and away, no doubt you'll bump into Philly, Jamie's dad, and his brother and mates at some point. They had seen the ups and downs of Jamie's career and they were always on hand to pick up my dad when things went badly for me.

Game fifteen was Portsmouth at Anfield. With twenty minutes on the clock, Bolo stuck the ball through Andy Griffin's legs on the left side of the box. As he went to sprint past him, Griffin stuck out an arm to stop him and Bolo went down. The referee, Peter Walton, pointed to the spot. My reaction was immediate. *I'm having this.*

I know what made me do it. It was all the frustration and hurt that had built up over the season – the taunts from rival fans, the long drives back home after training, fretting about where this goal was going to come from, the fears that I might not be good enough. No, of course I wasn't on penalties at the time. They were Stevie's job and he was good at them, but come on – Portsmouth at Anfield? A penalty in front of the Kop? This was the day I was going to smash any goalscoring hoodoo for good.

As I stood there with the ball under one arm, I could hear the tension in the stadium, the buzz. I could almost hear 40,000 Scouse voices murmuring, 'Go on Crouchy lad, stick this one away. Give us something to cheer about.' I put the ball down. I was good at penalties. I had stuck one past Portsmouth last season in the last minute for Southampton in the FA Cup, with Harry Redknapp on the touchline barely able to watch. I picked my side – keeper's right. Jamie Ashdown settled in the middle of his goal. I stepped up. Bang. *Get in there.* Ashdown saved it.

I had struck the ball hard. It came down and bounced up and, in that split second, so many feelings of embarrassment and pain ran through me that I didn't really react. Good job Bolo did. He was first to it and headed the rebound past Ashdown for the goal. Thank God for small mercies. I joined in the celebrations, of course I did, but inside I was broken up. This was getting beyond a joke. This was becoming a curse.

After the match, when our press officer Ian Cotton asked me if I would speak on camera, I made a point of going out there and putting a brave face on it. I wasn't going to shy away from it, however painful it was for me. 'I made the decision,' I told the BBC.

'Obviously I'm desperate to score at the moment, so I'll take any chance I can.' What else could I say? I was honest. I had a little smile when they asked me whether I would still be on penalty duty. That hurt but I wanted to show the fans I wasn't going to give up. I think I got a bit of credit for tackling it face on rather than hiding away.

I took a lot of stick in the newspapers, and from some commentators, too. That's a hazard of the job when you're a £7 million striker and not scoring goals. That's the way it goes, and up to a point, I probably deserved it, but certain people went over the top. Maybe it was because of the way I look, a soft target because I am different that people feel I am a much easier figure to take the piss out of – I suppose a 6ft 7in. footballer who isn't scoring goals is a lot more fun to take the mickey out of than a 5ft 11in. striker who isn't scoring goals. I accept the criticism but I thought some of it was too personal. Over the top. Unpleasant.

Of course, once the bad run was over and we were at the World Cup finals with England, the same journalists all wanted to be my mate again. One of the Liverpool-based reporters wrote something about me that so enraged Stevie and Carra that they gave him a load of stick when he came down to the tunnel after one game. At least the reporter in question had the decency to write me a letter of apology.

It wasn't just the newspapers. I was getting flak from every different angle. It was open season on Peter Crouch and some of the weirdest, least likely characters were weighing in. I can't recall exactly what it was I was watching – it may have been Sky News – but I was sitting at home with a cup of tea, just relaxing, when they cut to the Fifa World Player of the Year awards – at least, I think it was that. Eamonn Holmes was introducing it, with all the usual comments about the event being for the best players in the world. Then he made a little joke – 'So don't expect Peter Crouch to be here . . .'

What? I almost spat my tea across the room. I couldn't quite believe this. What the fuck did I have to do with this? Why was he bringing me into it and sticking the knife in? Had he been forced to put up with smaller breakfast servings in the Sky canteen that morning? What an idiot.

Some people find it difficult to accept me for their own reasons, and when I started to score goals and prove people wrong, it would have been nice for those same people who hammered me when I wasn't scoring to praise me, but it just doesn't seem to work like that. It's a shame.

As usual, my dad was a real strength. He would come home with me after games and talk about the match. A couple of times I said to him I had just had enough. Liverpool were a great club with great fans and great players but I wasn't enjoying myself. Not scoring was killing me, and I didn't like the constant jibes, or the massive press coverage, that came with playing for Liverpool.

'Right, that's it. I'm just not keen on it. I'm just not keen on being at the club,' I said to Dad. 'I want to get back to Southampton. I was enjoying life there and at this moment I'm not. At least at Southampton I was scoring goals.'

Dad wasn't having that. He wasn't going to allow me throw away my career and everything I'd worked for. So he came up to stay with me for a few days. At the time, I didn't even want to leave my flat because I felt that people were laughing at me – so much so that I didn't even want to go out for a drink in my local pub. That was the last straw for Dad.

'That's it, I'm not letting you get like this,' he said on one Saturday evening after a game. 'Get your coat on. We're going out for a few beers.'

A few beers turned into a good few more and we ended up having a massive night out, culminating in Brasingamens, a bar in Alderley Edge. That was where, in its previous existence as a pub, my dad met

Skinning Sami Hyypia for Southampton against Liverpool, 22 January 2005 (like I do every day in training!). We won 2–0 that day and Sami and I had a proper battle.

Stevie G looks on in awe at my finishing as I score the second against Liverpool that day. Carra, where were you?

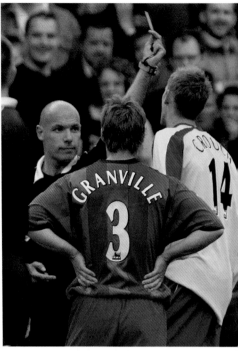

Jamie Redknapp, Henri Camara and I celebrate my goal from the spot against Crystal Palace, 7 May 2002. It turned out to be my last for the club.

Sent off by referee Howard Webb for a scuffle with Gonzalo Sorondo, I missed the last game of the season against Manchester United.

Harry Redknapp (*right*) and his assistant Jim Smith get that sinking feeling after Southampton draw 2–2 with Palace. We had to beat United to have any chance of staying up.

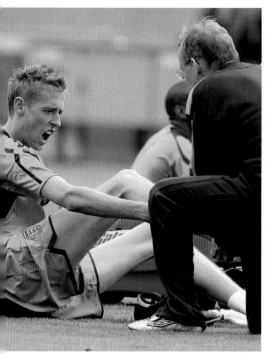

My England debut is postponed after I injured my ankle during training in Illinois, 27 May 2002.

Setting up Michael Owen for a hat-trick against Colombia at the Giants Stadium, New Jersey, 31 May 2002. I did it all with my feet!

Two slightly sheepish Crouchs holding the Big One in the Liverpool museum. I was worried what the Liverpool lads would think. I'd only just arrived at the club that day.

Taking instructions from the boss, Rafael Benitez, before a pre-season friendly against Olympiakos in Liechtenstein, 23 July 2005.

Clearing some hurdles in Japan during the FIFA club world championship, 13 December 2005.

Above: It's in! I'm out of the picture as my first goal for Liverpool after 18 games goes in on 3 December 2005 against Wigan. Some pundits tried to take it off me.

Right: Carra leads the celebrations with Finns (*left*) and Xabi (*right*) in pursuit.

Opposite page:

Above left: My first England goal, against Uruguay, 1 March 2006. I had No. 21 on my shirt and 12 on my shorts. The kitman asked me to keep it quiet, but I think a few people had noticed by then.

Above right: At the Beckhams' pre-World Cup party, 21 May 2006, with model Jodie Kidd and jockey Frankie Dettori. I don't think I'm the right height for a career in horseracing.

Below: Completing my hat-trick for England against Jamaica, 3 June 2006, was a fantastic moment, even if I did miss a penalty along the way.

Left: Showing the FA Cup to the fans at our post-match party in the Alma de Cuba restaurant in Liverpool, 13 May 2006. That turned into a big night.

Below: Hungover but happy, I can't believe how many fans have turned out to greet us on the open-topped bus tour. John Arne Riise (*right*) spots a friend. Luis Garcia is on the left.

Prince William seemed like a really good bloke and when Carra suggested I perform the robot dance for him, I could hardly refuse, 1 June 2006.

Caught in a World Cup wind-up by Rio Ferdinand (*left*) and his accomplice Robbie Fowler. The show was on ITV and the lads loved watching it while we were in Germany.

my mum all those years ago. At closing time, we didn't want to stop, so most of the people in Brasingamens came back to my place and we kept the party going.

In the morning, Dad said the flat looked like a scene from that Yellow Pages advert where the kid has a house-party when his parents are away on holiday. There were people asleep on the sofa, on the floor, in the hallway. I didn't know most of them. Some bloke who looked familiar was fast asleep in my front room. 'Isn't that Aaron Mokoena?' Dad said. It certainly was. The big Blackburn Rovers midfielder had turned up at the party at some point during the night. God knows when.

That night out did the trick. The next day I felt carefree. After being so down on the Saturday night, I went to training on the Monday morning, and worked hard again. Our way of getting round the difficult times was going out and having a good craic. Dad would say, 'Just forget about it. The goals will come.' And they did in the end. Looking back, I can say that's the test when you join a big club. No one can ever promise you that it's going to be easy. You have to accept that and learn to love playing for the club.

After Portsmouth, we played Real Betis at home. I had one of my best games of the season – a shot on the turn that was saved, a diving header that was just wide. I felt that the Betis defence couldn't live with me. But still no goal. By the time we played Wigan at Anfield on 3 December 2005, I had also started in the wins over Manchester City and Sunderland but still not scored. I was playing well and just one goal was all I needed. Just one.

I was heading for 24 hours on the pitch without a goal, going into that Wigan game. I just needed a bit of luck, something to go my way, and after 19 minutes, I got it at last. I chested the ball down on the halfway line, turned and ran at Wigan. They backed off so much that I got to the edge of the area – in range to have a go for goal. As I launched my shot, Leighton Baines got across, the ball screwed up off the outside of his foot and looped towards the goal. I watched and waited for what seemed like an eternity.

Stevie had followed the shot in, although in the end he didn't need to. The goalkeeper, Mike Pollitt, made a complete mess of it. He tried to flick the ball over the bar with one hand but got his angles wrong and pushed it into the back of the net. It was in. I'd scored. The place erupted. I sprinted off in celebration, my hands in the air.

I had said to the press that when I scored I would throw myself in the Kop but once I started running, I didn't want to stop. I ran towards the Kop and back along the main stand with most of my team-mates in pursuit. Carra got to me first. He threw his arms around my neck but he couldn't stop me. The wait was over. I was up and running and the best was yet to come. Three minutes before half-time, Finns launched a beauty of a ball from the right-back position. It split the Wigan defence and I was in on goal. I let it bounce in front of me and lifted a perfect little lob over Pollitt and into the goal.

I was buzzing. At last, what I had been waiting for, what I loved to do. I was scoring goals again. As we went in to the tunnel at half-time, Geoff Shreeves, the pitchside interviewer on Sky Sports, stepped out in front of me.

'Are you sure that first one is your goal?' he asked. 'They're saying in the studio it was an own goal.'

'Of course it's my goal,' I shot back at him. 'Are you joking?'

Carra pulled me aside as I walked into the dressing room.

'What did he say?'

'He said they're saying on telly that the first one wasn't my goal,' I said.

'He's taking the fucking piss,' Carra said.

We went out and won the game 3–0. Luis Garcia scored the third. After the match, Carra grabbed Shreeves in the tunnel and gave him the sort of bollocking only Carra can hand out. He was fuming.

'You fucking kidding? You fucking kidding?' he raged at Shreeves. 'Trying to take that fucking goal off Crouchy.'

Shreeves looked terrified. I was having my say and Stevie piled in as well.

'You're fucking out of order taking away his goal. You're taking the piss.'

The boys were fighting my corner, and that showed me what being part of Liverpool Football Club meant. Carra and Stevie knew what this goal meant to me, and they weren't going to let Sky get away with giving it as an own goal to Baines or Pollitt, but when I walked into the players' lounge and glanced up at the screen, Sky were giving the first goal as an own goal. I dropped my bag on the floor. I couldn't believe it. *People are trying to kill me here.* I thought there was some kind of conspiracy against me. Liverpool even put out a club statement from chief executive Rick Parry that said in the club's records the first would be my goal. It got that serious.

I tried to forget about it until it happened again – on Boxing Day, against Newcastle. I got up for a cross and headed it down into the corner to the left of Shay Given. It clipped the post and came out along the line, but the spin of the ball took it back over and into the goal. It was blatantly my goal, anyone could see that, but by the time I got home and turned on the telly, Sky Sports were giving it as an own goal. That was it for me. I was sure that someone at Sky Sports was having a go on purpose.

When there was a dispute about who had scored a goal, Sky Sports apparently put it to the 'dubious goals panel' to make a decision. The what? Who sits on this panel? Who makes the rules? When do they meet? And can I come along to put my case? As far as I was concerned, the dubious goals panel was the most dubious panel I had ever heard of.

'What the fuck is this dubious goals panel?' I asked Ian Cotton. I was not pleased and I wanted a phone number. I needed to speak to one of these people. I had been through eighteen games of hell trying to score my first goal for Liverpool and now they were trying to take goals off me. I just wasn't having it. Ian hunted around and found the name and number of the relevant person to talk to, so I rang Sky Sports and they put me through to the department concerned. From there, the conversation started to get a bit surreal.

'Ian Cotton gave me this name and I want to speak to the guy,' I said. 'If he's not there, whoever puts the names of the goalscorers up on screen. That's the bloke I want.'

'Well, we've got a researcher who does the graphics with the goalscorer's name.'

'Put me through to him.'

'Who is it?'

'Peter Crouch.'

'You what?'

'Peter Crouch.'

'You taking the mick, mate?'

It took me a while to convince him that I was who I said I was. The bloke at Sky Sports said that they made an immediate judgement while the game was live, but the final decision was up to the dubious goals panel, who met every month – just a group of guys (I assume) in a room. I'd love to know where they meet so I could sit in one day, and see them make these decisions. Thankfully, I have since been credited with both goals.

After the Wigan match, David Platt in his role as a Sky Sports pundit kept going on about the first goal not being mine, and he's brought it up since then. He likes having a dig at me. I don't know why he's so hostile – perhaps it's all those eggyboff challenges we got involved in with the Under-21s. The strange thing was that, a few days after he'd been slagging me off, I got a letter from him and some company he was representing, offering to look after my finances for me. Football's funny like that. I chucked the letter in the bin.

18

BOOED

Good old Sven. He didn't drop me from the England squad just because I hadn't scored a goal for Liverpool, or because I was getting the piss taken out of me on radio phone-ins. He stuck by me and I will never forget that. Like Rafael Benitez, he didn't make a big deal of the goalless run. He didn't pull me aside, but I was finding out that one-on-one chats with players weren't really Sven's style.

I played three games for England during my barren run for Liverpool, the first two a double-header against Austria and Poland at Old Trafford in October 2005, the third against Argentina in November. We faced an expectant nation, although many people were harbouring doubts about our chances at the World Cup finals, just eight months away.

I wasn't too daunted by the prospect of playing for my country. I looked at it this way – at least it gave me a break from the pressure I was under at Liverpool. And besides, Sven had problems of his own. While I had been out with my hamstring problems in August and September of 2005, the England team had been stuffed 4–1 in a friendly in Denmark, had beaten Wales 1–0 and then, in the worst result of Sven's reign so far, they were defeated 1–0 by Northern Ireland in Belfast in a World Cup qualifier. The boys said after that game Sven lost his temper, which wasn't like him. He singled out two or three individuals, telling them they hadn't been good enough.

For the last two qualifiers of the group, the heat was turned up and I was about to find out that there is a big difference between playing for England in an end-of-season tour in America and playing in a competitive match at Old Trafford. It was only when I joined up with the England boys that week that I realised the true magnitude of playing for your country. The pressure built up over the week leading up to the Austria game on the Saturday and Poland on the Wednesday. Wayne Rooney was suspended, Ashley Cole out with a stress fracture, Rio Ferdinand dropped from the team. The focus on everything we did was intense. This was different and I have to admit that I felt nervous.

When you play for England, the build-up around games is huge. The manager and the captain attend press conferences and, as a player, every now and again you are asked to face the media. The press conferences are held in the suites at Old Trafford and you don't get away with doing just one. There are three different rooms and three different audiences – television, radio and, at the end, the newspapers.

When you're relatively new to the squad, and the adrenaline is flowing just because you're there, it can be quite daunting to face the press. You get shoved up on a little stage to be confronted by a forest of microphones and a room full of experienced professional people – well, some of them anyway – who are all looking up at you. It's quite nerve-racking. One slip of the tongue and you're all over the back pages. That's just part of playing for England. The radio interviews are the most straightforward – I think to myself that the chances are I'm never going to hear the interview anyway. The television guys are OK, too. The newspaper reporters are the toughest. Mess that one up and they're on to you.

I found it very easy to get used to the atmosphere around the England team hotel. Some people who work behind the scenes have been there for years, especially in the massage room, where a lot of the banter goes on. The masseurs are Rod Thornley, Steve Slattery, Chris Neville and, of course, the legendary Billy McCulloch, aka 'Bill Blood'. The massage room is where a lot of the lads watch the Under-21s game the night before a match. It's a social place, as well as somewhere to go for a rub, that makes a change from killing time in your room. When it comes to massages, some of the lads swear by them – some have them every day. I only have them before a game, or if my legs feel stiff.

At the centre of it all is Billy, who works at Chelsea when he's not on England duty. He is a top masseur but that's not the only reason we have him around. He's famous for his gags and we love having him in the dressing room. He's hilarious. Jamie Carragher and Steven Gerrard are always trying to poach him for Liverpool, telling him that we'll offer him more money, but Billy's very close to the Chelsea boys, including John Terry, Wayne Bridge, Frank Lampard and Shaun Wright-Phillips. Billy's jokes are brilliant for getting the lads laughing and relaxed, but you would never expect Sven to find them funny. So it was a bit of a surprise to discover the boss loved them. It became a tradition in the months before the World Cup, and during the tournament itself, that at the end of a team-meeting, in the days before games, Sven would get Billy up to tell us a few of his gags. The lads loved it and Steve McClaren has kept that tradition going. Of course, Billy gets a load of stick for being Scottish. Before he was with England, Billy was part of the Scotland set-up under Walter Smith, but we nabbed him.

Rooney was suspended for the Austria game, and I was starting up front alongside Michael Owen. When I was asked if I found it frustrating that I would have to make room for Wayne Rooney after he'd served his suspension, my answer was simple. I was happy to be in the team and to be given the chance. I wasn't stupid, and I didn't think I would replace Wayne. Even if I played out my skin, he would come back in, but I wanted everyone to know I could play at that level. And I thought I did well against Austria.

We won 1–0 through a Frank Lampard penalty and results elsewhere meant that we had officially qualified for the World Cup before the Poland game on the Wednesday. Loads of my mum's side of the family – all the Manchester City fans – were in the stands at Old Trafford and I got the full 90 minutes. It was a proud day for all of us, and it couldn't prepare us for what was about to happen against Poland. You can go from amazing highs to real bad lows, and it happens when you least expect it.

I was a sub against Poland and, at 1–1, we were playing quite well when Sven told me to warm up. I was to replace Shaun Wright-Phillips, who was having a decent enough game. As he came to the touchline where I stood waiting to come on, I could hear a sound welling in the throats of the crowd. I could feel a weird vibe around the place, something not right. As Shaun came towards me I could hear the sound getting louder. What I had feared from the strange atmosphere that had blown up as I started to strip off my tracksuit was becoming a reality. I was coming on to the pitch to play for England, at home, for my third cap, in front of my family, and I was being booed by our own fans.

At first I felt terrible. I knew that up in the stands it would be killing my mum and dad. So this was what it was like playing for England, in England? It was a long way from Liverpool, where as long as the fans knew you were giving your all they were diehard behind their own players. Maybe I could have understood the reaction of the England fans if I'd been having a nightmare – a couple of terrible touches or missed a sitter. But I was just coming on to the field of play. They hadn't given me a chance. I was angry rather than upset, so I stuck to my tried and trusted approach in these situations and ignored them.

The fans are entitled to their opinion and, as players, we're big enough and well rewarded enough to take it, but that doesn't mean the spectators always get it right. They later booed Owen Hargreaves in the friendly with Hungary just before the World Cup, and three months later voted him England player of the year. When you play for England – in England – you get a different kind of person in the stand. I'm not saying all the fans are like it but a lot seem to be there just to be entertained. 'Go on,' they seem to be saying, 'put on a show.' I fully understand the frustrations that England fans have with the national team, and we didn't deliver at the 2006 World Cup finals, but their support is so important to us. They travel all over the world like no other nation's fans. I've been there and I know the massive difference it makes when they get behind me. And I can tell you, I respond a lot better to a cheer than the treatment I got at Old Trafford that night – or the abuse the boys got in Barcelona against Andorra.

Anyway, the job was done, we had beaten Poland 2–1 and we were going to Germany. The lads went on a lap of honour around the stadium but I just wanted to get back into the changing rooms. I would rather have got out of Old Trafford and not been associated with it. I was still boiling about the way I had been booed. How had I come to deserve that? Maybe a few other factors were involved, such as being a Liverpool player at Old Trafford, but as I drove home that night I was angry.

I was worried, too. Would Sven think twice about picking me? I was good enough to play for England at the World Cup but at the back of my mind I was anxious that the manager might not give me another crack. Maybe he would think the booing might affect me, or affect the way people viewed the team. I genuinely feared that I wouldn't be back in an England squad after that night at Old Trafford but on that score I had underestimated Sven – he didn't give a toss what people thought and he backed me all the way. I can't thank him enough for sticking by me.

The boys in the team had registered the booing – you could hardly miss it – but they didn't say anything. It's the old way in football, either laugh it off or don't bother talking about it. And with England, we all know that you experience the best and the worst of football – great highs, crushing lows. Every touch is scrutinised. Mess one up and those newspaper marks out of ten go down; make a good one and they go up. It's unspoken among the players but you just get on with it. If you believed all the things that get said or written, you would go mad. Things can change round so quickly. You can go from being the worst player in the world to being the fans' favourite, as Hargreaves did, in the space of a few months. Look at it that way and it's hilarious really. If Hargreaves let it affect him, if I let it affect me, it would be impossible for us to be footballers. I can tell you that, in the end, it's worth it – and I remember that every time I score for Liverpool or England, and a whole stadium is buzzing because of something I have done. The morning after the Poland game, I thought about the booing and just laughed it off.

When the England squad met a month later for the Argentina game in Geneva, I still had not scored for Liverpool. By that time, I was in complete media blackout mode. My usual policy was to read the newspapers when I was playing well and avoid them when I was having a stinker, but by this time I was cutting out just about everything to do with football apart from my training with Liverpool and playing matches. I wasn't even watching games on television. I didn't know anything about the Premiership, who was playing well, what the pundits were saying, what the big issues were in the newspapers. I played for Liverpool, I read the results and that was it. You have to do that because you have to run on that pitch believing you are a top player. I would rather go out there having built myself up than knowing I'd been knocked down.

So England's 3–2 win over Argentina was special for me, and it felt like real acceptance. We were 2–1 down when I came on after 81 minutes and we won the match with two goals from Michael Owen against a team that a lot of people had tipped as one of the favourites for the World Cup. There was a totally different atmosphere in the stadium too. As I warmed up, the crowd were clapping me, and although it was a little thing, it picked me up. Joe Cole had come on just before the hour and really changed things, and when I got on the pitch I felt that the Argentina defence had real problems with me. We were getting on top of them and five minutes later Steven Gerrard crossed for Owen to get the equaliser.

The winner came from a cross to the near post from Joe. I went flying in but Mo just nipped in front of me to head it in. I've got a picture of it somewhere – me on the floor while Mo is turning away in celebration. I would have loved a goal, I needed one then as much as anyone, but after that performance I was just buzzing to be involved. On that day, my mood about being an England player totally changed.

At last I felt I was getting taken a bit more seriously. Before I came on we were trying to play through Argentina and it wasn't working. After I came on we were more direct and got two goals out of it. That's not the way I want to be seen as a footballer – first and foremost, I much prefer the ball to my feet to allow me to bring players into the game, but I'm not blind to the fact that my height is an alternative. I don't care what you say about the right or wrong way to play football – if passing intricately through the opposition is not working, let's play it long. After that game, bringing me on was talked about as an option for the World Cup.

Coming back to win against a team of the stature of Argentina gave us a lot of confidence before the World Cup, and that was probably where the hype about us winning it came from. We knew full well it was a good result but people were getting a bit carried away. From my own point of view, I felt much more part of England, and more accepted, than I had during the games against Austria and Poland in the previous month. Before, I could sense that a few people didn't think I should be playing. Now that seemed to be changing.

Among the England boys I felt more established, too. The digital age and PlayStation games may have killed off the card schools, but the squad gets on well. On the occasional England trips, it's a nice change to mix with a group of English boys, who have been through the same experiences, and come from the same background. I know it's the same for the Spanish, Dutch and Norwegian lads at Liverpool when they join up with their national squads. What draws us together as England players is that shared experience of playing together in youth teams and the old school banter. It's a good group to be around.

By the time we played Uruguay in March 2006, our last friendly of the season, I was well on my way with Liverpool, having scored six goals, and I was raring to go for England. This international was going to be different because it was to be played at Anfield, where I knew the fans would be behind me. I was disappointed not to start alongside Rooney – by then Mo was out with a broken metatarsal – but I could understand why Sven wanted to give Darren Bent a chance. When I came on after 64 minutes I wanted to make sure my performance counted. We were losing to South American opposition again, 1–0 down, and again I felt that Joe Cole and I made the difference.

I have watched my first goal for England on video time and time again. Joe laid the ball back to Michael Carrick who put him in with a long ball down the left wing. Joe picked it up, doubled back and whipped a lovely cross to the back post where I was waiting. I got up well above the defender to head it down past the goalkeeper. What a special moment – my first England goal in front of the Anfield Road end. In injury time, Joe nipped in at the near post and got us the winner. We had beaten two South American sides, having come from behind both times. I was revelling in my first England goal and it wasn't until I got off the pitch that it was pointed out to me that the numbers on my shirt didn't match up.

On the front, the shirt had my squad number, 21, and on the back number 12. John Motson, commentating for the BBC, had spotted it as soon as I came on for Rooney, but I had no idea. When I'm named as a sub I go out to warm up, come back in, put on my shirt and then my jacket straight over the top. I'm not one to put my shirt on just before I come on. I always have it on ready. So I didn't have a clue about the mistake. The poor old kitman Tom McKechnie was really twitching. He came up to me and said that if I did an interview, I should take the shirt off and not mention it. But the story was already out so I decided to have a bit of a laugh with Tom and said in my post-match interview that he'd probably be in trouble. He wasn't of course, and the mistake probably makes that shirt as special as any other I have kept from my career. It was quite funny, a genuine mistake, but because it happened with England it became a big deal.

A few collectors have offered to buy that shirt from me, because it is such a one-off. But I couldn't put a value on the shirt I was wearing when I scored my first England goal and I want it up on the wall of my house. When I finally get round to settling in a house for more than a couple of years, I'll have to work out a way of displaying it. You really need to see the front as well as the back – perhaps some sort of rotating display cabinet is in order.

As a striker, you know certain team-mates are going to look for you first and you can come to a real understanding. Robert Prosinecki at Portsmouth was like that and Joe Cole is the same. He beats players, but when he is on the left and gets a chance to get the ball on his right foot, he whips it in. Yes, he does a few tricks, and he can be unpredictable, but more often than not he looks for me and it certainly helps the way I play. At Portsmouth, I discovered that getting in the rhythm of playing with the same players helped a lot, and it's hard to replicate that at international level.

Between the Argentina game in November and the Uruguay match in March, big changes had been taking place around the England team. In January, the *News of the World* broke the story of their sting on Sven, in which they had got him saying a few things he shouldn't have done to their undercover reporter. How had the reporter tricked him? By pretending to be a sheikh who was inter-ested in investing in English football clubs. The lads couldn't quite believe that anyone would go so far as that to stitch him up. It sounded hilarious, the sort of get-up that wouldn't have been out of place at Lee Hendrie's stag do. Surely this was all just a bit of a laugh?

Not for Sven, though. He'd had a few drinks with this bloke in the fancy dress and made some indiscreet comments about some of the England players that were secretly recorded. Over the next few days it turned into quite a big deal and he rang the players involved to sort it out with them but, as it turned out, worse was to come.

This may have been a massive story in the newspapers but if there was animosity between Sven and the players, I didn't see it. We were more in shock that he had allowed himself to get into that situation, especially when the second load of allegations came out the following Sunday. The quotes from Sven about corruption in football were even more damaging, and it seemed that he really could be on his way out. One of the lads said to me, 'Fucking hell, he's in trouble now,' and so it turned out. On the following Monday the Football Association announced that Sven would be stepping down after the World Cup that summer.

That started a big debate about whether he was suitable to lead the team to Germany, whether the players would respond to a manager whom they knew was leaving. That argument sounded pointless to me. Why would you not perform at a World Cup, regardless of who the manager is? It's your place that's on the line, and so many players in the country want to be in that England team, no one would toss it away. I was so proud to be in the England squad. Whoever the manager was after the World Cup was immaterial. I wanted to do as well as I could, and all the lads felt the same.

I did feel a bit sorry for Sven. It was daft to get involved, and I'm sure he was embarrassed about what he said, but for the players it was, as is normally the case, just a case of laughing at the whole set-up. I mean, a bloke dressed up as a sheikh? What's going on there? When we met up for the Uruguay game we had a meeting and Sven said briefly that we should not worry about the stories that had come out and that he had apologised to those who had been named. By that time, the story was more than a month old. That's a long time in football. We'd moved on.

I suppose we could have done without the constant stories about who was going to get the job after the summer, but you can't blame people for wanting to know. It seemed that the FA wanted Luiz Felipe Scolari, the Brazilian in charge of Portugal, and while I know as much about him as most football fans know, it didn't really seem that important to me. Having not been in the squad that long, I was more interested in playing than worrying about the hierarchy. That was the FA's job. All we wanted to do was go to Germany in the best possible shape for the World Cup.

If you could have listened to the boys in the England squad discussing who the next England manager was going to be, it wouldn't have been that much different from any group of lads in the pub talking about the same thing. We may know a bit more about the characters involved but as far as knowing who it was going to be is concerned, we read the same newspapers as the fans, and we guessed just the same. Before Steve McClaren was appointed, people in the street would stop to ask me who was going to be the next England manager. When I told them politely that I didn't know, I could tell they thought I was lying, or keeping something back.

It's the same when Liverpool fans ask who we are signing in the summer. I haven't got the foggiest idea. Not a clue. Most of the time, I don't even know if I'm playing on Saturday. That's the way it is.

19

THE CUP IN CARDIFF

'Bare Arse' is a legendary game at Liverpool for honing the talents of strikers, and I've become a devotee of it. Lose and you have to stand on the goalline while your team-mates ping the ball at your bare arse; win and you get to do the pinging. It's a regular game after training, although we have had to stop the tradition of actually baring your arse for the punishment.

In November 2005, a couple of weeks before the end of my barren run, someone sneaked a camera over the fences at Melwood and caught me on camera hitting the ball at Steven Gerrard's backside. We'd finished training and had a game of 'Arse', which Stevie had lost. The rules are simple. Everyone gets ten 'sets' – a ball laid off on the edge of the area – and the one who beats the keeper the fewest times has to drop their pants. The rest of us get to whack a ball at them from the penalty spot, but you have to be careful – miss the goal altogether and it's your arse that goes on the line next.

When the newspapers saw these pictures, it must have made their day. 'Crouch can't hit a backside with a banjo!' was the *Daily Mirror*'s spin on it. They assumed Stevie was so confident I would miss that he was even prepared for me to use his arse as a target. I found it quite funny really, especially as it was Stevie whose arse was on display when morning newspapers were opened over breakfast. From then on, though, the rules of 'Bare Arse' had to change. Until we know for sure that no photographers are lurking, we keep our shorts up.

At least there would be no more stories like that after the Wigan game. During December 2005, I scored five goals for Liverpool and started to feel a lot more confident. It's always the same – when you're not scoring, it plays on your mind constantly, and when you are scoring, the ball goes in so easily. My next two goals for Liverpool came in Japan in that strange mid-season tournament for the Fifa club world championship. The winners of all six Fifa 'confederations' – Europe, Africa, Asia, South America, North and Central America and Oceania – compete for the title of best club team in the world. Let's be honest here. I'd much rather win the FA Cup, but since we were there as European Cup winners, we wanted to get the job done.

Japan looked like a fascinating place, although we didn't get much of a chance to look around, and the Japanese seemed to be equally fascinated by me. Blond hair, blue eyes, extremely tall – I wasn't exactly what they were used to. I don't think they could get their heads round it when they saw me walking down the street.

They are such polite people, though. In England, autograph hunters don't hold back. You turn up at a hotel and it's, 'Sign this, mate, sign that.' They're straight in there. It wasn't like that in Japan. A few of us were walking around the enormous hotel where we were staying and were approached by some of the locals asking for autographs. I asked them if they would mind us doing it in about ten minutes or so. No complaints there. We wandered off again around the hotel, having a bit of an exploration, and a few minutes later one of the lads tugged my sleeve and suggested I look behind us.

There must have been more than a hundred people following us in absolute silence, waiting for us to finish so we could sign their pictures and autograph books. There were loads of them, but no pushing or shoving, no one trying to get to the front of the queue. Amazing. I kept getting little written notes passed to me, or gifts. They were very welcoming, but they never went over the top.

We didn't see much of the sights, and took just one trip to an electrical superstore, where I bought a camera, but I still haven't been able to figure out the instructions. One problem with playing on the other side of the world is jetlag, and I spent the whole time absolutely shattered. All the lads were affected by the time difference. I had to ask the doc for sleeping pills to get through the night.

In the tournament, I got two goals in the semi-final against Deportivo Saprissa, the Costa Rican champions, but was left out for the final, which we lost to Sao Paulo from Brazil. Although we would have loved to be crowned the best team in the world, we had bigger concerns at home. The Merseyside derby was coming up and all I could think about was Stevie's bit of wisdom about playing Everton.

'If you score against Everton, Crouchy, it counts as double,' he said.

I fancied a bit of that. Newcastle were first up and I scored against them. Then we put three past Everton at Goodison Park. Eleven minutes into my first Merseyside derby, I took a pass from Stevie and went round Nigel Martyn to score the first goal of the game. It was a great day although we didn't go out as a team to celebrate afterwards – there are some things you just can't risk. Incidents that some people aren't going to be happy about always occur in derby games. If you lose, you don't want to bump into your own fans in a bar because you don't want to be seen as not caring, and if you win, you will always get stick from the blue side of Liverpool. From my experience, it's best to avoid the city on derby days. Winning Merseyside derbies is an achievement to celebrate indoors.

After we came back from Japan we lost just four games in the Premiership all season. One was to Manchester United at Old Trafford, a real sickener in the last minute – unlucky on two counts, because it came from Rio Ferdinand and he never usually scores. Losing 2–0 to Chelsea at Stamford Bridge in February was made even worse by Arjen Robben's antics to get Pepe Reina sent off. His fall in that game was hilarious when you look back at it now. At the time, I said to the referee Alan Wiley, 'What he's just done is embarrassing.' When Robben looks back at it now, he must cringe.

We were getting beaten 2–0 and Pepe had scythed down Eidur Gudjohnsen by the corner flag. He was walking over to the ref when Robben got involved. Pepe put his hand up, pointing at Robben's nose like he had a gun, and down went Robben like a sack of spuds. I was right next to Robben and Pepe barely touched him, hardly connected with him at all. I was telling him to get up. It was embarrassing. Everyone could see it was a joke. Robben probably didn't care. Why should he? Pepe was sent off.

When you join Liverpool, you're left in no doubt that Everton and Manchester United are your two biggest rivals. About a month after we lost to United in the Premiership, we had them at Anfield in the fifth round of the FA Cup, but this time there was more of an edge to the game. After the Premiership game, Gary Neville had run the length of Old Trafford to celebrate right in front of our away fans. He hadn't held back and was not the most popular man on Merseyside come the FA Cup game in February.

I was one of the few Liverpool players who actually saw what Gary did because I was sat on the bench in the dugout, having come off during the game. *What is he doing in front of our fans?* Our supporters were going mad, although I can't recall the media making that big a deal out of it at first. It became an issue during the next few days, mainly because Sky Sports News constantly replayed the footage of it. They really stitched up Gary on that one. Suddenly, there were discussions on phone-ins and people seemed to be talking about it. It meant the game at Anfield was a lot more hostile.

Liverpool supporters and Gary will never see eye-to-eye and this is an emotional topic for both sides, but the incident does pose questions about the relationship between players and fans. As footballers we have to be on our best behaviour on the pitch and that's quite right. I've taken some shit from fans that I would never take from someone in the street, and I've developed a way of coping with it, but it isn't always easy.

It's a strange one. When people are singing something nasty about you, or your family, your natural reaction if you score a goal, or win the game, is to give it back to them about it. It's human nature to react. If fans came up to you in the street and started, let's say, insulting your mum, they know that they wouldn't get away with it. In the street it's not allowed but it is during a game. As far as some fans are concerned, when you're on the pitch, it's different. That's the injustice. If you want to be a footballer, you have to overcome it and you can't react as much as you want to. But we're all human and sometimes you just can't stop yourself. Everyone reacts differently.

None of that helped Gary at Anfield. I was standing beside him at one point when he was taking a throw-in and someone lobbed a cheeseburger at him. I picked it up and made as if I was going to take a bite out of it. Gary was laughing and, thankfully, that sort of missile wasn't going to hurt him – knowing the burgers you get at most football grounds, it would have done him less damage if it had hit him than it would if he'd eaten it.

Nineteen minutes had gone when Finns knocked a ball over from the right and I got my head to it first. It beat Edwin Van der Sar at his left post, rolled along the line and in. And so we beat Manchester United to reach the last eight of the FA Cup.

I'm often criticised for not scoring enough headers, but people who say that haven't followed my career closely. Loads of my goals at Portsmouth and Southampton came from headers, especially at

Pompey. Robert Prosinecki would cross the ball in front of me, rather than at me, so I could attack it – like the second goal of my hat-trick against Arsenal in March 2007, when Fabio Aurelio crossed a beauty from the left.

With Liverpool and England, we use the ProZone system that records every single walk, jog, run and sprint that you make during a game, and measures and times them. At the end of a game you've got a total figure for how much you have moved during a match. And I'm pleased that I always come out on top.

Surprised? I was too. I would have said that, for example, Stevie runs more than I do. It must be all that time I spent in Aston Villa's reserves, doing all that running for Juan Pablo Angel. I run on average 13 kilometres a game and the closest to me at Liverpool is usually midfielder Momo Sissoko, who tends to do about 12 kilometres. The norm for a forward is 8–9 kilometres. The stats tell me that I'm never standing still, but always running around. I don't know why. I'm always trying to offer myself for the ball, I suppose, which means I'm constantly on the move, making angles to receive it. I also try to close down the opposition, which is expected of everyone, and defend set pieces as well.

The importance that many coaches place on ProZone has helped my cause. Steve McClaren uses it a lot. He helped to develop the system when he was an assistant manager at Derby County, and after every England game we are sent DVDs of our performances – every shot, pass, tackle and touch is there. In the build-up to England games, the stats from the last game are displayed on a big board in the canteen. All your stats are broken down into categories – runs, sprints, passes, headers, tackles. Steve McClaren doesn't tell us to look at it because he knows that we will all have a good read. The lads are always surprised at the amount of running I do. Sometimes I wish I could show it to a few other people too.

Competition among strikers at Liverpool is intense, which is something I have had to get used to after my experiences at Queens Park Rangers, Portsmouth and Southampton under Harry Redknapp. Then I knew I was going to play every week. Now I can't be so sure. That's one of the sacrifices you make when you go to a big club and different people take it in different ways. In my first season at Liverpool, Djibril Cisse was one of those who was not happy about being rested – he wanted to play all the time. His character shall we say didn't quite suit Rafael Benitez. Djib was a decent bloke but completely daft. He got on well with all the lads and was obviously a goalscorer in the most basic sense of the word – he wanted to shoot from every angle. He wasn't much of a team player, but he was good to have around the place, and he will be remembered for his outrageous gear.

He'd bought Ridge Manor Estate in Cheshire, which came with a title, so Djib could legitimately call himself Lord of the Manor of Frodsham. It suited his style, to be honest. He would wear unbelievable stuff, even to training, to go with his tattoos, bleached hair and beard. But what I will remember most about Djib is his mobile phone. He had taken the handset off an old Bakelite telephone – the heavy style phones with a big dial – and got someone to customise it so it worked as an extension of his mobile phone. Every time the mobile rang, he would fiddle around plugging in a wire that connected his mobile to the old Bakelite handset. He'd have his mobile in one hand and speak into his old-school Bakelite handset in the other hand.

The FA Cup saved us that season. We had considered ourselves lucky getting Benfica in the first knockout round of the Champions League, and then they knocked us out, beating us home and away. As holders, that was hard to take, and we missed chances at Anfield, myself included. In the FA Cup we steam-rollered Birmingham City

7–0 and I got two, making it four in three games, which set up a semi-final against Chelsea.

That was a big one. After the lads had beaten them in the Champions League semi-final the season before, we had lost 4–1 to them at Anfield, 2–0 at their place and drawn twice in the Champions League. This time we wanted some payback, and we got it at Old Trafford. Chelsea may have had the better of us in the Premiership but, psychologically, in the cups we have the edge over them. John Arne Riise and Luis Garcia got the goals and we were on our way to Cardiff for the final. Luis was one of those players who seems to step up a gear in the big games, and as for Riise, well, the lads cracked up when we found an interview he had given to some magazine about his goal. Apparently, according to him, he had spotted a gap underneath the wall to the left and he had seen the keeper move to his right. So that's why he put the ball where he did. He even described it as a 'phenomenal' goal. I believe he was rather hoping that interview would never find its way into the hands of his team-mates. No chance.

If you grew up loving English football, you know how much the FA Cup means. As a kid, I would make mental lists of the things I wanted to do and top of each one was playing in an FA Cup final. Maybe now winning the Champions League takes precedence, but getting to the Millennium Stadium gave me a huge sense of achievement. It's difficult to explain to the foreign lads. How do you explain about watching the build-up to FA Cup final day on telly as a kid? About the captain introducing his team-mates, the camera on the team bus going to Wembley, the new suits, the new boots, sometimes even a new kit? If you revelled in those details as a kid – and I did – then FA Cup final day was magical. I may sound like a really boring old fart, but I was buzzing to get to the FA Cup final, and that day against West Ham was incredible.

I'd been to Wembley a few times with my dad to support Chelsea. We were there in 1994 when they beat Luton Town in the semi-final and then got done by Manchester United in the final. Dad and I went back in 1997 to see them beat Middlesbrough with a goal from Roberto Di Matteo after 42 seconds. But it's the last Wembley final, in 2000, before they demolished the old stadium, Chelsea v. Aston Villa, that always raises a laugh in the Crouch household. From our house in Ealing, we could walk to Wembley in about forty minutes. That day we stopped off for a beer or two in JJ Moons on Wembley High Road to meet a few mates and sing a few songs. A bit worse for wear, Dad and I continued on our way to the stadium.

Whatever he says, it was my dad's idea to take a cut through. He reckoned the house was empty and if we went through the garden and climbed over the back fence into the street, it would take about ten minutes off our walk. It turned out the fence was quite high, so he gave me a leg up. I scrambled over the top and dropped down to the other side, almost landing on top of a couple of police officers.

'What do you think you're doing?' they said.

I looked round for Dad but he was nowhere to be seen.

'We'd better take your name down, son,' the coppers said.

Over their heads, amid the bushes, I could just see Dad peering over the top of the fence, and signalled silently to him by shaking my head. He said later that he was worried that if he came over too, they might arrest us and we wouldn't get to see the game. That was his story anyway. I got well and truly done – name and address taken, the works. They even made me ring home on my mobile and then took it off me and spoke to my mum.

'This is the police. Is this Peter's mum?'

'Yes. Is he in trouble? Where's his father?'

'Where's your father, Peter?' the coppers asked.

THE CUP IN CARDIFF

I could hardly drop Dad in it then. I just made up some excuse and, after they'd gone, I called for him to come over the fence. He looked a bit sheepish about the whole thing.

At the Millennium Stadium, I was thrilled to be part of it all. The prestige of playing in an FA Cup final is tremendous. I even scored but the goal was ruled out for offside – wrongly, in my opinion. I'm not the type to dwell on goals that should have been, but that was a cruel one to get chalked off. We came back from two goals down and it was my touch that made the chance for Stevie's first. By the time he got his famous second equaliser I was already off, which seemed to be the way for me that season. I would have loved to be among the penalty-takers, although the manager picked them himself. There was no volunteering. We saw the very best of Stevie that day, especially the way he can carry the team in crucial times.

What really spurred us on at half-time? That stupid dance the West Ham players were doing when they scored. I know I'm a fine one to talk when it comes to stupid dances but we had already clocked Nigel Reo-Coker and Anton Ferdinand doing their celebration dances and we felt that, if they won it, our noses would definitely be rubbed in it. That was the way with West Ham – there seemed to be a lot of dancing going on. Even their manager Alan Pardew was into it at one stage. The talk in the dressing room was along the lines of 'We are Liverpool Football Club. This is the FA Cup final and we should be winning. We can't have the West Ham boys doing their little dance around the FA Cup.'

When we finally did win, we celebrated in style. It was great to lift the trophy and bring it back to Liverpool. We had booked the upstairs of the Alma de Cuba restaurant in the city for a meal and a few drinks after. A lot of our fans were in the club and, up on the balcony, we took turns holding up the Cup. Each time it was greeted with a roar. This was the thrill of winning, the thrill of my first major trophy – a great feeling. And then we proceded to get really quite drunk.

That was some night, and somehow I ended up in a casino at about 5 a.m. There was no time for lie-ins the next morning, though, because we were booked for the open-topped bus tour of the city. I have to admit, I felt like death. I'd had barely a few hours' sleep and the hangover was really kicking in. For the first half-hour of the trip, I was sitting down with my head in my hands, thinking about how much I would rather be in bed. I didn't expect too many fans to turn up anyway because they had come out in incredible numbers the year before when the lads had brought home the European Cup. But I had underestimated the Liverpool fans. They were there in their thousands – even when at one stage it started lashing down with rain – and, after a while, I started to perk up a bit.

Going round the city on that bus was an amazing experience and I took pictures that I will cherish forever. It showed me what football means to people in Liverpool, and how important they feel it is to mark every achievement. Liverpool is a close-knit city. When it comes to the way people interact, it can feel like a village. Everyone knows everyone, and everyone is friendly. It's the same with Liverpool FC – in my experience, they are a lot more close-knit than other clubs. You see it in the Liverpool lads in the team. Stevie and Carra live and breathe the club. It hurts them so much when we lose. People talk about players not caring but we do, we care a great deal, and no one more than the local lads in the team. Stevie and Carra talk about football all the time and Carra is the keenest student of the game I know. It's unreal how much he knows about the game in this country and in Spain and Italy. If he isn't suited to go into management after his football career, I don't know who is.

Many people in Liverpool are knowledgeable about the game and you realise that when you meet fans. It's one of the reasons I got through that run without a goal at the start of the season. The fans could see I was trying my hardest and they didn't just write me off. I still remember during my debut for the club, away in a Champions League qualifier against Kaunas in Lithuania at the end of July 2005, I thought that the fans were singing my name. I couldn't be sure, and I didn't want to take it for granted. After the game, Carra shouted across the changing room, 'Did you hear that, Crouchy? That's your song they're singing.'

It was too – 'He's big, he's red, his feet stick out the bed, Peter Crouch, Peter Crouch.' I love that song and as soon as I knew it was mine I started to feel accepted. And it took the fans just one game to come up with it.

20

THE ROBOT

I suppose it was in May of 2006 that life went a bit mad for me, and partly because of a little dance I did when I'd had a few drinks. It will always amaze me how quickly word of the robot dance spread, and how far and wide it went. I decided to do it in a split second at David Beckham's pre-World Cup party, as I walked across the dance floor on my way to the loo. I had no idea of the effect it would end up having.

I remember the build-up to the World Cup for my hat-trick against Jamaica and my goal against Hungary, but a lot of people, especially those who aren't particularly football fans, remember it for my robot dance. I got a taste of what it's like to be caught up in something basically trivial that becomes a big deal in the media. I had newspaper reporters camped outside my parents' house. I'm not complaining, but it was a weird time.

How long did it go on, and how far did it spread? After the World Cup had ended in July, I was on holiday in Miami with a few mates. Walking past a bar, I heard someone shout at me in an American accent, 'HEY, ROBOT BOY!' I would have ignored it but one of my mates looked round at where the noise was coming from.

'Isn't that Mickey Rourke shouting at you?' he said.

It certainly was. If hard-living old Hollywood stars had seen me do my robot dance, who knows how many more people had seen it? I couldn't resist going over to Mickey to say hello. I've got a photograph of us doing the robot together. He turned out to be a top bloke. These things seem to have a life of their own.

Before the FA Cup final, at the end of the season, England's World Cup preparations had taken a massive blow. On 29 April at Stamford Bridge, Wayne Rooney chased a ball with Paulo Ferreira, stumbled, fell and broke the metatarsal bone in the fifth toe of his right foot. It's a deadly injury. Michael Owen had done the same on New Year's Eve and was only just getting back to fitness at the end of the season. Wayne's injury was desperate for his chances of playing in Germany. Suddenly, the whole country was in a panic. If we didn't have Wayne, who was going to score the goals?

I was gutted for Wayne. I had got to know him well and I like him a lot. He's down-to-earth, hilarious at times, and certainly one of the characters in the squad. It never bothered me that he was selected ahead of me but my reaction when he was injured was the same as any other player's in similar circumstances – now he's out, does that mean I'm going to be involved? I'm not ashamed to say that. Anyone in my position would be the same. Wayne and Michael Owen were the first-choice strikers for England and now, unless they could both prove their fitness in time, Sven would have to do something different.

I remember it clearly, that first dawning of realisation that my place in the team could be changing dramatically. You can feel it. Your heart starts racing, and you start to think about what lies ahead of you. *I am going to be playing in the World Cup. I have got a massive opportunity.* You always hope that you will play in more than one major international tournament with England, more than one World Cup, but you never really know. It could be one of those once-in-a-lifetime opportunities. I wanted to take mine with both hands.

In the build-up to the World Cup squad announcement on 8 May, I found myself in a nice position. As newspaper and television pundits tried to predict the squad that Sven would take, it seemed that I was a definite on everyone's lists. As someone who has learned throughout his career never to take anything for granted, this was a new experience. It seemed my performances that season, less than a year after making my debut, had been enough. I felt like I was a veteran – and when the squad was announced, I really did feel old compared with some of those who had been brought in. Theo Walcott, aged 17, had never played a Premiership game, and so he was a surprise.

The Football Association couldn't have made it much worse for him by the way they unveiled the squad. I watched the announcement on television and, up on the stage in front of the cameras, the FA had twenty-three kids wearing the shirts of each of the players selected. It must have been a great day for the kids – they met Sven and were given a free England shirt – but it left poor Theo open to an easy gag. Was the kid wearing the Walcott shirt a schoolboy or was it Theo himself?

Theo's not the only one who has suffered with the business of mascots in football. At most matches, especially Champions League games and internationals, each player walks out holding the hand of a kid who is wearing the opposition team's strip. It's great for the kids, who get to stand in front of us when the anthems are played and have their pictures taken. We're only with them for a few minutes. Basically, they wait in the tunnel and you get assigned one just before you walk out.

It was a tradition when I was at Portsmouth, too, although one Saturday afternoon I got a bit more than I bargained for. In the tunnel before the game, I stuck out my hand without really looking for one of the kids to take before we walked out, and was surprised to find the hand that gripped it back particularly firm for your average nine-year-old. I looked to my right and there, looking back at me, holding my hand, was a fully grown man wearing the Portsmouth home kit. It took me a second to work out what the hell was going on.

'What you doing here, mate?' I asked – still holding his hand.

'I've won a competition to be a mascot.'

'I'm not sure about this,' I replied.

'But I've won a competition,' he said.

I was only 20 at the time and he must have been at least twice my age. He had a beard while I was barely shaving. As much as I'm open-minded about these things, there was no way I was going to walk out at Fratton Park hand-in-hand with this geezer, looking like one half of Hampshire's happiest gay couple. I took my hand away and thought to myself that this had to be a stitch-up.

It turned out that he really was supposed to be there and that the club had assigned him to me because I was the tallest and he'd look least out of place that way. But those kind of practical jokes are commonplace in football, although no one has ever gone to the lengths that Rio Ferdinand did in his 'World Cup wind-ups' programme that summer. Rio set up a number of elaborate practical jokes on members of the squad, which were secretly filmed for a television show. He had everything from David Beckham being kidnapped to Gary Neville being arrested by a fake copper, from Wayne Rooney being blamed for the death of a little boy's dog to Shaun Wright-Phillips inadvertently getting an over-friendly waiter the sack. In my case, the stitch-up involved one dwarf and three Russian gangsters.

It was a brilliant set-up. Robbie Fowler and Steven Gerrard were in on it and they lured me into the trap. Robbie was on at me for ages to come to meet some bloke who was doing discount properties for England players. I wasn't interested one bit but Robbie went on and on about it, and Stevie chipped in after training one day.

'This bloke's a top man, Crouchy,' he said. 'I'm involved. You should do it.' So, like an idiot, I went along with Robbie.

The rest you may have seen on television, but what you won't have been shown was how I sussed it halfway through. We went to the Radisson Hotel in Liverpool city centre where, unbeknown to me, the hotel room we were heading for had been rigged up with cameras. Rio and the television crew were watching in the next room. The basic plot was that an 'Indian businessman' and his assistant, who was a dwarf, were offering me an apartment in some posh Middle East development. Then we were to be interrupted by three 'Russian gangsters', demanding that the businessman pay his debts or have his finger cut off. Oh yeah, and two girls dressed in their underwear 'accidentally' showed up as well.

The dwarf was the first gag. He had a little stepladder that he used to see through the peephole in the door. When he let us in and I saw that, I had to fight not to laugh. I have nothing against small people. It's just that I was embarrassed, and Robbie was trying to make me laugh. I didn't want to hurt the bloke's feelings, so I was desperately trying to keep it all in. We sat on the sofa and waited for the businessman character to arrive. I hadn't smelt a rat at that point, but when the girls came in I did begin to get suspicious, and I said something I've never said before, or since, in my life. God knows why. These girls came into the room giggling, I was embarrassed and surprised, and for some reason I uttered one word in response – 'Wowser.' Wowser? I don't know where that came from, but the funny thing is that when we watched the programme together as a squad in Germany, it was me saying 'Wowser' that got the biggest laugh from my team-mates. They cracked up at that one.

When the 'Russians' came bursting in and started to threaten the 'Indian businessman', I knew it was a stitch-up. I was saying, 'Come on, where are the cameras?' The actors just ignored me and carried on and that bit was cut out of the show. If you watch the clip, you'll notice that towards the end we are talking about the 'property development' that I'm supposed to be interested in. The 'Indian businessman' shows me a picture of this offshore development and part of the gag is that it's shaped like, shall we say, a gentleman's private parts. A few minutes later, when I'm explaining to the 'Russians' what I'm doing there, I say, 'I only came here to look at these apartments that are shaped like a penis.' I used the polite term because by then I knew I was on television.

I loved the show and Rio did a great job. In fact, I was more than happy to be part of it because the night we sat down as a squad to watch it together was one of the best. We were roaring with laughter at the looks on different people's faces as they realised they'd been fooled. I thought the lads came out of it really well – Shaun desperately trying to persuade the restaurant manager not to sack the waiter, and Gary's honesty with the copper. I know that, to the fans, players can sometimes seem very distant and I think Rio's show revealed their human side.

Our first World Cup warm-up game was the B international against Belarus, which I started, and I did quite well. The B inter-national is a weird one. I thought those games had been abandoned years ago. It was played at Reading and we lost 2–1, but the point of the match was to give the squad players a run-out. Apart from Michael Owen playing, the only big story of the night was an awful injury to goalkeeper Rob Green. It was atrocious and we all felt terrible for him but, and there's no easy way of saying this, the way he did it was very funny. I know it meant that he missed the World Cup and I know it must have hurt, but football dressing rooms are cruel places and the lads take the mick whatever you've done to yourself. Poor old Rob wasn't spared.

He had only been on the pitch five minutes after coming on as a half-time sub when he went to take a goal-kick on the left of his area. He basically collapsed as he struck the ball and it just sliced off straight to the feet of Vitaly Kutuzov, the Belarus striker. Kutuzov took a couple of strides and rolled it into the net past Rob, who was still on the floor, writhing in agony, for the equaliser.

My first reaction? That he was taking the piss. That he had messed up the goal-kick and was pretending to be injured after giving away a comedy goal. Then I realised he really was hurt, and looked up in the stand to where Rio and Stevie were sitting. *Thank God that wasn't me.* All the players felt terrible for Rob but at the same time we were trying to suppress a laugh. That's the black humour of football. Sometimes it's the very worst things that are the funniest, and because you know you're not supposed to laugh that makes you want to all the more. Rob had the biggest lump where his groin had just torn. He needed an operation to sort it out.

The Sunday before our last week in England was the Beckham World Cup party at their house in Hertfordshire. It was a big do – P. Diddy, James Brown and Robbie Williams provided entertainment, and plenty of famous people were there, along with most of the World Cup squad. I was going on my own, or at least I would be walking up the red carpet on my own, but for the journey to the place known as 'Beckingham Palace', all the Crouch family came along – Mum, Dad and Sarah. And we managed to get there late.

As soon as Mum opened the car door a load of camera flashes went off, which caught her totally by surprise, so she shut it again. I said goodbye and walked up to the entrance while Dad made to turn the car around. He wanted to go out the way he had come in but the security guards wouldn't let him.

'Sorry, mate,' they said, 'the drivers have got to wait around the back.'

'But I'm not a driver. I'm Peter Crouch's dad.'

'Round the back please.'

I still give my dad stick about this now. While he was drinking tea out of a polystyrene cup around the back of the house with the rest of the chauffeurs, I was sipping champagne and having my picture taken with Jodie Kidd and Elle Macpherson. That's the way it goes sometimes.

It was surreal seeing all these famous people at a footballer's party – a bit different from a night out in Acton with the Queens Park Rangers boys. I was on a table with Nigel Reo-Coker, Stevie, Carra and Michael Owen, as well as their wives and partners. Our table was right next to the dance floor. The food was brilliant, the marquee was incredible and there was an auction for charity. Sharon Osbourne, Gordon Ramsay, Tom Cruise and Liz Hurley were among the guests, and they sat me next to Reo-Coker. Single lads get put together I suppose.

We had great craic, drinks were going down and I had started to forget that the whole thing was being filmed. I've got a bit of a thing for the dance floor at weddings and parties. It seems to draw me to it, especially after I've had a few drinks. I like to think I can encourage people to get out of their seats and on to an empty dance floor by doing a few moves. I got up to go to the loo but the dance floor, which was on the way, was too good to resist. I tapped Carra on the shoulder.

'Check out this move, mate. Watch and learn.'

Little did I know that, as I wandered off, Carra was getting everyone to look at me, most of all the cameraman, whom he told to follow me. I hadn't noticed any of that. I just hit the floor and did the robot. Why the robot? Well, why not? Everyone knows the robot. If you're pissed in a club, the robot is the one to do. It's just a stupid dance, up there with body-popping. I've always found it funny, but I wouldn't say it was my trademark. I suppose when you're as tall as I am, you look even funnier, but when I did it, I never had any intention for it to become as big as it did. I just did it to give Carra a laugh.

So there I was doing the robot and, as I swivelled round robot-style, the camera was right in front of me. I didn't really know what to do, so I did the honourable thing – kept on going. I finished off with a little kick and went on my way to the toilet. All the boys were roaring with laughter and clapping. By the end of the night I'd forgotten about it because things had become considerably livelier. At one point I recall that Andrew Flintoff and I were carrying Frankie Dettori around above our heads, although in our defence we'd had quite a bit to drink by then. I had never met Flintoff before but he's a top bloke.

It was a great night out. I'm a big believer in getting the lads together for an evening out. I have always found it brings everyone out of themselves and makes them feel more comfortable within the squad, and happy footballers train and play better as a team. At the Beckhams' party, everyone got together and it worked a treat. At the start of almost two months together, it gave the lads something to talk about as well, and if you're going away for that length of time, you need to get on with each other. The party was Becks' choice. He gets some stick for those sorts of things, but I felt it definitely brought us closer together as a squad.

The programme about the party was on television the night before the first of our last two warm-up games, against Hungary. Becks had said to me that his wife Victoria had been with the show's producers editing the programme, and they had some funny footage of me. Would I mind if they put it in? Of course I said go ahead, but I didn't really think anything of it.

In the last week before we left for Germany, we were in the

Lowry Hotel in Manchester while we trained at Carrington, Manchester United's training ground. We were interested to see what was in the programme about the Beckham party and most of the lads watched it. The footage of me dancing came right at the very end, just a five-second cameo really, and the sight of me doing the robot about one foot from the camera lens brought it all back in an instant. Immediately, I could hear roars of laughter coming from all the lads' rooms. My phone was going mad with calls and texts from people asking me if I had seen it. The lads in the squad loved it and from then on they were on at me. If I scored, I had to do the robot.

Against Hungary, we played a strange kind of formation, with Carra as a holding midfielder and Stevie as a second striker behind Michael Owen, and in the first half Frank Lampard missed a penalty. I was on the bench. John Terry and Stevie got a couple of quick goals before Hungary pulled one back and, with about 25 minutes left, I finally got on. Joe Cole was having another one of those days when the opposition couldn't get the ball off him. With six minutes left, he went on a mazy run, cutting in from the left wing across the front of the box. Joe delayed his pass right until the last minute, a beautiful little ball in to me on the edge of the area. I took one touch to control it and hit it on the turn into the far corner of the Hungary goal.

It felt so good to score at Old Trafford, the ground where I had been booed by the England fans eight months earlier. I was in a totally different place from where I had been then. I was flying, and as soon as the ball hit the back of the net I knew I was going to do the robot. I didn't intend it to be anything more than a bit of fun, something for the lads to laugh at and that would be it, but the next day it just went mad.

I suppose it caught people's imagination, but to a level that I would never have expected. The next day my robot dance was on Sky News and Sky Sports News, as well as on other news channels, including CNN. Some of the tabloids had it on the front page as well as the back. Since then, I have seen variations of it on websites, like YouTube, and I'm still at a loss to explain why people liked it so much. Even now people shout at me in the street to 'do the robot'. Perhaps it's partly because football, and especially the England team, is such a serious business. Everything we do is scrutinised. We have to be on our best behaviour at all times but, for once, everyone could see that we were having a laugh. The fact that we won the game probably helped. You could see the other players who came up to congratulate me laughing as well. If anything, I hope that it showed I can have a laugh at my own expense.

The day after the Hungary game, we had a special visitor at training. Prince William is president of the Football Association and he turned up to wish us all well for Germany. We were already on the pitch at Carrington and there were loads of press photographers and camera crews around. Even though he does it thousands of times, it must be hard for Prince William to have to make polite conversation with total strangers. This time he had to chat with twenty or so footballers who knew that if they said one thing they were going to get the piss taken by their team-mates later. It took David James to get the conversation started, and then I think it was Rio who asked the Prince why it was he supported Aston Villa. He explained that he had always liked them, from when he was a kid. Something approaching a proper conversation was getting going when Carra piped up, 'What do you think of Crouchy's robot then?'

'Oh, it was awesome, great to see,' said the Prince. He was grinning, and seemed to mean it.

Then Carra spoke up again, and I could have guessed what was coming.

'Come on, Crouchy lad, show him the robot. Come on, give him a bit of the robot.'

I really didn't want to. I don't mind making an idiot of myself when everyone's had a few drinks and we're on a night out, but at ten o'clock in the morning in a field in Manchester, in front of the future King of England, with reporters and photographers from all the nation's newspapers and television stations standing 50 yards away, lenses trained on us? No thanks. But I glanced around me, at the faces of my team-mates, and the man second in line to the British throne, and the realisation struck me that it would be a lot quicker – and easier – to get it over and done with there and then.

So I went for it – just a little one but it got them all laughing and me off the hook. And with that we got on with training. I couldn't quite believe I'd done it – the first time I'd met royalty and I'd ended up doing a dance.

When we finished training, a few of us – Frank Lampard, Steven Gerrard, David Beckham, Wayne Rooney, John Terry, Rio Ferdinand and I – were invited for a private chat with Prince William back at the hotel. We may have been footballers, and from totally different backgrounds from him, but we got on really well. We had more of a chat with him there than we'd had on the training pitch. I liked him a lot. He came across very well and I could see the lads were impressed with the way he conducted himself. He told us that he was going to get out to a game in Germany if possible. After a while I think a few of us even forgot we were talking to the second in line to the throne, it was all pretty informal. We asked him about his life, about his younger brother Prince Harry and his plans for the future. I suppose all of the footballers around that table had endured a bit of press interest in their private lives in the past but no-one apart from Becks will have had as much as William. And don't worry: I know the royal protocol, so I can't tell you exactly what was said between us and the man who would be king.

At home, things were getting a bit intense after the robot dance. Newspaper reporters not only camped outside Mum and Dad's house but also followed Mum to the park when she was walking Buster, the family dog. They were asking weird questions, such as, 'Is that Peter's dog?' All the neighbours got knocks on the door, so did my school and even my grandparents.

The funniest reaction to it came from Ivy, a very sweet old lady who lives a few doors down. She came round to see my mum one day. Ivy's known us since we moved to the area and she has always been very kind to Sarah and me. I wouldn't say she was the world's biggest football fan, although she had some idea that I had reached some level of fame by playing the game. Anyway, she was a bit worried.

'Jayne, I think I said too much to the newspapers about Peter,' she said. 'I hope I haven't given the game away.'

'What did you say?' Mum asked.

'I said, "I don't know anything about the dance but I know he's a lovely boy and he was nice to his sister when she was a little girl."'

That became a family joke: 'EXCLUSIVE! Ivy lifts the lid on Crouch family secrets – Pete was nice to his sister when he was a kid'.

It was unreal. The newspapers were after whatever they could get and I suppose I was the man of the moment. Locked away in the England team hotel I didn't realise until after the World Cup just how mad it had all become. With Wayne out injured, I guess the newspapers were looking for a story to fill the space, and for a while, a 6ft 7in. footballer with his own robot dance did the trick.

The best was yet to come, though. Two days before we left for Germany I scored a hat-trick against Jamaica at Old Trafford. It was a mad game played on a roasting hot day and I will remember it for the rest of my life. I've watched those goals on video enough times to know the moves for each one inside out. They are among the proudest moments of my career – and the penalty I missed when I was on two goals is one of the most embarrassing. I started the game, alongside Michael Owen, still full of confidence from the Hungary game, but when it came to the penalty, my judgement wasn't the best.

We were 2–0 up when I got my first on 29 minutes, a volley from Becks' corner. We were 4–0 up when I got my second, a tap-in from Carra's cross from the right. I was on a high – three goals in two games for England. The crowd were loving it and so was I. I didn't think I could do any wrong. So when Mo was brought down with eight minutes left, I grabbed the ball for the penalty. I wasn't actually supposed to be taking the penalties but this felt right. It felt like the moment I took the ball against Portsmouth in November in front of the Kop (although that one didn't go in either). This was it – my hat-trick for England. I was following in the footsteps of the greats – Geoff Hurst, Jimmy Greaves, Gary Lineker.

'Crouchy, what you gonna do?' asked Joe Cole.

'I'm going to dink him.'

'No way, mate! You can't.'

But I wouldn't be persuaded otherwise. I had visions of Ian Wright's great penalties for Arsenal. He would run up full pelt to the penalty spot and then hit a delicate dink down the middle as the keeper threw himself to one of the corners. That was the way I was I was going to do it. I was going to get this hat-trick in style. Never mind the robot, this would be the new Crouchy-style. Dinked penalties, casual as you like; 6–0 to England – or not.

I sent goalkeeper Donovan Ricketts the wrong way but the ball sailed over the bar and into the stand. I had got it totally wrong. The crowd groaned and it was like I had come round from the giddiness of my previous state. Then it hit home how stupid I had been. How many opportunities do you get to score a hat-trick for England? Not many. Only twenty-three other players in the history of English football have achieved it. I had got carried away with the robot dance and scoring two goals and done something really daft – trying to take the piss when I should have just stuck it in the corner.

I thought my chance had gone but with a minute to go I latched on to a ball from Michael Owen and curled it into the corner of the net. Thank God for that. I'd had an amazing day, an amazing week in fact, but in the end I was just grateful that the missed penalty was not the end of the story.

In the aftermath of the game, Sven said that he spoke to me about the way I took the penalty and – in a very rare moment for him – he actually criticised me to the press for messing about and not putting it away simply. I completely accept that I acted like an idiot, but the funny thing is Sven didn't pull me aside or have a go at me at all. In fact, I approached him.

The first person I saw when I walked into the dressing room was Steve McClaren.

'You know what you did with the penalty was wrong, don't you Crouchy?' he said.

'Yeah, I was stupid,' I replied. 'I should have taken it properly.'

Then I went to find Sven.

'Boss, I have got to apologise. I should have taken that penalty properly,' I said.

Sven didn't say much, just that it was OK, and then ten minutes later he was telling the press that he'd told me off about it.

'A golden opportunity to practise penalties,' Sven said to the press, 'and he joked about.'

He certainly didn't say that to me. That was Sven's last home game for England and the crowd gave him a proper send-off. We felt we were going to do well in Germany. There had been nothing wrong with our preparation for the World Cup and there was no problem with the squad's mood or confidence. Two days later, on 5 June, we flew to Germany expecting good things.

21

AT CASTLE GREYSKULL

Our team bus seemed to be heading for the middle of nowhere, high up in Germany's Black Forest where the road was barely wide enough for two cars to pass. The hotel that would be our World Cup home for the next month or so was a huge old building, the Bühlerhöhe Schlosshotel – or 'Castle Greyskull' as the lads called it. We were going to spend our days in the quiet countryside, well away from the World Cup madness that was taking over Germany.

The Football Association didn't let us down – the hotel was brilliant. When we arrived we all went straight out on to the terrace, from where you could see for miles and miles over the hills and mountains of southern Germany. That was after we had negotiated the welcome party that the locals from the village of Bühl had put on for us, with lots of banners, singing kids and dancing adults. It was very kind of them to go to such trouble, but you know what footballers are like. When the big bloke at the front started yodelling, or something like that, there were a few lads trying hard not to laugh.

This would be our base for the entire World Cup, although the night before a game we would stay near where we were playing. The hotel was a few miles outside the spa town of Baden Baden, where our families stayed and most of the press were based, and the FA had also hired a local stadium not far away in Bühlertal, where we trained and held press conferences. It was all extremely well organised. We had the whole hotel to ourselves and the FA had done everything possible to make sure our stay was comfortable and our preparations were spot-on. Flicking through the brochures in my room, I read that the place had been a hospital for injured German soldiers after the First World War; the good people at the FA had transformed it into a modern English footballers' paradise.

The games room was like Neverland, a Santa's grotto for grown-up kids, full of PlayStations and Xboxes as well as golf simulators and driving games. You would wander in there and find Joe Cole hunched over the steering wheel of a Mario Karts machine, trying to beat his personal best. We played a football management strategy game against each other and I dispatched a few people on the table-tennis table. People like Martin Grogan, our kitman, who turned up in Germany with his own bat and obviously fancied himself as a bit of a pro.

On the walls around the hotel, the FA had put up pictures of the England team, and on the door of everyone's room was an action shot of them playing, so you knew who was where. A lot had been made of the hotel having to order in a new big bed especially for me but I didn't notice that it was any longer than those at most hotels. I was just glad that we were well away from Baden Baden from where my dad was telling me that things were getting pretty mad right from the start. Paparazzi were parked right outside the hotel where the players' families were staying. If we had stayed there, or in any city, I don't think we would have got a moment's peace.

People said we would get bored, but I loved it up in the hotel in the mountains. On the tennis courts I showed the lads the skills I had honed at the Brentham Club all those years ago. On one occasion, Jermaine Jenas, Ashley Cole, masseur Rod Thornley and I got a real game going. Before we knew it we'd played a set and were sweating like mad. Sven was watching us from the balcony, then he disappeared and a few minutes later Sammy Lee showed up and told us to pack it in. We'd hardly noticed that we'd stepped up several gears. We're all sportsmen and in any competitive situation we want to win. The tennis had turned into a proper battle. The funny thing is, I can remember reading about Paul Gascoigne getting told off by Bobby Robson for playing tennis in the sun during the 1990 World Cup.

Everyone passed the time in his own way. A lot of the lads went down to Baden Baden to see their families if we were given an afternoon off, although not everyone did the same thing. Our goalkeeper David James – 'Jamo' to the lads – is a veteran of international tournaments. He is also a talented artist and spent a lot of his time working on portraits of the other players. That's his way of relaxing and Jamo isn't afraid to be different.

One morning of a day off, we were sat in the breakfast room, discussing going down into Baden Baden. Jamo had other plans.

'I'm going there today,' he said, pointing out across the terrace. We all followed his gaze towards the horizon.

'Where?' we asked.

'The chimney,' said Jamo.

If you looked carefully, you could just about see a single chimney miles away in the distance, among the trees, all on its own. We thought he was mucking about at first but that was where he went – deep into the countryside to draw the chimney. Jamo would often go off on his own to look at buildings, or visit an art gallery, around Baden Baden.

The mood of the team in training was good. We were sharp and looking forward to our first game, against Paraguay in Frankfurt, although all the talk had been about Wayne Rooney's broken metatarsal. Would he be fit to play? Would the doctors pass him? He had been named in the squad but the crunch came on 7 June when he flew back to Manchester for a scan.

The entire episode was mad. It seemed as though the whole country was talking about Wayne's foot but up in Castle Greyskull we tried to remain a little calmer. We all believed Wayne would play a part in the tournament but as for not being able to play without him, that wasn't the case. He was a very important player but we had enough talent in the squad to make sure we won the games we played without him. When a player is injured, the rest of you just get on with it. It's worse for the injured player, who usually gets shunted off to train on his own. We had a job to do, with or without Wayne, and that's how we saw it.

When he came back from Manchester, word was that Wayne's injury had healed but that he wouldn't be fit to play until after the group stage. We still felt confident. We had played well leading up to the World Cup and training had gone well. In the final sessions before the match against Paraguay, when we were concentrating on team shape, it became clear to me that I was going to start. I also noticed a hint of nerves around the lads, which was unusual – nothing major, just that some of the boys were quieter than usual. All the same, we felt that we would go on and have a good tournament.

That afternoon in Frankfurt was ridiculously hot. The ground was packed out with England fans, George crosses everywhere, and having come down from our perch up in the Black Forest, we were getting a taste of what it meant to be part of the World Cup at last. We had a great start – an own goal from Carlos Gamarra headed in from Becks' cross from the left in the fourth minute. Maybe people expected us to go out and win 4–0 but Paraguay were a decent side and hard to break down. If your club side wins 1–0 you're happy, but with England there is so much more pressure. We got a result and we were all pleased with that but we knew we could play better and we thought once we got going we would click. You don't really recognise the magnitude of the event when you're playing, but it was amazing just to be there, and getting the result was what mattered.

At the end of the game, we were dehydrated and had blisters on our feet. Playing in that kind of weather is draining, although we weren't rushing up and down the pitch like we do in the Premiership, when it's usually pouring with rain and cooler. English players are suited to colder climates and a more high-tempo game, and we got sucked into playing in a continental way, which is less intense and with a slower build-up. We have players with the ability to do that but we are better when we are attacking teams.

Back in the isolation of the team hotel we didn't really have much of an idea about what was going on down in Baden Baden, despite the bits and pieces reported to us by our families. We didn't have any newspapers at the hotel, so it was only when the lads went down to the town, and came across the papers, that they realised the impact the players' wives and girlfriends – WAGs as they became known – were making. The debate about whether the families should be there had already begun in the few articles I read. Personally, I thought it was a good idea but others were making a big issue of it. We weren't playing every day and there were five days between the group games. If you were back in England, you wouldn't be away from your family and friends for that length of time. We were in Germany five days before the Paraguay match and up until the Thursday before the Saturday of the game, I thought it was right that we did things as normal, which meant spending some time relaxing with our families. Come the Thursday, that's when we really went into game mode.

The way it looked in the newspapers, the Brenners Park Hotel – where the families stayed – seemed chaotic. The girls were on the front pages and we were on the back. It looked like a strange environment to be in but you wouldn't have known that speaking to Mum, Dad and Sarah. From the stories they were telling me, it sounded like they were having a great time. My sister absolutely loved it. She was on a girls' holiday. I'd ring them up and they would say they had been out with the Carragher family or the Nevilles or the Joe Coles. For Mum, Dad and Sarah, after watching me play in some of the pokiest grounds in the Championship, this was their reward and I was pleased that they were having a good time.

Some things never change, though. Apparently, at the Paraguay game Dad did get a bit fierce with a fan who was giving me a bit of stick. As a family, the abuse I have taken from the fans has become something we cope with, but Dad takes exception when it happens right under his nose. This bloke, who turned out to be German, was standing in front of him, shouting abuse at me even before kick-off. 'Why is that lanky so-and-so playing?' The usual stuff.

Dad tapped him on the shoulder. 'I think you'd better move, mate,' he said.

'Why?' the German bloke said. And then, Dad said, you could see him working it out. It slowly dawned on him who he was speaking to, and he moved.

There weren't that many bars in Baden Baden and apparently they had never seen anything like the number of people in town that month. Mum and Dad got to know Becks' mum, Sandra, who apparently had an incredible radar for when someone – usually an undercover reporter – was trying to stitch them up. I suppose if your son is one of the most famous people in the world, you get to know these things. They were out with a few of the families in a bar called Garibaldis one night when a couple sat down next to them and started speaking German. There was a bag left on the table. One of the parents turned to Dad and said, 'I bet there's a tape recorder in that bag recording us.' Dad was surprised – but he wanted to know. So when the woman got up, he picked up the bag, opened it and looked inside. He said he would have apologised and bought them a drink if he'd been wrong. Sure enough, there was a tape recorder and it was on. Dad smashed it on the floor, gathered up the pieces and dropped them back in the bag before the woman came back. That was his lesson to watch what he said, and where he said it.

As well as Jamo, I had got to know a few other members of the squad better during a break we had in Portugal before the friendlies against Hungary and Jamaica. The Algarve trip was a great bit of relaxation at the end of the season and the lads had been able to bring their families, so, as single boys, Owen Hargreaves, Stewart Downing, Rob Green and I knocked around together. Like Jamo, Greeny is another goalkeeper who isn't afraid to be a bit different. We were giving him some stick for living on his own in Norwich, which he was doing at the time and, as I knew myself, that could be a lonely experience. 'What do you do with yourself?' we asked him.

We were a bit surprised when he said he went to the pub every night. Surely he was joking. You can't go into training every morning with a hangover. But apparently that's not how it works for Greeny. He's at West Ham now but he told us then that, at Norwich, most nights he would wander into his local, give the landlord the nod and get a seat by the fire. Then he would open the book he had brought with him, the barman would bring him over a tea in a big Norwich City mug and Greeny would sit there and read. That's one way to pass the time in Norwich.

I really did feel sorry for Greeny when he was injured so close to the World Cup because he's a good bloke and great company. When we were in Chicago the year before with England, we'd been given one afternoon to look around the city and I'd gone out with AJ. As we waited at some lights an open-topped bus tour had pulled up with the tourist guide speaking into a microphone, telling people about the sights. 'Not my idea of an exciting afternoon,' I said to AJ. And as we looked up at the top deck of the bus, there was Greeny sitting at the front, taking it all in. Good old Greeny, he knows what he likes and he doesn't care what people think about him.

That week in Portugal was a different experience from our time in Germany. We chilled out. We could go to restaurants as a team for a meal. Again, I was on the singles' table with Downing, Greeny, Owen Hargreaves and Nigel Reo-Coker. Reo-Coker was a funny one. He was one of the back-up players and never went to Germany, but he definitely managed to get himself noticed at one of the dinners in Portugal. Sven's partner, Nancy Dell'Olio, was going round the tables and chatting, saying, 'Thanks for coming,' and that sort of thing. As she came over to us, Reo-Coker took one look at her and shouted 'BADDA-BADDA-BADDA-BING!' It's the catchphrase from the television show 'Soccer AM' and basically it means – and this is putting it politely – 'She's good-looking.' Everyone around us heard it. I looked at the rest of the lads, not quite believing what I'd heard. Judging by their expressions, the boys felt the same. *Has he really just done that?* I'm glad to say I don't think Nancy clocked it. She was a nice woman, very friendly towards my family, and when we finally went out of the tournament she was in tears. She took the time to get to know people and she was really upset when it all ended.

Wayne was the centre of attention again before our game against Trinidad and Tobago on 15 June. The surgeon flew out to Germany to examine him before the game and this time Sven decided he was fit enough to be named as a sub. The plan was to beat Trinidad and bring him back for the Sweden game, which was the last group match, but after an hour, Wayne was on the pitch. Once again we were struggling for goals against one of the weakest teams in the tournament. It didn't help that I had misjudged a volley from a cross from the right that would have looked spectacular if it had gone in.

It was the old scissor-kick and I had launched myself at it. I had scored them before and I have scored them since – that day it just didn't happen for me. Looking back on it, I know I should have brought the ball down and finished it – but it was instinctive. Thank God I've scored a couple since then, against Galatasaray and Bolton, so people know that I can put them away. At the time, I sensed the rumblings in the stadium, as though the crowd were saying, 'What's he doing?' The stick would have been a lot worse if we hadn't managed to turn the game around in the last ten minutes.

It's not what people want to hear when we're playing sides such as Trinidad, but they were hard to break down. They were well organised and had just about everyone behind the ball. There were nerves among the lads because everyone was planning on us pummelling them. If we had scored early, we would have gone on and got four or five, but that didn't happen and we didn't play well. Wayne and Aaron Lennon were on for the last half-hour as we pushed for the winner.

There were seven minutes left when Becks picked up the ball on the right wing, glanced up and put in one of his trademark crosses to the back post, just where I wanted it – far enough ahead so I could run on to it and attack the ball. *I'm going to get on the end of this.* I jumped, connected – 1–0 to England. The stadium in Nuremberg went crazy. I ran down the byline towards the corner flag and stopped in front of the England fans with my arms outstretched as the boys piled in on me. What a sweet moment. There are not many who get to play in the biggest tournament in the world, let alone score in it. I hope that I will get more in 2010 but, if not, at least I'll be able to say that I scored in the World Cup finals.

The relief when the ball went in was huge, and Stevie scored a brilliant goal in injury time to seal it. I didn't have a clue about the controversy surrounding my goal. As I had gone up to head the ball, the cameras caught me pulling the hair of the Trinidad defender

Brent Sancho. It happened in a split second and I didn't remember a thing about it. In the English media the incident was virtually ignored – but not in Germany. All the other nations' television stations were going mad about it.

The German interviewer who spoke to me after the game was getting really excited, asking me about cheating. I had to stop him and ask him what he was talking about. They were calling it the 'Hand of God' for a joke, so I asked to see the replay to find out what all the fuss was about. They had a point. Sancho had long dreadlocks and as I went up for the ball I had given them a sharp tug. If you watch it closely, you can see his head snap back as I give his dreads a pull. The referee couldn't see what happened because Sancho's hair was hanging low down his back. I didn't think anything of it. None of the English reporters even asked me about it but when we got back to the team hotel, the staff were laughing and miming me pulling Sancho's hair.

With Wayne back in action, there wasn't much debate about him playing alongside Michael Owen against Sweden. That was just the way it went and, although I wanted to play as much as anyone, I accepted it. I got on really well with Mo. We knocked around the hotel together and played a few games of cards. That was us yearning after the lost days of the much-missed England card school. Mo's great but I wish he hadn't complained after the Trinidad game that we were playing too many long balls. They're not much good for Mo but, as I've said before, that's not the way I like to play either, and it came across that he was blaming it on me. I was just as keen for us to play the ball to feet.

Pretty soon things turned really bad for Mo. His injury against Sweden was horrific. The second he went down I could tell it was bad. He just went down so awkwardly, bounced up and then went down again – it didn't look good at all. It happened in the first minute of the match, which is weird when you're a sub because your mind isn't quite ready to be thrown into the action. I know you should be ready at any moment but subconsciously you're thinking you'll be on at half-time at the earliest, or more likely around the hour. Then suddenly the manager was turning to me. *Christ, I'm on.* Of course, after those few seconds I was raring to go, although I don't think anyone could be happy about the circumstances in which I came on for that game. Damaging the cruciate knee ligament is a terrible injury and it cost Mo just about all the next season. Everyone was gutted for him. Wayne had just come back and now Mo was out. It was horrible. In the stand, his missus was crying.

When a team-mate is injured, you come in at half-time and ask how he is, but as a professional you have to concentrate on your own game. We were 1-0 up through a brilliant goal from Joe Cole and playing the best football we had played since we got to Germany. I was playing higher up the field as the last man, with Wayne just off me. The ball was being played in to me while he dropped off deeper. It was the same way I had played with Stevie that season with Liverpool and it had worked well.

Sweden came flying back at us in the second half. The pressure was so intense that they had 12 corners after half-time and got an equaliser through Markus Allback. Stevie delivered what we thought was the winner until Henrik Larsson scored an equaliser for them at the death. We had won the group but we should have won that game. We were getting more stick about our performance – we had thrown it away in the second half, we were not yet hitting the heights.

We had Ecuador in the next round and this time we had to destroy them. The television pundits certainly seemed to think so. Back at the hotel I remember watching the BBC with a few of the lads, and the panel, including Lee Dixon and Gavin Peacock, were slaughtering us. It seemed we couldn't do anything right. I like Gavin and I respect his opinion but I was sitting with Becks, Frank Lampard, Stevie, Wayne, and they all had looks of utter dismay on their faces.

'Hang on a minute boys,' I said. 'Fuck this lot. When they were players, they weren't good enough to lace your boots.'

We accepted criticism when it wasn't going well, and everyone's entitled to their opinion, but sometimes you have to step in and say enough is enough, for the sake of everyone's sanity.

22

RAY WINSTONE AND THE END IN GELSENKIRCHEN

Life was getting pretty mad down in Baden Baden with the WAGs, the families and the paparazzi. How mad? Put it this way, there was even a Peter Crouch impostor doing the rounds.

After the Sweden game, I came down from the team hotel to the town to meet Mum, Dad and Sarah for a meal. We'd gone to a nice restaurant. Wayne and Coleen were there, and so were Gary Neville and his wife. As we were finishing, I noticed this bloke sitting just by the door. In fact, he was hard to miss because he was as tall as I am and, even though it was about 10 p.m., he was dressed in full England kit. He must have been aged about 20 and I didn't think he was there for an autograph.

The longer you spend in football, the more attuned you become to things like this. I didn't know what the kid was after but it looked like a stitch-up in some shape or form. I pointed him out to my dad and he agreed it didn't look right. When the bill came, I asked the waiter if I could slip out through the kitchens, and I rang the FA car that was going to take me to Castle Greyskull to tell the driver to meet me round the back. Mum, Dad and Sarah went out through the front door, past this bloke in the England kit, and it became obvious what was going on. The tall kid would walk alongside me as I came out of the restaurant, where a photographer was waiting to take our picture.

To be honest, it would probably have made a funny picture but, at the time, I didn't want to play along with any stitch-up. I don't take myself too seriously, and I know my height makes a difference – why pretend otherwise? – but I was out for a meal with my family and I thought I deserved to be left alone. Anyway, they didn't have a prayer as soon as Dad man-marked the photographer to stop him taking any pictures. I jumped in the car as this poor lanky kid came jogging round the corner to the back of the restaurant. He was English and he had clearly been bunged a few quid to do it. When he saw me in the car, his shoulders slumped. I put the window down.

'Look at you, mate. They're taking the piss out of you and you're going along with it,' I said. 'You've got to take a look at yourself. Have some self-respect.' It was just a bit of advice from one tall bloke to another tall bloke. The kid looked completely crestfallen.

I had played just about every minute of the three group matches and now that Mo was out I thought I would definitely play in the next game against Ecuador. Sven had brought four strikers – Wayne, Mo, Theo Walcott and me. I rate Theo highly, and he will be a great player one day, but he just wasn't ready for a World Cup. With the exception of Wayne and Mo, I don't think another player in the squad would have been ready at that age. When I was 17, I could hardly get in the Tottenham reserve team.

It was hard on Theo because he is a kid with so much potential as he showed the following season at Arsenal. He is very quick, and at the level he had played up until then, that pace had probably been enough to take him past defenders, but in international football, you need to do more. Against John Terry and Rio Ferdinand, you will struggle to go straight past, however quick you are. I certainly wouldn't try it myself. Theo will learn that and as he gets older he will know when to hold on to the ball and when to lay it off. Top-class defenders such as JT, Rio and Sol can muscle the most experienced players off the ball, and in international football it's so important to keep possession. It was difficult for Theo, especially as he was so young, but we were all impressed by the way he handled himself. Such a big fuss was made of him being in the squad and he conducted himself really well. The lads respected that.

Even though just two forwards were available for the Ecuador game, from the team shape we practised in training, it seemed that I wasn't going to be involved. Instead, we were going for a five-man midfield, with Michael Carrick in the side as the holding midfield player and Wayne on his own up front. That was really frustrating. I could accept being left out for Mo and Wayne but a 4–5–1 formation with just one striker seemed so negative. After the way we had played against Sweden, I thought the natural progression was to go on and try to batter Ecuador.

A lot of the lads said to me that they felt I should have played against Ecuador, and most of them thought that we should have been playing two up front, which was good for me to hear – I just wish the manager had been saying it, too.

There were more nerves before the game in Stuttgart – not enough to harm anyone's performance, but they were there. It was under-standable – we were in the knockout stages and there was no longer any margin for error. Back home, the country was expecting great things, while we seemed to be grinding out results. That does happen sometimes. We would have loved to go out and smash someone 4–0 but it just didn't seem to be going that way for us.

To get us all going we got into the habit of having a huddle in the dressing rooms before going out on to the pitch. The idea came from JT. He said they did it at Chelsea and it got them going for every game. In the huddle JT would shout and swear in the middle of it, really geeing the boys up. Becks would say a few words too, although a bit more quietly. Before the Ecuador game, Becks pointed out that quite a few of the players might not get another chance to play in a World Cup and we had to go out there and give it our all, and not leave anything on the pitch. He talked about what a big game it was, and said that with all our families in the crowd, and millions of people watching back home, we mustn't let anyone down. It was serious stuff.

But sometimes a few laughs were to be had in the huddle. Before one game, Rio was giving the speech and he got really into it – 'We've got to do this lot, let's fucking win this one,' and all that. He was shouting, 'We have to have pride in the shirt, we gotta do this, we gotta do that,' and then he paused. Something must have interrupted his flow and he lost his thread – either that or he didn't have anything more to say. After a split-second delay he just shouted, 'Come on, let's just fucking do them!' In the huddle, the rule seemed to be if in doubt, swear a lot.

I know that the huddle works for a lot of the boys but I'm not really the type to shout and scream, or to respond to it. I prefer to think about my own game and go out there and do it. This was the World Cup and I was pumped up anyway. It's just a different approach and some of the others, including Mo, were the same as me. The videos work well for me. Steve McClaren shows us videos on the team bus – basically, tackles, saves, goals all put to music. I enjoy that and it gets my mood right before a game. It was before the Ecuador game that we were sent a video message from Ray Winstone, who was out in Germany watching a few of the games and doing some work for the FA with the fans. Now that was brilliant. Ray's a great actor, the lads love his films and JT and some of the Chelsea boys knew him.

I have tried hard to track down a copy of what Ray said but I haven't been able to find it. Maybe he made it up as he went along. It was a speech about never giving in, fighting to the end, about the pride of the English people. It was like a war-cry, all spoken by Ray in that harsh Cockney accent of his. The lads loved it. It was all about the history of the English people, about our never-say-die attitude. One line was something like, 'When they say we're beaten – fuck it, we're not beaten.' It was inspiring. He was trying to get across the fans' perspective, and how those people who had come out to support us were seeing it – how they wanted us to play with our hearts on our sleeves. I was surprised by how much it got to me. On the day of the game, the speech was printed out and pinned to the dressing-room wall.

We got the result. Becks scored with a free-kick on the hour. It was the one game of the tournament I didn't play in. Of course, I was disappointed but I wasn't going to complain to Sven. I didn't think that would be right during a World Cup, when the squad has to stick together. Besides, plenty of people weren't playing at all and most important, we had won and were in the quarter-finals against Portugal.

For some time it had been fair game to have a go at Sven, but my relationship with him was always good. He had stood by me and I had got used to his style of management. He was quiet, relaxed and nothing seemed to faze him. It was quite refreshing not to have a manager barking orders at you during training, and allowing you to settle down to work. You weren't looking over your shoulder at the manager all the time. Some people prefer it if their boss shouts and screams but Sven didn't do that. It wasn't his style. The only time he ever approached giving anyone a bollocking was after the defeat in Belfast.

A lot of managers I have played for – including Graham Rix and Harry Redknapp – would take me aside after training and say, 'You did this well on Saturday,' or, 'You could have done that better,' and I would go home knowing exactly what they were thinking. That wasn't Sven's way and, to an extent, it isn't the way that Rafael

Benitez operates at Liverpool, either. Both of them may tell you how the team has played, but neither would necessarily tell you how you have done individually.

Sven would keep his cards close to his chest. He wouldn't let you get to know him that well, and only now and again did we see the private side of his character. I'll always remember a great moment at the Lowry Hotel in Manchester, where we were staying during the pre-World Cup friendlies. We had just beaten Hungary and Sven said to us we could have a few drinks in the bar. Most of the players met their wives or girlfriends but there were a few single lads in the squad. I think Sven must have been given a tip-off that some kind of newspaper stitch-up was in the offing, probably involving women. He got us single lads in a room and said, 'You have to be sensible tonight. You can have a few drinks but nothing major.' Then he added, 'Listen, you boys like what I like, but just don't do it tonight.' Everyone creased up at that one. I am sure he had a sense of humour but he was just very private.

During training in the days before we took on Portugal in Gelsenkirchen, it became clear to me that I wasn't part of the manager's plans again, and that we were sticking with 4–5–1 with Wayne on his own up front and Owen Hargreaves, rather than Michael Carrick, playing the holding midfield role. Although it was great to be involved at all, I was disappointed and frustrated not to start. This was the first real test. Portugal have some top players. It turned out to be one of those games where we did OK in parts but never really played as well as we would have liked. They looked good, although neither side looked like they were going to score.

The stadium was incredible but with the roof closed it felt strange – like playing on Astroturf – because you were indoors. Thousands of fans with their flags created an incredible atmosphere, and we all felt an almost overwhelming sense of expectation. When you step into a stadium like that it can be a bit daunting at first but it soon gets the adrenaline going. Everyone knows the stakes that you're playing for. One mistake and you get punished – and you'll get slaughtered for it forever more – but, on the other hand, you can go out there and be a hero. That game was made for someone to be a real hero. Shame he didn't turn out to be English.

The big moment came on about 62 minutes. Wayne tussled for a ball with Ricardo Carvalho and then came the stamp – not a big one, but a stamp all the same – that changed England's World Cup. Wayne probably did lose it for a second, and retaliate against Carvalho. It was one of those things. No one really blamed him. In a tough, tense game with a defender who just wouldn't stop chipping away at him, it was a heat of the moment reaction. Sat on the bench, things happened very quickly for me. When Wayne got the red card, Sven had to get another striker on and I replaced Joe Cole. As I stood up, that usual feeling of excitement and nerves came over me. *I'm coming on here. Get focused. Time to stand up and be counted.*

We were fuming because of the way the Portugal players, including Cristiano Ronaldo and Armando Petit, had stood around the referee encouraging him to produce a red card. I hate that. Getting players sent off just isn't the English way. I don't think I have ever seen an English footballer giving it the card mime – you know the one where a player holds up an imaginary card to the referee. It's gamesmanship, pure and simple, and it worked for Portugal. There was no denying their players wanted to get Wayne sent off and it obviously worked.

The Portuguese were diving all over the place and it seemed that every time I got the ball they were appealing for me to put it out so one of their supposedly injured players could have treatment. When one of them hit the deck and I didn't put the ball out, they went mad

Above: Under Sven-Goran Eriksson's watchful eye, Wayne Rooney and I train at the Frankfurt stadium, 9 June 2006, the day before our first World Cup match, against Paraguay.

Above right: Signing autographs for local kids at our World Cup training ground in Buhlertal, hidden away up in the Black Forest hills.

Below right: My sister Sarah (*right*) becomes a WAG for a few weeks with the lovely Coleen McLoughlin (*left*) and her friend Claire at the World Cup.

Below: Mum with the great Ray Winstone at the World Cup. He recorded a brilliant video message for the lads that we watched in Germany.

I give Brent Sancho's dreads a tug and head in our first goal against Trinidad and Tobago, 15 June 2006 in Nuremberg. A World Cup goal – as Dad said, 'They can never take that away.'

Wayne Rooney and I work well together against Sweden in the last group match, 20 June 2006. The lads wanted Sven to play two up front, but against Ecuador it was 4-5-1.

'Why did you get him sent off?' Cristiano Ronaldo is a great player but I lost patience with his antics in the quarter-finals, 1 July 2006.

Penalty hell. We lose in another shoot-out, this time against Portugal. Funnily enough, Sven never asked me to take one. That must have been because of the dink I attempted against Jamaica.

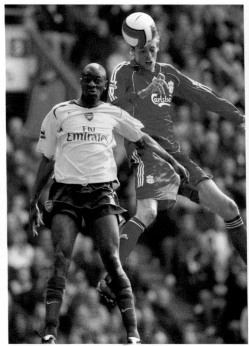

Bloody hell! I take one in the face from Rob Hulse against Sheffield United, 24 February 2007. I needed a major operation on my nose to put it right.

The second of my hat-trick goals against Arsenal, 31 March 2007 – the first club hat-trick of my career.

The best goal of my professional career – against Galatasaray, 27 September 2006. I got a similar one against Bolton.

In goes the third against Arsenal. After the operation on my nose, I was back on song.

Three at Anfield – a brilliant feeling.

We got off to a flier against PSV Eindhoven in the first leg of the Champions League quarter-final, 3 April 2007. This is my goal in a 3–0 win that virtually saw us into the last four.

Daniel Agger's goal levels the tie against Chelsea in the semi-final second leg, 1 May 2007. Stevie, Bolo Zenden, John Arne Riise, Dirk Kuyt and I celebrate. I knew we could do it from then on.

Becks is back! Scoring against Estonia from another great David Beckham cross, 6 June 2007. We had to win that game to keep on track for Euro 2008 – and finished it 3–0.

It was great to have Becks back in the England team against Brazil and Estonia. The precision of his crossing is vital for me.

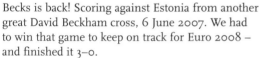

Out-pacing Brazilians in my Pumas, 1 June 2007, during the first England international at the new Wembley stadium.

Left: Celebrating scoring for England against Estonia. By the summer of 2007 I had 19 caps and 12 goals for my country. I'm pleased with that ratio.

Below: The Ealing boys I grew up with (*left to right*): Ed Aitken, Herms, Julesy, me and Ben Fitzgerald. Rob Aitken and Greg Chapman must be at the bar.

once the referee had stopped play. They crowded round me telling me I should put the ball out. Carvalho was shouting at me in broken English, 'CROUCH! CROUCH! OUT! OUT!'

'If you stop cheating, I'll put the ball out,' I said. 'At the moment, I can't tell whether he's injured or not.'

They were diving to get the result, which is not the way we play the game. I think that situation needs to be discussed. Look at how hard Wayne tried to stay on his feet when he was getting kicked in the seconds before he was shown a red card. If a stupid tackle's coming in and it's going to be an obvious penalty, I think as a striker you should go down – even if you don't absolutely need to. But there were a lot of times in that game when there was no contact and the Portugal players were rolling around like they were in agony. At the end of the day, the emphasis is on results. They wanted to win and they did it their way.

It's a shame that it takes away the praise that Portugal deserve. They are a top side and Cristiano Ronaldo is a fantastic player, a joy to watch. He has to be one of the best players in the world and in 2006–07, I voted for him as my PFA player of the year. He can change a game in an instant and, in terms of ability, I have great respect for him. You only had to see how casually and confidently he took his penalty to win it in the shoot-out. He ran up, stopped a bit and then put it in. He never looked like he was going to miss.

We had practised penalties every day in training since we joined up, and I can assure you that Carra was on fire, absolutely brilliant. In training he didn't miss one the whole time we were in Germany. As for Stevie and Lamps, you'd have put your house on them scoring. And yet in the end, only Owen Hargreaves scored in the penalty shoot-out. Afterwards, we all felt deflated. I was knackered from chasing every ball on my own up front in a team of ten men, and I never got a shout to take one of the penalties. I would have been well up for it. Sven had a list of the penalty takers ready and I think I was probably somewhere after Paul Robinson. Going for the dink against Jamaica obviously hadn't helped my cause.

Cristiano Ronaldo kissed the ball then slammed it in the net, and we were out. Heartbreaking. All those England fans in the stadium, my family among them and my old mates Greg, Herms and Rob, who had come out for the game, I felt as though I'd let them all down. That hits you straight away, the magnitude of the situation. For so long the World Cup, and the chance of going all the way, had been built up in our minds. That was it now. Over. We were going home.

The dressing room after the game was a horrible place to be. Wayne was already changed, just sitting there quietly. No one really said anything. A lot of the lads were upset. Rio was crying, JT was in tears. It means a lot to the players, although I know some people don't think it does. We knew we hadn't played well and the lads were as gutted as any fan. There was a lot of silence. Sven came round and said, 'Well done, unlucky.' It was over for him as well.

'I won't be here next year but you'll do well,' he said. 'I'll look out for you in the future and maybe some of our paths will cross again.' You could tell he was devastated.

Wayne was angry more than anything and I think he was embarrassed at what had happened. The stamp was nothing really, and on another day the referee might just have ignored it. One thing that was certain was that Carvalho wasn't hurt one bit. Wayne was fuming about Cristiano Ronaldo, too. 'What was he getting involved for?' he kept asking. The initial anger was directed at Cristiano Ronaldo. It wasn't until later that we looked at the tournament as a whole and saw that we had come up short. At the time, Cristiano Ronaldo was a scapegoat. It was a bit of an escape for us all to blame him. Wayne wanted to wait by the coach and have it out with him face to face there and then.

When they got back to Old Trafford that August, they clearly worked it out and credit to both of them because they have been fantastic for United. In the heat of the moment, incidents such as that are magnified. If you are playing against your mate and it's a 50–50 ball, you smash each other and have a big argument. Afterwards you laugh about it and put it behind you.

We had a few beers in the hotel that night and watched the highlights. The mood was very low. The atmosphere with England after a defeat is different from at club level, and I know that other players have commented on this. Perhaps sometimes we aren't as blunt with England team-mates as we are with our club-mates. There is a lot of mutual respect among the England boys and it takes a strong character to come in and start barking orders around. The captain has a right to pull people into line but it is difficult when you have so many characters who are top players at their own clubs. I would say that there are not as many bollockings among the England players as there are at Liverpool. As much as you try to get a club atmosphere at international level, it's not the same, and will never be the same. With your club you are together day in, day out, all the time. The odd harsh word won't linger. When you're not going to meet up for another two months, it's difficult to call someone a twat.

The flight home the next day stopped at London to drop a few of us off before taking the rest on to Manchester. I got off in London and apparently the flight up north was horrific. Rio, Carra and Stevie thought it was coming down because the turbulence was so bad. In the end it got so violent that the flight was re-routed to Liverpool. The boys still say to this day that after losing in the World Cup going down over the Irish Sea would have just topped it.

23

THE PARROT

Squad rotation is the manager's philosophy at Liverpool. For a traditional English footballer, that was hard to accept at first, but I have learned. When the manager is as successful as Rafael Benitez, you know that there is a reason for what he does, however hard it is to sit on the bench.

I played 49 times for Liverpool in the 2006–07 season, 30 of them starts and I scored 18 in all competitions as well as five for England. Although I have been left out of games that I have been desperate to play, I know that in the long term it has benefited me. As I got to the end of the season, I felt fresher than I had in years, especially the seasons at the clubs where I played week in, week out. Most of all, I felt hungrier than ever to score goals. There is nothing that sharpens the appetite of a striker more than sitting on the bench – not that I want the gaffer to make a habit of dropping me.

A lot was made of our manager's rotation policy in the 2006–07 season. When Dirk Kuyt and Craig Bellamy – 'Bellers' – arrived in the summer of 2006, it was obvious that Robbie Fowler and I were not going to play all the time. We had four forwards and you cannot keep everyone happy all the time. I liked the competition but I wanted to play. The English player's mentality is that the manager picks his best XI every single week until a player is injured or totally burns out. That's the way we have always been brought up. When you are pulled off or on the bench, it is seen as a black mark. Our manager's philosophy is to play the best XI for each particular game, using the strengths of our squad and weaknesses of the opposition's team. I suppose that is what I have come to accept. Rafael Benitez has even said in interviews that I have learned the benefits of the rotation system. I can't say that I will ever like sitting on the bench but I have learned that the system is there to benefit the team by keeping me fresh. Every time I'm left out, I'm desperate to get back in.

We started the season well. I scored the winner against Chelsea in the Community Shield at the Millennium Stadium, a back-post header from Bellers' cross, and I was on a run – eight goals in six games for Liverpool and England. I was flying, and had none of the problems in scoring that I had gone through at the start of the previous season. The goals were coming from all over, starting with two against Greece in Steve McClaren's first England game in charge. There was another against Maccabi Haifa in the Champions League, another against West Ham, two against Andorra and the winner against Macedonia. That made 11 goals for England in just over six months.

I wasn't in the original team to face Greece, but came in as a replacement for Dean Ashton, who broke his ankle in training, a bad injury that ruled him out for the entire season. You knew as soon as he went down that he was in agony. He was loud. Even the defenders working at the other end of the Old Trafford pitch turned round to see what the fuss was about. Shaun Wright-Phillips and Dean had just sort of run into each other. That innocuous challenge cost Dean so much.

We beat Greece 4–0 with goals from new captain John Terry, another one from Lamps and I got the third after their keeper had saved Lamps' shot. My second, the fourth of the game, was a strange one. Gary Neville whipped in a great cross from the right but I just couldn't get my feet off the ground. Somehow I couldn't get them working quickly enough to get in a leap. On the replay it even looks as though I ducked under Gary's cross, and he wasn't happy about it. He was shouting at me in frustration, hands on his head. He even turned round to the crowd with a 'What's he playing at?' look. I got myself back onside and when Stewart Downing's cross came in I put a simple downward header in the corner. When I looked over at Gary, he still had his head in his hands but he ran over to me and gave me a friendly slap on the back of the head for messing up his cross. Maybe he was on an assists bonus.

Just a month and half earlier we had been knocked out of the World Cup in Gelsenkirchen. In the rain at Old Trafford that night against Greece we couldn't have been any better. No matter what has happened since then, I still believe that is our true form. When we are playing at our best and attacking, we get results like that.

I was left on the bench for the first Premiership game of the season but I got the winner in the next one, at Anfield against West Ham, from Luis Garcia's pass. My confidence was high, goals were coming, and against the next opposition, Andorra, I fancied my chances of a few more.

I have never played a worse football team than Andorra in all my professional career – and that includes the Championship years. Andorra certainly wouldn't survive in that division and I wouldn't want to do a disservice to League One by saying that they would be OK at that standard. Andorra were at Old Trafford for the day out and they came to defend. We still prepared for the game as if we were playing against Portugal in the World Cup quarter-finals. Steve McClaren wouldn't have it any other way. I have to say I didn't know much about Andorra before the squad met up but I did by the time I came to play against them. They were as bad as I imagined and good for my goal tally.

Andorra played with eleven men behind the ball. Their only tactic was for their one player who was a bit tricky to go on mazy dribbles. The problem for him was that none of his team-mates would go with him, so he would end up turning into a corner and we would take the ball off him. Seriously, that was as far as they got forward. They barely crossed the halfway line, and they never had a shot. It is odd playing teams like that and it can be strangely difficult unless you get an early goal, as we did that day, because if you don't those teams can grow in confidence.

Four days after the Andorra game, I scored the winner against Macedonia in Skopje, my fifth goal for England in three games. Macedonia were a decent enough side, and the pitch was bobbly, but we got the job done. Three wins out of three was a pretty good start to Steve McClaren's management era, and we felt confident.

The Merseyside derby brought me back down to earth with a painful 3–0 defeat at Goodison Park. I don't think anyone watching would say that we were three goals worse than they were, although on the day Everton probably were the better side. Thankfully, we win the majority of derby games but when Everton do win, they tend to rub it in a lot more than we ever do. The Liverpool lads couldn't believe it when we found out that, days after the game, Everton had rushed out a DVD of the match and were selling it in the club shop. They even had players signing copies of it. It was obviously a big moment for them.

Come our first Champions League group game of the competition proper, I had gone five games without a goal, including two that I had sat out on the bench. But I started against Galatasaray, from Turkey, and nine minutes into the game, got on the end of a Fabio Aurelio cross from the right to put us a goal up. Luis Garcia got the second but it was my third that I will remember the longest – an overhead kick, the sort of goal you dream about scoring.

The best goal of my career is how I would describe it, scored in front of the Kop on 52 minutes. Finns burst down the right and put in a cross at about my shoulder height and behind me. It wasn't like the effort against Trinidad, when I had a chance to pull the ball down and take a touch. This was a no-lose situation – if the overhead kick had gone ten feet over the bar at least I would have got an effort in. In the event, it worked out a lot better than that. I threw myself into it, caught it sweetly with my right foot and in it flew. I do try them occasionally in training and I have definitely got that one in the locker when it's needed. To perform that difficult technique on a Champions League night was just about perfect.

We won the game 3–2 and I was still on a high on the way home. Dad drove me back to my flat and as soon as we pulled into the car park outside I knew something was wrong.

'The car's gone,' I said to Dad.

The car was an Aston Martin, a DB9 that I had treated myself to at the end of my first season at Liverpool. As soon as I saw it was gone I realised that I'd been burgled. I'd parked it behind a gate, and they would have needed the keys to get it started. There was no sign that they had smashed a window. We walked into the building and my front door was open. While I had been scoring two goals against Galatasaray, my flat had been ransacked.

They had come in through a window and done a professional job. All the pictures on the walls had been taken down in their hunt for cash and safes. They had unscrewed skirting boards because – the police told me later – that is often where people hide money. They had even ripped out the fireplace looking for a safe. It might sound like I wasn't taking it seriously enough, but, the more I thought about it, I wasn't too concerned. So what? I had lost the car, which was expensive, but it was insured. No one had got hurt. Apart from the car, I reckon that the burglars must have been very disappointed. If they were expecting one of those flashy 'cribs' you see on the television, they were in for a shock. With my relaxed attitude towards tidiness, my place looked more like a student's house than that of a professional footballer.

Unfortunately for the burglars, I don't have expensive tastes. I'm not really bothered about jewellery and watches. They must have got really desperate in their hunt for cash because they nicked a money-box my mum had bought me as a stocking filler one Christmas. I think it had about forty quid in it – not much of a haul. Mum bought me another one that Christmas.

The worst thing was that they took a few of my Liverpool and England shirts, including the one that I had worn in the FA Cup final. Generally, I don't keep my memorabilia – shirts and balls etc – at my flat. They are all somewhere safe so I can decide what to do with them when my career ends. What I felt terrible about was Bobby Zamora's FA Cup final West Ham shirt. Bobby had given it to me months earlier to get the Liverpool lads to sign and I had forgotten to do it. Instead, I had left it lying around my flat and now it was gone. How was I going to tell Bobby that I had lost the shirt he wore in the most important match of his career?

I decided to leave it a few days and, thankfully, Merseyside police, who were brilliant about the whole thing, caught the bloke who had burgled my place. He had made a habit of breaking into footballers' home and had done Jerzy Dudek, Florent Sinama Pongolle and Daniel Agger as well. When you look at the photographs the police took of the bloke's house with all our stuff in it, you can just see Bobby Zamora's West Ham shirt lying under a bed. Clearly the burglars didn't think they could make much money out of selling it. Bobby doesn't actually know how close I came to losing it, and I made sure I got it signed and back to him as soon as possible.

I even got the Aston Martin back, although I have to say I never drive it, and I'll probably get rid of it soon. I just loved the car, and I had always wanted one, so I decided to splash out. It was the one time I have really treated myself. I realise that as professional footballers in the Premiership, we earn great money and, of course, it makes a difference. But I'm not obsessed with money. I can't remember the last time I checked my bank balance. I'm happy as long as I can do what I want to do. If I want to go on a holiday, I can. If I want to go out for a meal, I can. Other than that, I'm not too concerned. There's nothing I really want. I have bought a couple of houses as investments and I quite enjoy looking at the property market and deciding what would be a bargain.

I appreciate how lucky I am to have money to spend on my family and friends but I don't think I ever go overboard. I love being able to treat my family at birthdays and Christmas, and every summer I go on holiday to America with my old mates from Ealing and I pay for the flights and hotels. I don't do that because they need the help – they've all got jobs. I do it just because it's a nice thing to do.

The debate over footballers' pay is difficult. Of course nurses and teachers should be paid more. I know poor pay is unfair on people who do important jobs and I can see why it gets people's backs up that we earn a lot. But there is so much money in the game from television deals alone and I truly believe that people would prefer to see it go to the players who create the enjoyment rather than anyone else.

When contract negotiations come round, I'm no different from anyone in any walk of life. I want to get the best deal for myself and for my family. Other than that, I carry on doing my job like any other person. As footballers, we all know we are in a privileged position and earning good money, but I would say that the majority of players I know aren't driven by money at all. If a bloke working in a bank is offered a job at a different bank for, say, double his original salary, he would go, no contest. Yet when people do move for money in football, everyone tells them how greedy they are. In any other job, it wouldn't be an issue. OK, football is different from working in a bank, but most footballers I know would put salary very low down on their priorities when it comes to moving clubs. So many other factors are more important, such as loyalty, how much you enjoy playing for your club and your relationship with the fans. All that comes into it.

I have never had stick from fans about the money I earn as a professional footballer and I hope that is partly down to the fact that I always give everything on the pitch and partly that I don't show off. I try to keep that to a minimum. If I am out on the town, I'll have a pint, although I have seen players get the champagne out and sit on the top table. Some players don't help themselves, and a small minority are in it for the money. Newspapers, of course, are more interested in players who provide them with good stories than someone like Paul Scholes, for instance, a player you never hear about away from football. He has won everything in the game and must have earned a lot of money but he would never be seen flashing it around. Those players are heroes to the fans.

It is a similar situation with Carra. He's a brilliant footballer who just won't have any fuss. Even in this day and age, Carra won't go anywhere near a coloured boot. He wears black Pumas and blacks out any white bits because he thinks defenders shouldn't wear any colour on their boots. It just cracks me up when I see him fussing over his boots but I know what he means and I know what he represents. And I have only respect for him.

By October 2006, we had lost to Chelsea, Everton and Bolton in the Premiership and keeping pace with Chelsea and Manchester United at the top was proving difficult. At the start of that month I was back in an England shirt and life was about to get harder. At Old

Trafford, Macedonia put up another good fight and held us to a 0–0 draw. We were still confident, we had been on a winning run of three games since the World Cup, but we couldn't break them down. We really needed to win and it was a frustrating day. Four days later, we played Croatia in Zagreb.

That 2–0 defeat was probably one of the worst I have been involved in. It was a bad day. As a team we didn't play at all well and we deserved the criticism we got. We let Steve McClaren down that night.

As we came out of the stadium to get on the coach, a few England fans were leaning over the back of the stand, giving us stick. As much as they could, the boys were ignoring it, although Wayne Rooney didn't ignore it quite as much as everyone else. He was walking slowly, looking up at the fans, and you could tell he was upset. We got him back on the coach and he was all right. The fans were angry and rightly so. We hadn't performed. Sometimes, various outside factors can affect the way we play, but there were no excuses for that game in Croatia. Right from the start, we didn't play well.

Even in that hostile atmosphere, we should have been able to grind out a result, but our passing wasn't there and Croatia grew in confidence. When they scored it was downhill for us. We didn't really have a decent attempt on goal. A bad game in an England shirt feels terrible because you don't get too many games to impress. After the Croatia game we didn't play again until February – with our club sides we have a bad result and three days later we get the chance to put it right. That night, as ever with England, the whole nation was watching us and we turned in a bad performance. We knew that we were going to get stick and we knew the fans weren't going to be happy. We take the glory and prestige of playing for our country and we have to take the criticism when it goes badly.

From October to Christmas Liverpool were flying in the Champions League but we fell behind in the Premiership. We dropped four points to Blackburn, lost at Manchester United, and drew with Portsmouth and Middlesbrough. With United and Chelsea so consistent, if we lost a game it put us three points further behind them. Draw and that was still another two behind. It just built up. It's a fine line and you can't afford to slip up.

Christmas is probably the worst time for a footballer. You can't really take part in the celebrations at all. There are so many games over the Christmas period that you spend most of the time just trying to recover. Everyone else is out enjoying themselves and we're training – although I'm not for a moment suggesting that we get a raw end of the deal. We still get our Christmas lunch with the girls who work in the training ground canteen, although that's normally on 10 December. We got the afternoon off on Christmas Day to be with our families and I went to my gran's in Macclesfield for a bit of turkey. I didn't even bother getting changed out of my tracksuit and headed straight back to Liverpool afterwards to our team hotel.

One tradition that never gets ignored is the club Christmas party – and we had a proper do this time round. Robbie Fowler came up with the idea of fancy dress – he loves a costume. I think he spent about three grand on outfits for the last Christmas party. Having turned up as a shark for the Portsmouth Christmas party, and a chicken for Lee Hendrie's stag do, I was on the look-out for a really good costume this time. I found one that I thought would be a winner. It was a woman carrying a baby and the way the costume was designed meant that the wearer's head was on the baby's body. I thought that one would be it but I came up against the usual problem I have buying clothes – it was just too short. I like costumes that make me look really ridiculous. I hate it when people turn up as, say, one of the Blues Brothers. Take off the shades and the hat and you're just a bloke in a suit. Where's the fun in that? So if I couldn't be the baby on the woman's back, it had to be the next best option – the parrot.

We had hired Aldo's, John Aldridge's bar in Liverpool city centre, but a few of us went to the Grapes pub in Mathew Street first. A few of us turned up to have a beer with the locals. As Liverpool footballers, we normally get a bit of attention but the regulars in the Grapes that night won't have seen anything like it. I was dressed as a parrot, Stephen Warnock was dressed as a penguin, Bellers was Chewbacca from 'Star Wars' and Robbie had come as, he said, 'a pervert' – you'll have to see the pictures of that one. There was never any chance of us getting away with it and a few photographers were waiting outside Aldo's. The effort that the lads put in was brilliant, especially the young boys. As the first team, we took responsibility for picking the reserves' costumes for them. Nabil El Zhar as the Incredible Hulk had painted his face completely green.

It was a great night – a few bevs and a good laugh, and a bit of karaoke too. My tune is 'You can't touch this' by MC Hammer, and I throw in a few moves when I'm on the microphone. Christmas parties are a good blow-out and it is not often all the players are together. Also, having so many nationalities at the club can make it difficult to find something that everyone's going to enjoy, but the fancy dress idea really worked. The boss knows it's an English tradition to have a Christmas party, and he goes along with it. He can see the value in us all getting together. We were talking about that one night for weeks.

For five of the six games we played in December I was a sub, and in the newspapers there was a bit of speculation that I could be sold in the January transfer window. Newcastle seemed to be declaring their interest quite strongly. It's a weird feeling to pick up a paper and read a story that could have a major effect on your life. For a moment, you ask yourself, 'What's actually going on here?' I wanted to stay at Liverpool, I always have, but at the back of my mind I'm aware that changes in your career are often decided by other people. When it really started to heat up, the manager pulled me aside and told me there wasn't any chance of me leaving.

'Don't be concerned about anything you read,' he said, 'and don't worry about any players coming in because you are still part of my plans.'

It was nice of him to do that. He didn't have to, and he doesn't often do those sorts of things. I have to say I was relieved. I told him that there was no way I wanted to leave. More recently, he has told me that he considers me important to the team. That means a lot to me. Liverpool are a fantastic club and I want to be challenging for trophies with them.

My career has had more turnarounds than most. December 2006 wasn't a great month but then against Bolton at Anfield on New Year's Day I scored with another scissor-kick. This time it was Jermaine Pennant's cross from the right, a touch behind me but I caught it just right and it flew past Jussi Jaaskelainen. It was my first Premiership goal in 11 games, although in my defence I had been sub in six of them and hadn't played 90 minutes in any. That's always been the way with my career. I go a few games without scoring and it's, 'He's crap, what's he doing in the team?' Then I go on a run of goals and turn it around again. I don't mind as long as the ups outweigh the downs.

At the start of January we were sent crashing back down again with two Cup defeats in a row at Anfield by Arsenal. First the FA Cup, in which I played, then the Carling Cup, for which I sat on the bench. Having won the FA Cup in Cardiff the previous season, losing at home was hard to take. In the Carling Cup we scored three but they scored six. As a team, we just weren't at the races.

I got two goals against Watford in January and was desperate to stay on for my hat-trick. Up until then I had never got a club hat-trick in my whole career although I had got loads of twos. I was pretty sure

I would have got one before if I had managed to stay on the pitch a few times, and that day at Vicarage Road was no different. I still had 40 minutes left when I scored my second and I was so anxious that I had a quiet word with our first-team coach, Alex Miller, to make sure I stayed on. Big mistake. I'm sure that was enough to make sure I came off. Alex was grinning as I came to the bench. 'Sorry about that, mate!' he said.

In January we beat Chelsea in the Premiership for the first time since Rafael Benitez took over at Liverpool. It was a great victory with a really classy second goal by Jermaine Pennant, his first for the club. I like Jermaine, whom I've known since playing for the England Under-21s. He was a £2 million footballer as a teenager, and he would admit that he has made a few mistakes in his career, but I certainly think he has played his best ever football at Liverpool. He gets the micky taken out of him for all his various past misdemeanours. When we went go-karting one time we even told him he had to stand and watch because he's had that many driving bans. I have to say his crossing ability has really benefited me.

After a 0–0 draw in the second Merseyside derby of the season, England duty resumed on 7 February. The friendly against Spain was a big one for the English lads at Liverpool because we have a Spanish manager, Spanish staff and a lot of Spanish players – and we dish out the stick to them quite a bit. We're forever telling them that the Premiership is so much better than *La Liga*, that their national team will never win anything and so on. Xabi Alonso and Carra are at it quite a bit, especially as Carra watches all the matches, Spanish, Italian, you name it, on television. So to lose to an Andres Iniesta goal at Old Trafford was a real blow. We wanted to make amends for the Croatia result, but it didn't go as well as we hoped. We started strongly and it seemed to be going well, and then we just fell away. A goalless draw would have been a fair result, but they snatched a winner after the hour.

At Liverpool, we'd get our chance to show that we could beat Spanish opposition. In the Champions League we had drawn the holders, Barcelona.

24

ATHENS

I would love to say that I played a key role in our two famous wins against Barcelona that put Ronaldinho, Samuel Eto'o, Lionel Messi, Deco and company out of the Champions League. And one day I'll tell my kids that I hit the bar in the Nou Camp and the post at Anfield. The truth is that I played about one minute in both games as a sub and, between the away and home legs, I smashed up my nose.

I was absolutely buzzing when we won 2–1 at the Nou Camp, but although I was involved, it is difficult to celebrate in the same way as everyone else when you have not played a full part. That's just the way football is. In those circumstances, you feel on the margins. The boys had done a great job to beat what most people felt was the best football team in the world, and our manager had been spot-on with the tactics.

Then for the return leg at Anfield, which we won 1–0, I was frustrated to be left on the bench, but I could understand the manager's feelings. I was having trouble breathing – a result of getting volleyed in the face by Sheffield United's Rob Hulse three days after the first-leg match. As injuries go, it was one of the nastiest, although I have to admit I did look hilarious when my nose blew up to about four times its normal size. Just 23 minutes into the game against Sheffield United at Anfield I bent down to head the ball and Hulse smashed me in the face with his foot. It wasn't intentional but I could feel the bleeding immediately. I had a cut above my left eye and my nose was even more painful. I just couldn't get up.

When the physio came on to the pitch to treat me, I tried desperately to get up and walk off because I feel such a twat being carried on a stretcher. But my head was all over the place and eventually I agreed to get on the stretcher. Or at least I think I did. The memories of those moments are still a bit hazy. By the time I arrived in the treatment room, I had an idea that my nose must be bad. As usual, Doc Waller, the club doctor, was fantastic. He kept telling me I was fine as he put twelve stitches in my nose. All the staff who came in to see me said, 'You're OK, nothing serious.' I was beginning to feel a bit better. Then my dad turned up. He'd come down from the stand.

'BLOODY HELL, LOOK AT YOUR FACE,' he blurted out.

'Really?' I said. 'Is it that bad?'

Out the corner of my eye I could see Doc Waller frantically trying to indicate to Dad to play it down and keep me calm. My nose had swollen up all across my face and my eyebrow was virtually hanging off. The doc still laughs about Dad's reaction now. He reckons his bedside manner needs some work.

I told the doc not to worry – I knew it was bad. At half-time a few of the lads popped in to see me – Robbie, Stevie, Carra, the manager – and they were surprisingly sympathetic. Afterwards, I lay back on the bed and prepared to watch the second half on the television in the treatment room. On telly I could see the lads standing around the centre circle waiting for Sheffield United to come out. Stevie was pointing to his nose and laughing a lot. You could just tell what he was saying – 'What about the state of Crouchy's face? It's all over the place!' All the lads were pointing to their noses and cracking up with laughter. So much for sympathy from my caring team-mates. I was known as 'Hooknose' for the next four weeks.

I told the boss that I would be able to play the next game even though I was having trouble sleeping. I could hardly breathe through one nostril and the other was shut. Most nights I kept waking because of problems breathing. I've still got a picture of my face that I took with my mobile phone just half an hour after it happened and sent to a few of my mates. It's very funny but I look a right mess. I convinced myself I could play, even though the medics thought I would need an operation to sort it out. We had Manchester United and then Barcelona in the second leg at Anfield and I was desperate to be involved. The boss had different ideas.

The coaching staff didn't think I was fit enough to play and I was a sub in both of the games. Losing in the last minute to United was a choker, beating Barcelona was fantastic, but after that I decided that I couldn't wait until the end of the season to get the operation done. It would mean missing a trip to Villa Park with Liverpool but, worse, I also missed the England Euro 2008 qualifiers against Israel and Andorra. Steve McClaren was great, constantly in touch to find out how I was. I felt there was a chance I might play but the operation didn't turn out as well as I hoped.

I know what you're thinking – it's just a broken nose, what's the problem? But this one was more complicated than normal. The doctors kept me in hospital for two nights and I was coughing up blood most of the time. I had little blue plastic splints put in my nose, as well as packing and stitches, and had to keep them in for a week. It was murder. I went back to Mum and Dad's in Ealing and didn't leave the house for a week because I couldn't go out with all the bandaging around my nose.

One night my dad came in to check on me and found me half-asleep making a strange gurgling noise. My nose had started haemorrhaging and instead of the blood coming out it was going back down my throat as I slept. In turn, I was coughing it up in my sleep and the bedroom looked like a horror movie had been filmed there. Dad woke me up just in time. There was no chance of being ready to play for England. I sat on the sofa and tried not to feel sorry for myself, just hoping that the boys would get six points against Israel and Andorra.

We desperately needed to win against Israel and we didn't play well. There's no denying that – we should have done better. They may not have the same football history as us but Israel are still a good side. They drew twice with France in the qualifiers for the 2006 World Cup. It was a difficult game and the boys got quite a bit of stick at the end from the crowd. That was a sign of things to come when they played Andorra in Barcelona. Of course, as players we all accept that you deserve stick if you don't play well – but this time it got a touch personal.

Like many England fans, I watched the game on television. I could see the Andorrans growing in confidence the longer we went without scoring, and I could hear the crowd getting on top of the England players. You didn't have to be in the Olympic Stadium that night to tell that this was not an easy evening to be an England player. Stevie got us off the hook with a couple of goals and David Nugent got the third but 3–0 was never going to be enough in the circumstances. The attitude of the fans towards the manager and the players at the end was clear. They were disillusioned with the performance and getting angrier and angrier. It was a delicate situation. Sitting in my parents' front room in Ealing, I thought about how I might have handled the fallout after the game, and I thought that no one cut to the heart of it better than John Terry. He said that the fans had paid good money to watch the team and if they wanted to get their feelings off their chest and boo the players and the manager, then so be it. They were perfectly entitled to their opinions. But, as JT added, when you're trying to win a football match – it doesn't help.

I would love to have been involved in those games, despite how they turned out. I would never even consider not playing for England. It is an honour to pull on your country's shirt and every time I do it I feel the same excitement as I did for my first cap in New Jersey in May 2005. I know there were rumours after the Andorra match that some players wanted out. I don't believe that. In the aftermath of a match all sorts of things are said. In the cold light of day, the England lads want to play for their country and they want to get it right.

It's weird how football works. When I returned from injury against Arsenal at Anfield on 31 March, I hadn't played 90 minutes for Liverpool for almost two months, I hadn't scored since the West Ham game at the end of January and I'd been in for surgery in the meantime. I swerved the last appointment with the nose specialist to make sure he didn't advise me to miss the Arsenal game. My luck was about to change. The older you get, the more you realise not to despair during the bad times, because they're never as bad as you think. And you appreciate the good times because they don't last forever.

Arsenal at Anfield – my first club hat-trick. I scored with a right-foot shot, a header and my left foot – a great way to mark my comeback. My all-round game was good that day. I was playing against two centre-halves, William Gallas and Kolo Toure, and making their lives difficult. We got an early goal when Jermaine Pennant crossed from the right and I tucked the ball in at the near post. Fabio Aurelio put in a great cross for me to head in the second but I was most pleased with the way I pulled away from Gallas and Toure to bury the third. I got the match ball and all the boys signed it. 'You'd never have done it without me,' was Pennant's take on the game.

Arsene Wenger was generous with his praise after the match and when I turned on my phone there were loads of texts from friends congratulating me. The one that meant the most was from Robbie Fowler. 'You were a joy to watch today, mate,' he said. Robbie's a top bloke and he's still a legend in the game, someone I look up to a lot. He sent another text – 'But you'll still be dropped next week.' I asked him why. 'It's happened to me before after I've scored hat-tricks,' he replied. 'Three times.' He does like to remind me that he's scored a few hat-tricks in his time.

Robbie was wrong about me getting dropped. I played in our next Champions League game, which was the first leg against PSV Eindhoven, and scored the third in a 3–0 win that set us up nicely for the second leg. I got the only goal in that game as we strolled to a place in the semi-finals.

The team is not the only thing Rafael Benitez likes to keep on a rotation basis. It's the same when it comes to hotel room-mates. On various occasions I've been paired with Robbie and with Jermaine Pennant, and in the second half of 2006–07 I was paired with Javier Mascherano. He's a great person, and learning English quickly, but I can't say the banter between us was exactly flying. I've never known anyone to study English so hard, and when he finally finishes *The Count of Monte Cristo* maybe he can read this book. Javi and I had to pull our single beds further apart at the hotel we stay in outside Liverpool before home games. One wrong move while I was asleep and I would wake up with one of my long arms wrapped around my Argentine room-mate.

Before the first leg of the Champions League semi-final against Chelsea on 25 April all the talk was about what a big game it would be, about the atmosphere and excitement – especially since Liverpool had beaten Chelsea at the same stage of the competition two years earlier – but in the end it was an anticlimax. I don't think the Chelsea fans really raised the roof at Stamford Bridge. In fact, it felt more like a Premiership match even though it was the biggest club game of my career up to that point. I came on for Bellers after 52 minutes when we were already one down to Joe Cole's goal. A lot of my friends and family were at the game, including my QPR-supporting mates from Ealing, and they were all in the Liverpool end, hoping Chelsea would lose.

We were disappointed to lose that game but I never doubted that we would win in the second leg. At Anfield it would be different. The boys had told me about the atmosphere at the semi-final in 2005, about the noise and intensity of the place being like nothing they had ever experienced before. I was at Southampton then and had watched the game on television. It was difficult to imagine that Anfield could be even noisier than it was on those raw, passionate European nights I had already experienced. But when I came out of the tunnel on 1 May, I knew what Stevie and Carra had been talking about. This was really loud. The mood was totally different from anything I had ever known. If Stamford Bridge had seemed like a Premiership game, at Anfield that night you knew you were in a Champions League semi-final. A big game – and our fans expected us to deliver.

Before the first leg at Chelsea I had been selected to do the official Uefa pre-match press conference, a sure sign, or so I thought, that I would be playing. That was how it had worked all season in the Champions League. Whoever was alongside the boss in the press conference before the game was in the team. Not this time. My selection was a decoy, intended to sell Jose Mourinho a dummy. Dirk and Bellers were in and I was on the bench.

Before the second leg I had a strong feeling that I would be in the side, although I don't take anything for granted these days. But being left out of the squad to play Portsmouth on the weekend between the two semi-final games seemed like a good sign and, against Chelsea at Anfield, I started up front with Dirk. When Daniel Agger scored after 22 minutes to level the score on aggregate, our fans raised the roof.

Anfield could sense a seventh European Cup final. From then on, I felt confident that we would be solid enough to keep a clean sheet and win the game.

The goal was brilliantly taken by Agger, just the way our manager planned it. Rafa Benitez has us working on those free-kicks in training all the time. Stevie took the free-kick on the left wing and, while Chelsea expected a deep cross to the back post, he side-footed the ball to the near side of the box from where Agger curled it in with his left foot. That's just the way Teddy Sheringham used to get corners played in to him at the near side, and it worked perfectly. In fact, it worked a lot better than it ever does in training. The manager often says that set-pieces will be the difference in games and that time he was proved absolutely right.

Playing against John Terry is always one of the toughest battles of my season, although I feel that I hold my own. There is a bit of needle between us at times. We go in hard and we challenge for every ball in the air. A Champions League semi-final is a massive game with so much at stake. We might be team-mates with England but in the weeks leading up to this match – and during the match itself – we exchanged not a word about the game. I tried to pressurise Michael Essien, who was playing as a makeshift centre-half, because I knew I had the beating of him in the air. Dirk dropped deep and it worked well for us that night.

The game ended all square on aggregate and so went to extra time. In the second period, Bellers came on for me, which meant that, after the previous season's FA Cup final and the World Cup, I was going to miss out on another penalty shootout. Robbie Fowler, however, wasn't about to get away so easily. With about two minutes of extra time left, the boss turned to him and told him to warm up.

'Robbie, get yourself ready,' the manager said. 'You're coming on for the penalties.'

'Oh cheers boss, thanks for that,' Robbie whispered to me as he got up. But he knows he's the man when it comes to penalties. In training he tucks them away better than anyone. Robbie was down to take the fifth and final penalty on the list but in the end we didn't even need to go that far. It would have been great to see him score the penalty that took Liverpool into the Champions League final. It just turned out that Pepe Reina was on such top form that Robbie didn't have to.

From the very start of the penalty shootout we just never looked like losing. Bolo put the first one away confidently and that set the tone for us. In front of the Anfield Road end, Xabi and Stevie scored our next two penalties while in goal Pepe was the star. He is a penalty-saving specialist and – apart from Frank Lampard, who was the only Chelsea player to score – he seemed to psych out Chelsea. He saved their first penalty from Arjen Robben and their third from Geremi. That left Dirk with the fourth penalty to take us to Athens and when he put that one away, the stadium just exploded with noise.

In the stands our fans were in heaven, and later, in the dressing room, we celebrated loud and long. During the season Pepe had taught us a Spanish song – more of a football chant really – about Diego Maradona. It's become our theme tune. Pepe puts it on the stereo before games to get us going and, when we're celebrating after matches, we sing it loud and swing our shirts above our heads the way you see Spanish fans do with their scarves. The changing room was rocking that night. George Gillett came in and immediately got drenched in champagne by Robbie. Our new American owner stood there with his nice suit wet through, his glasses all steamed up, and you could tell from his face that he was absolutely loving it. What a time to take over the club. We had just won the semi-final of the Champions League and we had beaten Barcelona and Chelsea to get there. He must have thought he'd hit the jackpot.

There is a little secret about the Anfield dressing room that only the players know. If a manager really shouts at his players in the away dressing room the noise drifts through to us in the home dressing room from an air vent and vice versa apparently. We heard one Premiership manager completely lose his rag with his team after one game. He was shouting so loudly we could hear it through the vent. So after the semi-final win, no doubt the noise from our dressing room could be heard in theirs – which made us sing that little bit louder. When the players gathered for the England camp at the end of the season I spoke to Joe Cole about it and he said that they could hear us singing afterwards. That's football. You have to accept it. If we had lost, I'm sure they would have rubbed it in.

That night the party continued at the Sir Thomas Hotel in Liverpool. It was a great Liverpool FC night. All the players were there, the staff, our families and most of Carra's mates as well. The place was packed out. George Gillett's son Foster turned up to have a few beers and sing some songs. I even bumped into the actors Jude Law and Clive Owen, who had come up for the game. You could hardly move for all the people helping us celebrate another famous win. The city was buzzing with the excitement of a seventh European Cup final.

We still had two games of the Premiership season left before the final in Athens on 23 May, although by then everything was geared towards the game against AC Milan. The night after we knocked out Chelsea, they beat Manchester United 3–0 in some style. I wasn't even in the squad for the Fulham game and in the last match of the season, against Charlton, I got just two minutes as a sub. The manager was keeping us fresh for the match in Athens, although predicting what team he would select was proving as difficult as ever.

After a week in La Manga – when I acquired the scars on my leg from the go-kart incident as a memento – we arrived in Athens two days before the game. As usual, our fans came in their thousands any way they could. Getting flights to Greece wasn't easy – let alone tickets for the match. I know how hard it can be to get to these games because my family have to do the same. Mum, Dad and Sarah eventually managed to get a flight to the island of Mykonos and then, the day before the game, they came over on a flight to Athens. Plenty of other Liverpool fans did the same kind of thing. Dad said the flight to Mykonos was the weirdest mix of passengers he's ever seen on the way to a match – Liverpool fans going to the final and gay couples going on holiday.

As players, we miss out on all the excitement that goes on in the build-up to big games, and sometimes I only remember if I have already played in a certain city when I recognise the hotel we are staying in. Kiev, Eindhoven, Bordeaux, Istanbul, Barcelona – once you're in the hotel for an away match, you might as well be anywhere. Those of my mates and my family who are there to see the game keep me up to date with what's going on in the city.

The hotel we were allocated outside Athens was atrocious, like an old people's home, and the rooms were terrible. I've still got a picture on my phone of Robbie in Bolo Zenden's bathroom. It was so small that he could sit on the toilet seat and wash his hands in the sink with one leg in the shower – all at the same time. Rafa Benitez came in to see what we were laughing about and decided that was the final straw. We were all moved to better rooms.

I thought I had a chance of starting the game but the manager kept us guessing right up to a couple of hours before kick-off. In the hotel he said we were playing one up front and Stevie off the striker and I knew then I was probably out because he always plays Dirk ahead of me. He told us the team when we got to the ground and I was gutted. I had played with Stevie just off me against Arsenal and scored a hat-trick. This time I would be watching from the bench. I felt flat. How many chances do you get to play in a Champions League final? But this was a big game and the team was more important than any one player. You have to get over the disappointment and be ready to come on.

The final did not live up to its billing – neither team really got into their stride. AC Milan nicked a goal before half-time, an Andrea Pirlo free-kick that deflected in off Filippo Inzaghi. I came on for Javi Mascherano with 12 minutes left and Inzaghi scored a second four minutes later. When I finally got on I was so desperate to make something happen that I must have looked like a headless chicken. I was trying to do the best I could to get into the game – I had one decent shot, and it was over.

The atmosphere was great, our fans were brilliant, and it had been fantastic to be part of an amazing run to the final, but when you lose a game like that you don't want to dwell on it. It's better just to put the runner-up medal away and think about winning the trophy next time. I just wish I had been given more of a chance to show what I can do. Watching from the side of the pitch, I thought AC Milan were there for the taking. They are a great team but, although I don't think we played as well as we could, we were the better side. If we had gone at them more, we would have won.

It was a quiet dressing room afterwards. I was finding it hard to come to terms with the fact that I had watched so much of the game from the touchline. And then to top it all I was selected to do a drugs test. I know they're an important part of the way sport is governed, but I seem to be doing them all the time. I walked to the testing room past the AC Milan dressing room and heard their music, singing and laughter. Just like us when we beat Chelsea. Just as we would have been if we had won that night in Athens. When you lose a game like this, you want to get out of town as quickly as possible.

I pushed open the door to the testing room and found one other person in there. And of all the people in the AC Milan team it had to be Gennaro Gattuso – still wearing his winner's medal. I groaned to myself. I didn't know the bloke personally but from what I had seen of him on the pitch I didn't much like him. He always seemed to be around when there was trouble, always shouting the odds.

I slumped in a chair and lost myself in my thoughts. There would be no open-topped bus journey around Liverpool this time. No glory. All we would be taking back to Liverpool and to our loyal fans was a load of regret. Then Gattuso piped up.

He had learned English during his time in Scotland with Rangers and we chatted about the game. He turned out to be a great bloke, very knowledgeable about English football and full of praise for how Liverpool had got to the final. He had even seen a few of my goals and said he was surprised I wasn't in the starting XI. The drugs-test room was the last place either of us wanted to be. I wanted to get back to England, he wanted to get back to his team-mates and celebrate. Gattuso was buzzing about the win but he didn't rub it in. We shook hands before he left. It's funny how you can be wrong about some people.

On my way back to the dressing room I saw the AC Milan kitman on his way to our dressing room with a load of shirts to exchange for ours. I picked one out as my one memento of the evening – 'Inzaghi 9'. He scored two goals and will want to remember that night for the rest of his life. It's not quite the same for me. Half an hour or so after the game, it was already a bit of a blur. We went back to the hotel and tried to raise our spirits but in that terrible place even a victory party would have been a struggle.

Somehow I feel I'll be back. I've got the taste for it now. After two seasons at Liverpool Football Club I know what it means to be part of this team, part of this tradition. Five European Cups is some heritage. I'd love to be part of the team that wins the sixth.

25

BECKS COMES BACK

After Athens came the final test of the 2006–07 season – an England double-header that we could not afford to mess up. First a friendly against Brazil at the new Wembley Stadium and then, on 6 June, the crunch match for Euro 2008 qualification, an away game in Estonia that we just had to win. And if the stakes were not high enough already, the return of David Beckham to the squad made things even more interesting.

Rumours that Becks was coming back had circulated before the last two games, against Israel and Andorra, but an injury he picked up in Spain had put an end to that. This time there was a definite sense that Steve McClaren was going to pick him in the squad he named on 26 May. One day later Becks walked back into the England team hotel after eleven months away. No drum roll, no big fuss – in fact Becks tried to be as innocuous as possible and slip in under the radar. As much as David Beckham can ever slip under the radar.

Around the squad Becks was quiet. He kept his head down, content just to be one of the lads. He got on with his job, although in training you could see that he had a point to prove. In that first session, on a cold windy afternoon at Arsenal's training ground in Hertfordshire, he was definitely putting himself about. There was a picture in a few of the newspapers of the moment he smashed me in a tackle. You could tell he was keen to make an impression and he certainly did that. Over the two games there was no doubt he was our best player.

I would have loved to start against Brazil at the new Wembley but it was Alan Smith who got the nod to play alongside Michael Owen in the attack. Although I came on with seven minutes left, I was gutted not to be in the team. That's international football. You have to prove yourself with every single game. We drew 1–1 after Brazil equalised in injury time.

I had been on the bench for two crucial games at the end of the season for club and country. Now all I could hope was that Steve McClaren would not overlook me for that must-win game in Estonia.

We arrived late on the Tuesday, the day before the game, after our flight was delayed from Luton airport. As we drove away from Tallinn airport that evening, some of the lads spotted a bloke in a 4x4 speeding up alongside the coach and waving up at us. I suppose you could call him Estonia's biggest David Beckham fan. He had his hair shaved in the same style as Becks, he was wearing identical earrings, tattoos and a Real Madrid shirt. To top it all, his car registration was 'Becks 23', and nothing would stop him from trying to attract the attention of his hero. He was hammering along the wrong side of the road, waving at us like a lunatic without keeping his eyes on the cars coming towards him. It reminded you of the hysteria that follows England's most famous footballer wherever he goes. Becks must have encountered some mad people in his time.

Beating Estonia was vital if we were to have a chance of qualifying from Group E the following season. It was also the last game of the season – a match in which you are always desperate to play well. It can be a killer if you lose that last game and have to spend the whole of the summer thinking about it. During the season, when I lose or play badly I want to put it right as soon as possible and I did not want to go off on my summer holidays dwelling on what might have been.

Steve McClaren gave me my chance, selecting me with Michael Owen. From the very start we never looked like failing. It took us a while to get our first goal but after Joe Cole scored on 37 minutes we were cruising and it could have been four or five. I felt my all-round game was good that night. The ball was played in to me a lot and I thought I did a good job of laying it off and bringing players into the game. All I wanted was a chance to put one away. I hit one wide in the first half but when Becks swung a cross in from the right on 54 minutes, I knew I was in. With the goalkeeper in no-man's land, I headed the ball over him.

As it stood at the end of the 2006–07 season my goalscoring record for England was pretty good. I had 12 goals in 19 caps – but of those games only 12 were starts.

I was buzzing with excitement right up until the moment I got myself booked. We were 3–0 up after Mo got a third and there was no need for me to make the tackle. What an idiot! The yellow card meant that I would miss the game against Israel at Wembley on 8 September. For the first time in the game, I had a bad first touch and lost the ball. Chasing after it, I just lost my head and lunged in without thinking. Steve McClaren, Terry Venables and Bill Beswick all said to me afterwards, 'What were you doing?' Missing England games through suspension is a risky business because there is always someone who wants to take your place. Don't be in any doubt – we're desperate to qualify for Euro 2008.

As for the 2007–08 season, I'm happy to be at Liverpool as we go after the Premiership title again. The manager made it quite clear to me that he wanted me to stay, even before he signed Fernando Torres. He said that he wanted a player who would complement me and, from what I have seen of Torres, I think we will work really well together. He's got a bit of everything – he's quite tricky, he's quick and he scores goals.

You could see at the last World Cup finals that Torres is a top player and, given the fee the club have spent on him, the manager obviously has great faith in him. We need that level of signings to compete with Manchester United and Chelsea and I hope Torres will be another piece of the jigsaw in making Liverpool successful. As players, we want to bring the Premiership title back to Liverpool just as much as the fans want to see it come back. Everyone knows the importance of winning that title after seventeen years without it.

From what he has told me, Rafa Benitez sees Dirk Kuyt as similar to me, and Andriy Voronin and Torres as similar to one other, so when he picks his front two I think it will be a case of one from either pair. Nevertheless, I have shown that I can play with Dirk and I believe I can play with either of the two new boys, too. I'm hoping to get as many games as I can but the manager will rotate the squad to cope with the demands of another big season.

I feel I have established myself at Liverpool over the first two seasons and I'm ready to push on and win trophies. So far my football career – going all the way back to that first day as a 14-year-old at Queens Park Rangers – has brought me some fantastic moments. It's a job I love and I'm at a club that has great tradition and real ambition. I still believe that, for Liverpool and England, the best times are yet to come. And you can be certain I'll give everything to make sure that happens.

CAREER RECORD
PETER JAMES CROUCH

Born Macclesfield, 30 January 1981

PLAYING CAREER

Second figure is substitute appearances. Figure in brackets is goals.

	League	FA Cup	League Cup	Europe	Other	Total
Tottenham Hotspur (Signed professional 2 July 1998)						
1998–99	0	0	0	0	0	0
1999–2000	0	0	0	0	0	0
Dulwich Hamlet (Signed, loan, February 2000)						
1999–2000	6 (1)	0	0	0	0	6 (1)
IFK Hässleholm (Signed, loan, June 2000)						
1999–2000	8 (3)	0	0	0	0	8 (3)
Queens Park Rangers (Signed, £60,000, 28 July 2000)						
2000–01	38+4 (10)	3 (2)	1+1	0	0	42+5 (12)
Portsmouth (Signed, £1.25m, 11 July 2001)						
2001–02	37 (18)	1	1 (1)	0	0	39 (19)
Aston Villa (Signed, £4m, 28 March 2002)						
2001–02	7 (2)	0	0	0	0	7 (2)
2002–03	7+7	0	0	4	0	11+7 (0)
2003–04	6+10 (4)	0	1+1	0	0	7+11 (4)
Norwich (Signed, loan, 8 September 2003)						
2003–04	14+1 (4)	0	0	0	0	14+1 (4)
Southampton (Signed, £2m, 14 July 2004)						
2004–05	18+9 (12)	5 (4)	1	0	0	24+9 (16)
Liverpool (Signed, £7m, 20 July 2005)						
2005–06	27+5 (8)	5+1 (3)	1	8	1+1 (2)†	42+7 (13)
2006–07	19+13 (9)	1	1 (1)	8+6 (7)	1 (1)‡	30+19 (18)

	League	FA Cup	League Cup	Europe	Other	Total
Totals						
Tottenham	0	0	0	0	0	0
Dulwich	6 (1)	0	0	0	0	6 (1)
Hässleholm	8 (3)	0	0	0	0	8 (3)
QPR	38+4 (10)	3 (2)	1+1	0	0	42+5 (12)
Portsmouth	37 (18)	1	1 (1)	0	0	39 (19)
Aston Villa	20+17 (6)	0	1+1	4	0	25+18 (6)
Norwich	14+1 (4)	0	0	0	0	14+1 (4)
Southampton	18+9 (12)	5 (4)	1	0	0	24+9 (16)
Liverpool	46+18 (17)	6+1 (3)	2 (1)	16+6 (7)	2+1 (3)	72+26 (31)
TOTALS	187+49 (71)	15+1 (9)	6+2 (2)	20+6 (7)	2+1 (3)	230+59 (90)

†World Club Championship
‡Community Shield

GAMES

1999–2000

Dulwich Hamlet

Date	Opposition	Competition	Result	Goals
4–3–2000	Billericay (h)	Isthmian Premiership	L 1–2	1
7–3–2000	Hampton & Richmond Borough (a)	Isthmian Premiership	L 0–3	
11–3–2000	Carshalton (h)	Isthmian Premiership	L 1–3	
18–3–2000	Harrow Borough (a)	Isthmian Premiership	L 0–1	
25–3–2000	Heybridge Swifts (a)	Isthmian Premiership	D 1–1	
1–4–2000	Aylesbury Utd (h)	Isthmian Premiership	W 3–0	

IFK Hässleholm
Unknown

2000–01

QPR

Date	Opposition	Competition	Result	Goals
12–8–2000	Birmingham (h)	Division 1	D 0–0	
20–8–2000	Crystal Palace (a)*	Division 1	D 1–1	
23–8–2000	Colchester (a)*	League Cup	W 1–0	
28–8–2000	WBA (a)*	Division 1	L 0–1	

*substitute

CAREER RECORD

Date	Opposition	Competition	Result	Goals
6–9–2000	Colchester (h)	League Cup	L 1–4	
9–9–2000	Preston (h)*	Division 1	D 0–0	
13–9–2000	Gillingham (h)*	Division 1	D 2–2	1
16–9–2000	Barnsley (a)	Division 1	L 2–4	
23–9–2000	Wimbledon (h)	Division 1	W 2–1	1
30–9–2000	Sheff Utd (a)	Division 1	D 1–1	
14–10–2000	Watford (a)	Division 1	L 1–3	
17–10–2000	Grimsby (a)	Division 1	L 1–3	
21–10–2000	Burnley (h)	Division 1	L 0–1	
25–10–2000	Sheff Wed (h)	Division 1	L 1–2	
28–10–2000	Tranmere (a)	Division 1	D 1–1	
31–10–2000	Bolton (a)	Division 1	L 1–3	1
4–11–2000	Portsmouth (h)	Division 1	D 1–1	
11–11–2000	Stockport (a)	Division 1	D 2–2	
18–11–2000	Huddersfield (h)	Division 1	D 0–0	
25–11–2000	Wolves (h)	Division 1	D 2–2	
2–12–2000	Sheff Wed (a)	Division 1	L 2–5	2
16–12–2000	Nottingham Forest (h)	Division 1	W 1–0	1
23–12–2000	Birmingham (a)	Division 1	D 0–0	
26–12–2000	Norwich (h)	Division 1	L 2–3	
30–12–2000	Crystal Palace (h)	Division 1	D 1–1	1
6–1–01	Luton (a)	FA Cup	D 3–3	2
13–1–01	WBA (h)	Division 1	W 2–0	
17–1–01	Luton (h)	FA Cup	W 2–1	
20–1–01	Norwich (a)	Division 1	L 0–1	
27–1–01	Arsenal (h)	FA Cup	L 0–6	
31–1–01	Fulham (h)	Division 1	L 0–2	
3–2–01	Bolton (h)	Division 1	D 1–1	
17–2–01	Barnsley (h)	Division 1	W 2–0	1
20–2–01	Gillingham (a)	Division 1	W 1–0	
24–2–01	Wimbledon (a)	Division 1	L 0–5	
3–3–01	Sheff Utd (h)	Division 1	L 1–3	
7–3–01	Watford (h)	Division 1	D 1–1	
10–3–01	Fulham (a)	Division 1	L 0–2	
17–3–01	Grimsby (h)	Division 1	L 0–1	
24–3–01	Burnley (a)	Division 1	L 1–2	
31–3–01	Nottingham Forest (a)	Division 1	D 1–1	
7–4–01	Blackburn (h)	Division 1	L 1–3	
10-4-01	Crewe (a)	Division 1	D 2–2	1
14–4–01	Portsmouth (a)	Division 1	D 1–1	
16–4–01	Tranmere (h)	Division 1	W 2–0	1
21–4–01	Huddersfield (a)	Division 1	L 1–2	
6–5–01	Wolves (a)	Division 1	D 1–1	

*substitute

2001–02

Portsmouth

Date	Opposition	Competition	Result	Goals
11–8–01	Wolves (a)	Division 1	D 2–2	1
18–8–01	Bradford (h)	Division 1	L 0–1	
21–8–01	Colchester (h)	League Cup	L 1–2	1
25–8–01	Stockport (a)	Division 1	W 1–0	
27–8–01	Grimsby (h)	Division 1	W 4–2	2
8–9–01	Gillingham (h)	Division 1	W 2–1	
12–9–01	Wimbledon (a)	Division 1	D 3–3	1
15–9–01	Crystal Palace (h)	Division 1	W 4–2	1
18–9–01	Walsall (a)	Division 1	D 0–0	
22–9–01	Coventry (a)	Division 1	L 0–1	
25–9–01	WBA (h)	Division 1	L 1–2	
28–9–01	Barnsley (a)	Division 1	W 4–1	1
12–10–01	Rotherham (a)	Division 1	L 1–2	1
20–10–01	Sheff Utd (h)	Division 1	W 1–0	
3–11–01	Sheff Wed (a)	Division 1	W 3–2	2
10–11–01	Burnley (a)	Division 1	D 1–1	1
17–11–01	Man City (h)	Division 1	W 2–1	1
25–11–01	Watford (a)	Division 1	W 3–0	
28–11–01	Nottingham Forest (h)	Division 1	W 3–2	
2–12–01	Norwich (h)	Division 1	L 1–2	
8–12–01	Crewe (h)	Division 1	L 2–4	1
13–12–01	Millwall (a)	Division 1	L 0–1	
22–12–01	Stockport (h)	Division 1	W 2–0	1
26–12–01	Gillingham (a)	Division 1	L 0–2	
29–12–01	Grimsby (a)	Division 1	L 1–3	1
5–1–02	Leyton Orient (h)	FA Cup	L 1–4	
12–1–02	Bradford C (a)	Division 1	L 1–3	
17–1–02	Wolves (h)	Division 1	L 2–3	
2–2–02	Barnsley (h)	Division 1	D 4–4	
9–2–02	Sheff Utd (a)	Division 1	L 3–4	1
16–2–02	Rotherham (h)	Division 1	D 0–0	
23–2–02	WBA (a)	Division 1	L 0–5	
26–2–02	Coventry (h)	Division 1	W 1–0	1
2–3–02	Walsall (h)	Division 1	D 1–1	1
5–3–02	Crystal Palace (a)	Division 1	D 0–0	
9–3–02	Millwall (h)	Division 1	W 3–0	
12–3–02	Wimbledon (h)	Division 1	L 1–2	
16–3–02	Crewe (a)	Division 1	D 1–1	1
23–3–02	Sheff Wed (h)	Division 1	D 0–0	

*substitute

Aston Villa

Date	Opposition	Competition	Result	Goals
30–2–02	Bolton (a)	Premiership	L 2–3	
2–4–02	Newcastle (h)	Premiership	D 1–1	1
6–4–02	Middlesbrough (a)	Premiership	L 1–2	
13–4–02	Leeds (h)	Premiership	L 0–1	
20–4–02	Leicester (a)	Premiership	D 2–2	
27–4–02	Southampton (h)	Premiership	W 2–1	
11–5–02	Chelsea (a)	Premiership	W 3–1	1

2002–03

Aston Villa

Date	Opposition	Competition	Result	Goals
21–7–02	FC Zurich (a)	InterToto	L 0–2	
27–7–02	FC Zurich (h)	InterToto	W 3–0	
31–7–02	Lille (a)	InterToto	D 1–1	
7–8–02	Lille (h)	InterToto	L 0–2	
18–8–02	Liverpool (h)	Premiership	L 0–1	
24–8–01	Tottenham (a)	Premiership	L 0–1	
28–8–02	Man City (h)	Premiership	W 1–0	
1–9–02	Bolton (a)	Premiership	L 0–1	
11–9–02	Charlton (h)*	Premiership	W 2–0	
22–9–02	Everton (h)	Premiership	W 3–2	
28–9–02	Sunderland (a)*	Premiership	L 0–1	
26–10–02	Man Utd (a)*	Premiership	D 1–1	
3–11–02	Blackburn (a)*	Premiership	D 0–0	
18–1–02	Tottenham (h)*	Premiership	L 0–1	
8–2–02	Fulham (a)*	Premiership	L 1–2	
22–2–02	Charlton (a)	Premiership	L 0–3	
3–3–02	Birmingham (h)*	Premiership	L 0–2	
22–3–02	Southampton (a)	Premiership	D 2–2	

2003–04

Aston Villa

Date	Opposition	Competition	Result	Goals
16–8–03	Portsmouth (a)*	Premiership	L 1–2	

*substitute

Norwich City (loan)

Date	Opposition	Competition	Result	Goals
13–9–03	Burnley (h)	Division 1	W 2–0	1
16–9–03	Gillingham (a)	Division 1	W 2–1	1
20–9–03	Stoke (a)	Division 1	D 1–1	
27–9–03	Crystal Palace (h)	Division 1	W 2–1	
30–9–03	Reading (h)	Division 1	W 2–1	
15–10–03	West Ham (a)	Division 1	D 1–1	1
18–10–03	WBA (a)*	Division 1	L 0–1	
21–10–03	Derby (h)	Division 1	W 2–1	
25–10–03	Sunderland (h)	Division 1	W 1–0	
1–11–03	Walsall (a)	Division 1	W 3–1	1
8–11–03	Millwall (h)	Division 1	W 3–1	
22–11–03	Preston (a)	Division 1	D 0–0	
25–11–03	Coventry (h)	Division 1	D 1–1	
29–11–03	Crewe (h)	Division 1	W 1–0	
6–12–03	Millwall (a)	Division 1	D 0–0	

Aston Villa

Date	Opposition	Competition	Result	Goals
12–12–03	Chelsea (h)*	League Cup	W 2–1	
6–1–04	Portsmouth (h)*	Premiership	W 2–1	
18–1–04	Arsenal (h)*	Premiership	L 0–2	
27–1–04	Bolton (h)	League Cup	W 2–0	
31–1–04	Leicester (a)	Premiership	W 5–0	2
7–2–04	Leeds (h)*	Premiership	W 2–0	
28–2–04	Everton (a)*	Premiership	L 0–2	
14–3–04	Wolves (a)*	Premiership	W 4–0	
20–3–04	Blackburn (h)*	Premiership	L 0–2	
4–4–04	Man City (h)*	Premiership	D 1–1	
10–4–04	Bolton (a)	Premiership	D 2–2	1
12–4–04	Chelsea (h)	Premiership	W 3–2	
18–4–04	Newcastle (h)	Premiership	D 0–0	
24–4–04	Middlesbrough (a)*	Premiership	W 2–1	1
2–5–04	Tottenham (h)	Premiership	W 1–0	
8–5–04	Southampton (a)*	Premiership	D 1–1	
15–5–04	Man Utd (a)	Premiership	L 0–2	

*substitute

2004–05

Southampton

Date	Opposition	Competition	Result	Goals
14–8–04	Aston Villa (a)*	Premiership	L 0–2	
25–8–04	Bolton (h)*	Premiership	L 1–2	1
28–8–04	Chelsea (a)*	Premiership	L 1–2	
13–9–04	Charlton (a)*	Premiership	D 0–0	
19–9–04	Newcastle (h)*	Premiership	L 1–2	
22–9–04	Northampton (a)	League Cup	W 3–0	
2–10–04	Man City (h)*	Premiership	D 0–0	
20–11–04	Norwich (a)*	Premiership	L 1–2	
27–11–04	Crystal Palace (h)*	Premiership	D 2–2	
11–12–04	Middlesbrough (h)	Premiership	D 2–2	1
18–12–04	Tottenham (a)	Premiership	L 1–5	1
26–12–04	Charlton (h)	Premiership	D 0–0	
1–1–05	Man City (a)*	Premiership	L 1–2	
5–1–05	Fulham (h)	Premiership	D 3–3	
8–1–05	Northampton (a)	FA Cup	W 3–1	1
15–1–05	Newcastle (a)	Premiership	L 1–2	1
22–1–05	Liverpool (h)	Premiership	W 2–0	1
29–1–05	Portsmouth (h)	FA Cup	W 2–1	1
2–2–05	Birmingham (a)	Premiership	L 1–2	
6–2–05	Everton (h)	Premiership	D 2–2	1
19–2–05	Brentford (h)	FA Cup	D 2–2	
22–2–05	WBA (a)	Premiership	D 0–0	
26–2–05	Southampton (h)	Premiership	D 1–1	1
1–3–05	Brentford (a)	FA Cup	W 3–1	2
5–3–05	Tottenham (h)	Premiership	W 1–0	
12–3–05	Man Utd (h)	FA Cup	L 0–4	
20–3–05	Middlesbrough (a)	Premiership	W 3–1	2
2–4–05	Chelsea (h)	Premiership	L 1–3	
9–4–05	Blackburn (a)	Premiership	L 0–3	
16–4–05	Aston Villa (h)	Premiership	L 2–3	1
19–4–05	Bolton (a)	Premiership	D 1–1	
30–4–05	Norwich (h)	Premiership	W 4–3	1
7–5–05	Crystal Palace (a)	Premiership	D 2–2	1

*substitute

2005–06

Liverpool

Date	Opposition	Competition	Result	Goals
26–7–05	FBK Kaunas (a)	CLQ	W 3–1	
2–8–05	FBK Kaunas (h)	CLQ	W 2–0	
10–9–05	Tottenham (a)	Premiership	D 0–0	
13–9–05	Real Betis (a)	CL	W 2–1	
18–9–05	Man Utd (h)	Premiership	D 0–0	
24–9–05	Birmingham (a)	Premiership	D 2–2	
28–9–05	Chelsea (h)	CL	D 0–0	
2–10–05	Chelsea (h)	Premiership	L 1–4	
15–10–05	Blackburn (h)	Premiership	W 1–0	
22–10–05	Fulham (a)*	Premiership	L 0–2	
25–10–05	Crystal Palace (a)	League Cup	L 1–2	
29–10–05	West Ham (h)*	Premiership	W 2–0	
1–11–05	Anderlecht (h)	CL	W 3–0	
5–11–05	Aston Villa (a)*	Premiership	W 2–0	
19–11–05	Portsmouth (h)	Premiership	W 3–0	
23–11–05	Real Betis (h)	CL	D 0–0	
26–11–05	Man City (a)	Premiership	W 1–0	
30–11–05	Sunderland (a)	Premiership	W 2–0	
3–12–05	Wigan (h)	Premiership	W 3–0	2
6–12–05	Chelsea (a)	CL	D 0–0	
10–12–05	Middlesbrough (h)	Premiership	W 2–0	
15–12–05	D Saprissa (Japan)	FCWC	W 3–0	2
18–12–05	Sao Paulo* (Japan)	FCWC	L 0–1	
26–12–05	Newcastle (h)	Premiership	W 2–0	1
28–12–05	Everton (a)	Premiership	W 3–1	1
31–12–05	WBA (h)	Premiership	W 1–0	1
2–1–06	Bolton (a)	Premiership	D 2–2	
7–1–06	Luton (a)	FA Cup	W 5–3	
14–1–06	Tottenham (h)	Premiership	W 1–0	
22–1–06	Man Utd (a)	Premiership	L 0–1	
29–1–06	Portsmouth (a)*	FA Cup	W 2–1	
1–2–06	Birmingham (h)	Premiership	D 1–1	
5–2–06	Chelsea (a)	Premiership	L 0–2	
8–2–06	Charlton (a)	Premiership	L 0–2	
18–2–06	Man Utd (h)	FA Cup	W 1–0	1
26–2–06	Man City (h)	Premiership	W 1–0	

*substitute

CAREER RECORD

Date	Opposition	Competition	Result	Goals
4–3–06	Charlton (h)	Premiership	D 0–0	
8–3–06	Benfica (h)	CL	L 0–2	
12–3–06	Arsenal (a)	Premiership	L 1–2	
15–3–06	Fulham (h)*	Premiership	W 5–1	1
19–3–06	Newcastle (a)	Premiership	W 3–1	1
21–3–06	Birmingham (a)	FA Cup	W 7–0	2
25–3–06	Everton (h)	Premiership	W 3–1	
1–4–06	WBA (a)	Premiership	W 2–0	
9–4–06	Bolton (h)	Premiership	W 1–0	
22–4–06	Chelsea (Old Trafford)	FA Cup	W 2–1	
29–4–06	Aston Villa (h)	Premiership	W 3–1	
7–5–06	Portsmouth (a)*	Premiership	W 3–1	1
13–5–06	West Ham (Cardiff)	FA Cup	D 3–3	

2006–07

Liverpool

Date	Opposition	Competition	Result	Goals
9–8–06	Maccabi Haifa (h)*	CLQ	W 2–1	
13–8–06	Chelsea (Cardiff)	CS	W 2–1	1
22–8–06	Maccabi Haifa (a)	CLQ	D 1–1	1
26–8–06	West Ham (h)	Premiership	W 2–1	1
9–9–06	Everton (a)	Premiership	L 0–3	
17–9–06	Chelsea (a)*	Premiership	L 0–1	
20–9–06	Newcastle (h)*	Premiership	W 2–0	
27–9–06	Galatasaray (h)	CL	W 3–2	2
30–9–06	Bolton (a)*	Premiership	L 0–2	
14–10–06	Blackburn (h)	Premiership	D 1–1	
18–10–06	Bordeaux (a)	CL	W 1–0	1
22–10–06	Man Utd (a)*	Premiership	L 0–2	
25–10–06	Reading (h)	League Cup	W 4–3	1
28–10–06	Aston Villa (h)	Premiership	W 3–1	1
31–10–06	Bordeaux (h)	CL	W 3–0	
4–11–06	Reading (h)	Premiership	W 2–0	
12–11–06	Arsenal (a)	Premiership	L 0–3	
18–11–06	Middlesbrough (a)*	Premiership	D 0–0	
22–11–06	PSV Eindhoven (h)	CL	W 2–0	1
25–11–06	Man City (h)	Premiership	W 1–0	

*substitute

Date	Opposition	Competition	Result	Goals
29–11–06	Portsmouth (h)	Premiership	D 0–0	
5–12–06	Galatasaray (a)*	CL	L 2–3	
9–12–06	Fulham (h)*	Premiership	W 4–0	
16–12–06	Charlton (a)*	Premiership	W 3–0	
23–12–06	Watford (h)*	Premiership	W 2–0	
26–12–06	Blackburn (a)	Premiership	L 0–1	
30–12–06	Tottenham (a)*	Premiership	W 1–0	
1–1–07	Bolton (h)	Premiership	W 3–0	1
6–1–07	Arsenal (h)	FA Cup	L 1–3	
13–1–07	Watford (a)	Premiership	W 3–0	2
20–1–07	Chelsea (h)	Premiership	W 2–0	
30–1–07	West Ham (a)	Premiership	W 2–1	1
3–2–07	Everton (h)	Premiership	D 0–0	
10–2–07	Newcastle (a)*	Premiership	L 1–2	
21–2–07	Barcelona (a)*	CL	W 2–1	
24–2–07	Sheff Utd (h)	Premiership	W 4–0	
3–3–07	Man Utd (h)*	Premiership	L 0–1	
6–3–07	Barcelona (h)*	CL	L 0–1	
31–3–07	Arsenal (h)	Premiership	W 4–1	3
3–4–07	PSV Eindoven (a)	CL	W 3–0	1
7–4–07	Reading (a)	Premiership	W 2–1	
11–4–07	PSV Eindhoven (h)	CL	W 1–0	1
14–4–07	Man City (a)*	Premiership	D 0–0	
18–4–07	Middlesbrough (h)	Premiership	W 2–0	
21–4–07	Wigan (h)	Premiership	W 2–0	
25–4–07	Chelsea (a)*	CL	L 0–1	
1–5–07	Chelsea (h)	CL	W 1–0	
13–5–07	Charlton (h)*	Premiership	D 2–2	
23–5–07	AC Milan (Greece)*	CL	L 0–1	

England U20

Date	Opposition	Competition	Result	Goals
11–4–99	Japan (Nigeria)*	WYC	L 0–2	

England U21

Date	Opposition	Competition	Result	Goals
26–3–02	Italy (h)*	F	D 1–1	
16–4–02	Portugal (h)*	F	L 0–1	
17–5–02	Switzerland (Switzerland)	EC	W 2–1	1
20–5–02	Italy (Switzerland)	EC	L 1–2	
15–10–02	Macedonia (h)*	ECQ	W 3–1	
28–3–03	Portugal (a)	F	L 2–4	

*substitute

England B

Date	Opposition (h/a)	Competition	Result	Goals
25–5–05	Belarus (h)	F	L 1–2	

England

Date	Opposition (h/a)	Competition	Result	Goals
31–5–03	Colombia (USA)	F	W 3–2	
8–10–05	Austria (h)	WCQ	W 1–0	
12–10–05	Poland (h)*	WCQ	W 2–1	
12–11–05	Argentina (Switzerland)*	F	W 3–2	
1–3–06	Uruguay (h)*	F	W 1–0	1
30–5–06	Hungary (h)*	F	W 3–1	1
3–6–06	Jamaica (h)	F	W 6–0	3
10–6–06	Paraguay (Germany)	WC	W 1–0	
15–6–06	Trinidad & Tobago (Germany)	WC	W 2–0	1
20–6–06	Sweden (Germany)*	WC	D 2–2	
1–7–06	Portugal (Germany)*	WC	D 0–0	
16–8–06	Greece (h)	F	W 2–0	2
2–9–06	Andorra (h)	ECQ	W 5–0	2
6–9–06	Macedonia (a)	ECQ	W 1–0	1
7–10–06	Macedonia (h)	ECQ	D 0–0	
11–10–06	Croatia (a)	ECQ	L 0–2	
7–2–07	Spain (h)	F	L 0–1	
1–6–07	Brazil* (h)	F	D 1–1	
6–6–07	Estonia (a)	ECQ	W 3–0	1

CL	Champions League
CLQ	Champions League Qualifier
CS	Community Shield
EC	European Championship
ECQ	European Championship Qualifier
F	Friendly
FCWC	FIFA Club World Championship
WC	World Cup
WCQ	World Cup Qualifier
WYC	World Youth Cup

*substitute

INDEX